# The Heritage of Spain

*An Introduction to Spanish Civilization*

## Nicholson B. Adams

HENRY HOLT AND COMPANY · NEW YORK

# Preface

Spain is not an easy country to know well, and through indifference or pride she has generally not taken the trouble to explain herself to foreigners. The world has been somewhat more interested in her since the establishment of the Second Republic in 1931 and the banishment of the late Alfonso XIII, but that interest has not always been unto knowledge. Ignorance might help to explain the extraordinary behavior of the democracies, England, France, and the United States, which allowed Franco, a rebel against a duly constituted republican Spanish government, to establish a Fascist dictatorship, with the applause and aid of Hitler and Mussolini. For that ignorance and for that policy of appeasement we are now paying heavily.

Spain has interested me ever since my early childhood memories of the Spanish-American War. I hope that others may be interested in what I have learned about her since then. I have tried to set down simply in this brief book the main facts about Spain's history, culture, and art, with emphasis on her still too-little-known literature. I hope it may be of aid, too, to those who wish to be good neighbors with Latin America. It was men from the Iberian Peninsula who spread their civilization from the Southern United States to Tierra del Fuego.

Those who want fuller information will find numerous suggestions in the bibliographies at the end of this volume.

I wish to express my gratitude to Lt. Thomas J. Wilson, III, U.S.N.R., and to Agatha Boyd Adams.

NICHOLSON B. ADAMS

Chapel Hill, N. C.
May, 1943

# Contents

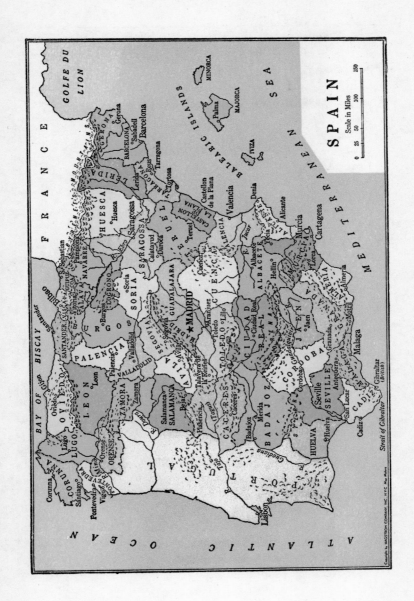

**SPAIN**

Scale in Miles

0  25  50  100  150

# I

## Spain Is a Country of Diversity

### CLIMATE AND TOPOGRAPHY

WHAT sort of a country is Spain? A desert made to order for the pilgrimage of ascetic and idealistic Don Quixotes? A lush land in which the lurid passion of Don José and Carmen reaches ecstasy and tragedy? Is it the land of the emaciated saints of El Greco or of the rich-fleshed *majas* of Goya? A country of castanets, guitars, love and laughter or a region of cruel and sanguinary civil wars? It is all of these, and more, for its chief characteristic is diversity, and generalizations about it are usually untrustworthy.

The sun burns the south and east with tropical fervor, while the Pyrenees, five hundred miles north of Malaga, are hoary with snow. A few sections are well watered and very fertile, while much of the country is ill favored and desert.

The rich and low-lying region around Valencia, filled with rice-swamps and well-irrigated truck farms, is bounded on the west by rugged mountains. To the north lies Catalonia, agriculturally favored and industrially energetic and prosperous. From east to west in the extreme north of Spain are Navarre, the Basque Provinces, and Asturias and Galicia, mainly taken up by the Pyrenees and their continuation, the Cantabrian Mountains. To the south of them lie León and Old and New Castile, forming a high, uneven table-land, parched in summer and swept in winter by icy winds. The stern hills of Castile are picturesquely lovely in a violet sunset, but the whole arid region gives one an impression of solemn desolation. Between Old Castile and Catalonia is the stubborn ancient kingdom of Aragon. South of León lies Estremadoura, famous for its

1

cattle. Andalusia, Granada and Murcia, while not lacking mountains, offer large regions for farming. They are the home of the orange, the fig and the olive.

Those who like figures may care to know that Spain has an area of about 190,000 square miles. Portugal has about 33,000. The Iberian Peninsula is, then, not quite so large as the state of Texas. Spain's population is estimated at about 26 million, Portugal's at seven million. Barcelona and Madrid have over a million inhabitants each, Lisbon 600,000.

To support the population Spain has theoretically over a hundred million acres of productive land, of which only about half is under cultivation. Over 4½ million acres are in olive orchards, 3½ million in vineyards and somewhat more than a million in fruit, mainly oranges. Production naturally fell after the beginning of the civil war of 1936-39: wheat, for example, from 186,834,000 bushels in 1935 to 121,490,000 bushels in 1937, and other cereals in proportion. At least Spain still produces more than 20 million gallons of wine per year. The annual production of olive oil is around 350,000 tons. Spain draws wealth not only from her soil, mines and streams, but also from the seas around her, for 130,000 men are engaged in fishing. The mineral wealth of the Peninsula is considerable: iron, lead, copper, zinc, mercury and other minerals, plus coal, all of which produced in the 1930's a total income of about a hundred million dollars a year. Sites for hydroelectric power (up to two million horsepower) are available, but largely undeveloped. Manufacturing, especially of textiles, is important in Catalonia, but Spain's balance of trade has long been decidedly adverse. She has been hampered by insufficient transportation facilities, for she has only about 10,000 miles of railroads, and 70,000 of highways, with less than 200,000 registered motor vehicles. (New York State has more than 2½ million.) In a word, Spain has sufficient resources, but they are largely undeveloped. The civil wars of the nineteenth and twentieth centuries have decidedly retarded normal progress.

With such diversity of climate and topography, with the difficulty of communication over mountain barriers, is it any wonder that the various regions of Spain, quite properly called in former times

*Las Españas,* developed each in its own peculiar physiognomy and character, and that it took long, long centuries for the country to achieve even a nominal unity? It is not to be forgotten that regional differences have by no means been composed to this very day, and that separatist tendencies will surely plague Spain for a very long time.

## THE PEOPLE OF SPAIN

Is there, then, any common denominator for the very different types of people who occupy the Spanish peninsula: the sentimental though shrewd Galician, the sturdy and conservative Basque, the hard-headed Aragonese, the industrious though somewhat fractious Catalan, the easy-going but passionate Andalusian, the strong and proud Castilian? Even the above regional generalizations about Spaniards may be proven false in many individual instances, and need modification.

A few general statements, however, may be hazarded about the Spanish variety of humanity. The Spaniard is above all an individualist, and greatly prizes personal autonomy. He is a born anarchist, and it is difficult to make him conform to systems and rules. He prefers to absorb from them what suits himself, to appropriate it and modify it according to his personal whim. Spanish writers, for example, pay very little attention to the dictates of the Spanish Academy. It has often been remarked that Spanish soldiers, in the days when personal valor was a preëminent requisite, were the best in Europe. When armies became more like machines, Spaniards lost their military power. The tendency of any Spanish organization, army, political party, economic association or what not, is to fly into as many sections as there are individuals composing it.

Is that centrifugal tendency a racial characteristic? It is hard to tell, for no one really knows very much about the primitive inhabitants of Spain, who are called Iberians. Perhaps the Basques who now live around the Pyrenees in northern Spain are descendants of this race, or perhaps of another race existing before the Iberians. It is known at least that a highly respectable civilization existed in

the south and southeast of Spain more than a thousand years before the Christian era. Subsequently the Peninsula was swept by
waves of invasion, colonization and conquest of very diverse origins. The Phoenicians came to trade and not to conquer, and they
established many colonies besides Cadiz, founded about 1100 B.C.,
and Tartessus (Tarshish), whence ships took to King Solomon
"gold, and silver, ivory and apes, and peacocks." In fact, these
Spanish Tyrians were reputed to be the richest traders in the world,
and their arts and civilization spread from the coast to the tribes
of the interior. The Greeks founded their colonies mainly on the
east coast, partly for purposes of trade and partly because they had
been driven from home by political upheavals. The permanent influence of both Phoenicia and Greece was very limited, because the
Phoenicians and Greeks seem to have remained in their trading-
posts and mixed little with the native population. The Celts from
the north were, however, real invaders, and they came in much
greater numbers. They remained particularly strong in the northwest (Galicia and Portugal), and were gradually fused with the
Iberians there and in the center of the country. This Celtiberian
mixture made a sturdy fighting stock whose valor is emphasized
by the Roman and Greek historians from whom we derive most
of our knowledge of them. Judging from the recent Spanish civil
war, Spaniards still possess the same toughness and vigor.

# II

## Spain Is Romanized

### A TRANSITION PERIOD

THE Romans were a sturdy, adventurous and rapacious people, who could not rest until they had overturned and conquered the ancient world. Spain was one of the regions which they transformed, and to Spain they gave a new language, new customs and laws, a new political organization. They left in the Iberian Peninsula impressive material structures, as well as their blood, for Spain was not dominated without a long and sanguinary struggle.

Spain has seen a great deal of fighting. The earliest about which we possess any accurate historical accounts was the great struggle between Rome and Carthage called the Punic Wars, in which Spain was an important battleground. Carthaginians, pursuing an aggressive expansionist policy, had come to Spain, supposedly invited by their Phoenician cousins there to help fight the Celtiberians. They attempted to conquer the country and to use its resources in their wars with Rome. With the First Punic War (264-241 B.C.) Carthage lost part of Sicily. Further fighting was inevitable.

Carthage, for all her military genius, could not cope with Fate's favorites, the Romans. Carthaginian power was crushed in Spain and in Africa by Scipio with the close of the Second Punic War (206 B.C.). The Romans were aided by their adoption of the two-edged Iberian sword as their standard weapon. In the ensuing six hundred years Spain became gradually Romanized. The first two centuries were difficult for the conquerors, because the fierce independence and vigorous local patriotism of the Celtiberians made

5

it necessary for the ultimate victors to win each hamlet, each valley, each pass, each hillock separately, sometimes by sheer brute force, and not infrequently by cruel treachery. In both procedures the Romans proved themselves adept. Southern and eastern Spain were subdued by 179 B.C. In the west the Romans found the going harder. A federation of tribes under a Lusitanian (Portuguese) shepherd named Viriatus held off and defeated Rome's best legions for ten years, but Viriatus was at last assassinated (140 B.C.) by hirelings bought with Roman gold. The Celtiberians continued their resistance in the city of Numancia, near modern Soria, which was successively besieged with signal unsuccess by five Roman consuls and their armies. Finally Rome sent her best general, Scipio Emilianus, who pressed the city for sixteen months. The inhabitants, worn by famine and pestilence and seeing all hope gone, destroyed all they had and fell on their own swords. Hardly a handful of prisoners were taken to grace the Roman triumph (132 B.C.). That bitter resistance was paralleled when Napoleon's troops besieged Saragossa in 1808, and in the sieges of Toledo and Madrid in Spain's most recent civil war.

Fifty years after Numancia, the Romans had another serious military problem in Spain. The fighting occasioned by the revolt of Sertorius, a Sabine with a Spanish mother, took place mainly in Spain, where Sertorius was murdered in 73 B.C. Pompey crushed what was left of his forces, and Julius Caesar, after Pompey's death in Africa, practically completed the pacification of Spain. It is worthy of note that Africans were involved in a great deal of the fighting in Spain even in Roman times. A serious incursion of Berbers had to be coped with between 180 and 170 B.C.: an instance of the danger of invasion from the continent across the Mediterranean, which has for three thousand years or more been a poignant reality in Spanish history. General Franco, for example, found the "Moors" of northern Africa most useful when he brought them to aid his rebellion in 1936.

## THE ROMAN OCCUPATION

The Roman occupation of the Iberian Peninsula was the most important single fact in its history. Spain became the most thoroughly Romanized province in the Empire outside of Italy. Roman law and administrative procedure, the Latin language, Graeco-Roman culture, Etruscan-Roman architecture, the Christian religion and even Roman social behavior were adopted almost universally. During the Empire Rome was drawing upon Spain not only for soldiers and material resources, but even for emperors, teachers and writers. Among the greatest successors of Caesar Augustus were Trajan, Hadrian, Marcus Aurelius and Theodosius, all Spaniards or of Spanish blood. The most important writers of the Silver Age of Latin literature were also Spaniards. The two Senecas, Marcus Annaeus and Lucius Annaeus, were born in Cordova. The tragedies and essays of the younger Seneca were popular not only in the Middle Ages but also during the Renaissance. Lucan, nephew of Lucius Annaeus Seneca, was also a native of Cordova. In the rather high-flown diction of his *Pharsalia* many critics have seen a suggestion of the floridity of another "Swan of Cordova," the great seventeenth-century poet Góngora. Martial the satirist (42-104 A.D.) was born in Bilbilis (Calatayud), and the orator and preceptist Quintilian (35-96) was a native of Calahorra. Pomponius Mela, the geographer, was a native of Tingentera, and Columella, the agronomist, of Gades (Cadiz).

Those were pagan authors, but there were many Christian authors too. Among Spanish churchmen who wrote in Latin were Juvencus, the poet, and St. Damasus, who rose to be Pope from 367 to 384; and the hymnologist Prudentius, born in 348, whom Erasmus considered the greatest Christian Latin poet.

It is to be understood that the Latin employed by the authors of the fourth and fifth centuries of our era was a somewhat artificial language modeled upon that used by classic authors such as Cicero and Vergil. The speech of the Romans in Spain at the time was quite different. It is called Vulgar Latin (*sermo plebeius*), and formed the basis of all the Romance tongues. No one can say with absolute precision just when Latin became Spanish. From the tenth century onward the vernacular speech (then called *romance*) becomes increasingly evident in documents, though the first literary monuments date from the twelfth century. There are now four languages spoken in the Iberian Peninsula, three of which are based upon the Latin. Basque, heard in northern Spain and southern France, is not a Romance language, not even Indo-European. Unlike any other language in Europe, it is thought by many to be a development of the language spoken by the primitive Iberians. Portuguese and its dialect Galician are spoken in the west; Castilian in the center, and Catalan and its dialect Valencian in the east. Castilian is usually called Spanish, and, with comparatively slight modifications, is spoken throughout Latin America by some sixty million people. The total number of those who speak Spanish in the world is estimated at somewhat over a hundred million. Portuguese is spoken in Brazil, the largest state in South America and a former colony of Portugal.

Although Spanish is a development of Latin, other languages have enriched its vocabulary. Arabic, though spoken in the Peninsula for about eight hundred years, has contributed only about 650 words, many of which begin with the Arabic article *al*. French, Italian, English and other languages have made their contribution. Mexican, Central and South American Indian languages have added a very large number of words to Spanish dictionaries, mainly names of flora and fauna, and likely to be rather local in use.

The Romans left in Spain much more than their language. Those who studied Roman history in the good old-fashioned way probably read something like this: *Q*. How did the Romans expand their power? *A*. 1) they founded colonies; 2) they built roads. They did indeed, and some of the many roads which they built in their Spanish colonies, as well as elsewhere, are still in use today. They also built temples, theaters, arenas and aqueducts, as well as walled towns. Their fortified camps became cities: (*Castra*) *Emerita* is Mérida, called "a second Rome" and noted for its aqueduct and other Roman remains; *Caesarea Augusta* is Zaragoza (Saragossa);

*Asturica Augusta* is Astorga; *Pax Augusta* is Badajoz and the *pax* is etymologically pleasant and historically ironical, since Badajoz was the object of horrible siege and capture by the Duke of Wellington's troops in 1808 and by Franco's in 1936. At Itálica, near Seville, are the ruins of an amphitheater capable of seating forty thousand spectators, of baths, old walls and an aqueduct. It is a little startling today to enter a peasant house in the adjacent village of Santiponce, to step upon a Roman mosaic floor, and to purchase for a few cents one of the numerous Roman lamps dug up in the fields nearby. After all, Itálica was once an important city, the birthplace of the emperors Trajan and Hadrian and of the poet Silius Italicus. Much more grandiose are the aqueducts of Tarragona and Segovia. The latter, still in use today, brings water from a spring more than ten miles distant, and is nearly a hundred feet above ground at the highest point. Considering its solidity—it is built of granite blocks dry, without mortar or cement—it gives an impression of singular lightness and grace. The bridge across the Tagus at Toledo, built by the Romans and repaired by Moors and Christians, is likewise an admirable combination of utility and beauty. This functional quality of Roman structures is constantly evident in Spain as elsewhere, and it is paralleled by the efficiency of the institutions which Rome bequeathed to all the peoples which she conquered.

# III

## *The Visigoths Come to Spain*

### THE GERMANIC INVASIONS

THE political and military control of the Eternal City over Spain was not eternal. The Romans were succeeded by Germanic tribes of great vigor but inferior culture. Spain's lot from 409 A.D. to 711 was not a happy one. The Visigothic kings, with their unpronounceable names, were only occasionally good sovereigns. However, a period of three hundred years in the life of a nation cannot be merely brushed aside.

In the very early years of the fifth century A.D. the Vandals and the Alans began their migration from central Europe, and, joined by the Suevians, crossed the Rhine and devastated France. They passed into Spain in 409, and encountered very little resistance, for Spain had been relatively peaceful for about four hundred years, and her best warriors had been drafted into the Roman legions to fight in distant parts of the Empire, from northern Britain to the Danube provinces. Galicia was apportioned to the Suevians and to a group of the Vandals; the Alans and the rest of the Vandals took southern Spain, to which the latter gave their name: Vandalusia > Andalucía.

The Visigoths, who had gone from Scandinavia to the Black Sea, across the Danube to Imperial territory, were already allied to Rome in the fourth century. They had been converted to Christianity and had become at least partly civilized. Getting into a dispute with the Roman emperors, they proceeded to wage war on their allies, and under Alaric captured and ravaged Rome in 410, the first sack of the Eternal City in eight hundred years. Alaric's successor Ataulf led the Visigoths out of Italy into France, nominally as allies of the Romans; but southern France was too tempting and they took it for themselves. The Visigoths made their first entry into Spain in 414, capturing Barcelona. The Vandals in southern Spain, when attacked by the Visigoths, left Spain for Africa (429). Theodoric and Euric captured practically all the Peninsula for the Visigoths. Euric, one of the few early Visigothic kings to escape assassination, was decidedly one of the most powerful sovereigns of his time, ruling from the Loire to Gibraltar. Toledo became the capital during the reign of Athanagild (554-567). The greatest of the thirty-five Visigothic rulers of Spain was Leovgild (573-586). His son Reccared, along with many of his Gothic compatriots, accepted Roman Catholic Christianity, which was the religion of the Hispano-Romans who constituted most of the population.

## GOTHIC INFLUENCE IN SPAIN

Amid the anarchy of the Visigothic period in Spain, the greatest stabilizing factor was the Christian Church, already long established there. There is a tradition that St. Paul preached in Spain. At any rate, Spaniards early accepted Christianity, and by the time of the persecution of Christians by Diocletian (284-305 A.D.), many Spaniards were ready to suffer martyrdom for their faith. The first church council, at Elvira, near Granada, was held in 306, and was attended by nineteen Spanish bishops and many priests and deacons. Until that date the clergy had freely married, but the council then declared for absolute celibacy of the priesthood.

The second council, at Saragossa, 380, dealt with heresy, and the third, Toledo, 400, unified doctrine on the basis of the Nicene Creed. At the highly important council of Nicaea (325), the Cordovan bishop Hosius had greatly helped Athanasius to triumph over Arius, who held that Jesus was begotten of God, but not coeternal and consubstantial with Him. The Visigoths, alas, were Arians, and were by Spanish Catholics regarded as heretics, and the Spanish church has never been tolerant of heresy. Witness what happened to Priscillian, a Galician who had become Bishop of Avila. Bishop or not, Priscillian held that the world was created and ruled, not by God but by the Devil, and made other dark professions. Consequently he was executed. Some have thought that he was not a heretic, only exaggeratedly ascetic. It was fortunate for religious unity, then, that Reccared and his Visigoths thus freed themselves from the taint of heterodoxy. It was also most fortunate for the power of the Church in affairs temporal and spiritual. The Church was the most important single unifying force in a time of disorder. Its ministrants served it with enthusiasm, and it has continued to be, not only throughout the Middle Ages and the palmy days of the Inquisition, but right up to this present moment, a vastly significant factor of Spanish life.

Secular education as such did not exist in Visigothic Spain, but the Catholic Church has at all periods sheltered men who had real scholarly aspirations. Just after the first incursion of Germanic tribes into Spain, a churchman named Orosius made an attempt to write a universal history from a Christian point of view. He called his work *Seven Books of History against Pagans* (418 A.D.). A much more gifted and diligent scholar was St. Isidore of Seville (ca. 570-636), one of the greatest compilers who ever existed. His *Etymologies,* divided into twenty books, touch all branches of human knowledge: a real mediaeval encyclopedia. St. Isidore wrote numerous other works, all in Latin, of course, and he is still venerated, not only as a saint but also as a man of enormous scholarly achievement. Another famous saint was Ildefonso, who wrote a book on the perpetual virginity of Our Lady. St. Mary, as a reward for his devotion, appeared to him and gave him a chasuble woven by angels. The subject became popular in painting.

The Romans left impressive structures all over Spain, but the Goths left comparatively few artistic monuments. So-called "Visigothic" architecture is a highly controversial subject, and opinions differ as to whether it is Roman or Oriental in origin. The horseshoe arch, already seen in Spain in the second and third centuries A.D., was also employed in Visigothic times. The completely restored Church of St. John, at Baños, still bears the dedicatory inscription of King Recceswinth (mid-seventh century).

Jewelry and architecture show the use of Oriental motifs, which

Sorolla: "Leonese Peasants."

Sorolla: "Ayamonte." Fish caught
in the Gulf of Cadiz.

Sorolla: "Galicia." Peasants resting in the northwest corner of Spain. The musical instrument is the *gaita*, like Scotch bagpipes.

Sorolla: "Sevilla." The dance. The rhythm of the dance is accentuated by the guitar, castanets, and swirling skirts.

Sorolla: "Castilla." Peasants in religious procession.

Sorolla: "Guipúzcoa." Basque peasants bowling.

Sorolla: "Valencia." A gay wedding procession in Spain's warm east-coast province.

Sorolla: "Extremadura." A village in Spain's western province.

Sorolla: "Andalucía. El Encierro."
Corraling the bulls.

Woman in wedding costume.
Province of Salamanca.

Ceremonial peasant costume. Province of Salamanca.

The famous *Dama de Elche*, a remarkable example of early sculpture discovered in the Province of Alicante. The eternal type of Spanish woman?

Prehistoric drawings discovered on the walls of the Cave of Altamira.

came to Spain from Byzantium (Constantinople, Istanbul). Byzantine Romans had been sent by Emperor Justinian to aid the Visigothic King Athanagild, and held parts of Southern Spain. It was only natural that their artistic ideas should spread. Crude but barbarously splendid Visigothic crowns and jewels can be seen in the *Armería* of Madrid and in the Cluny Museum in Paris.

Was the irruption of the not very civilized Gothic tribes into Spain a misfortune? No. They at least gave Spain an infusion of fresh, vigorous blood, and the religious and legal organization which they developed served in the end to reinforce Roman civilization. Their contribution in the realm of jurisprudence was highly significant. The code of laws promulgated by kings Chindaswinth and Recceswinth, called the *Lex Visigothorum* and later the *Fuero Juzgo,* was most useful and served as a basis for later compilations. Unfortunately the whole Visigothic period was marked by numerous civil wars, and the nobles were fractious and rebellious. The kings were elected by the nobles, and many elections were attended by sanguinary contests. The central royal authority was only occasionally strong, the various social classes had too few common bonds and the country was in no condition to unite efficiently against a common foe. A large degree of disintegration was evident when Spain was invaded from Africa in the early eighth century.

# IV

## The Moors Enrich Spain

### EARLY MOSLEM INVASIONS

PEOPLE whose religion was Mohammedan and whose complexion was dark, indiscriminately called Moors, were in the Iberian Peninsula for nearly eight hundred years. In other words the Christian Spaniards did not show great speed in driving them out during the period known as the Reconquest. The presence of the "Moors" was by no means an unmitigated disaster, because their culture was rich and splendid, and they contributed much to Spain and the rest of Europe.

Arabia in the seventh century A.D. was inhabited by a number of warlike tribes, many of whom were quite uncivilized and had no national consciousness. They were converted to Mohammedanism after the Hegira (622) and became its chief sword-bearers. By the early years of the eighth century they had overrun, in addition to other regions, nearly all of Syria and North Africa, putting the Berbers, who were Semitic in race and had an admixture of Vandal blood, under their rule. In the time of the Visigothic King Wamba (672-680) an attack by North African Moslems was even made on the eastern coast of Spain; but it was repulsed, as was a later attack.

However, the Visigothic monarchy was growing weaker. One king, Wamba, was strong, but he displeased various nobles and churchmen, who finally seized him, gave him a narcotic, tonsured him, and forced him to end his days in a monastery. Erwig was put on the throne, soon to be ousted by Wamba's nephew Egica. The latter was succeeded by his son Witiza, whose succession was favored by the church. The Gothic nobles, however, had another candidate, Roderic, who made good his claim by force of arms. Not for long, however. Oppas, Bishop of Seville, intriguing with the sons of Witiza for the overthrow of Roderic, invited Count Julian, the Eastern Roman Emperor's governor of Ceuta, to send African troops over to crush Roderic. It is likely that the oppressed Spanish Jews had a hand in the matter also. An Arab chief, Musa, authorized by the Caliph of Damascus, had, in 710, already sent a force under Tarik to reconnoitre in Spain, and the coming of African Moslems would have been inevitable even if Oppas had never summoned them.

In 711 Tarik and about seven thousand Berber troops landed at the spot now called Gibraltar (i.e., *Tarik's Mountain*). Roderic, with a force of sixty thousand, hastened to meet the enemy, and they joined a battle which lasted for three days, at the junction of the Guadelete and Guadalquivir rivers. Roderic would have won, but the troops of Oppas and of Witiza's sons turned against him (some say they merely deserted), and Tarik was joined by Julian and five thousand more Berbers. Roderic and his Goths were overwhelmed, and Roderic himself was never heard of again. His disappearance is thus described in the First General Chronicle of Spain: "No one knows what befell King Roderic in this mêlée; but his crown and his clothes and his royal insignia and his shoes of gold and of precious stones and his horse Orella were found in a mudhole by the river Guadelete, but not his body."

Legend puts the matter more picturesquely. Roderic is supposed to have let his royal eyes rest on the beautiful form of Count Julian's daughter as she bathed in a patio which could be seen from his palace window. Admiration was swiftly followed by seduction, and when Julian in cold fury sought the aid of Oppas and brought Africans to Spain in irresistible numbers, his vengeance was accomplished. It is further related that Roderic did not really die in battle near the Guadelete, but escaped to a solitary hermitage in Portugal to lead a life of dreadful penance. There is a concomitant legend that Roderic opened a forbidden chest in a locked house in Toledo, only to find in the bottom a cloth with a picture of a swarthy man, and the statement that Spain would be conquered by his like if anyone dared to violate the secret of the chest. Roderic's legend flourished luxuriantly, appearing in all sorts of forms in ballads, novels and dramas up to our own times. Southey's *Roderick* is the version probably best known to English readers.

## THE MOSLEM OCCUPATION

The Moslem conquest of the Peninsula was rapid, and by 718 was complete except for small mountainous regions in the far north. Spain was organized under an emir subject to the governor of Moslem Africa, who in turn owed obedience to the caliph of Damascus. Such was the official theory, but in fact the Spanish Moslems enjoyed a high degree of independence. The subject Christians were not on the whole treated very harshly, even though a fifth or more of the lands were confiscated and various taxes were imposed. Yet Catholic Spaniards were in the main allowed to practise their own religion. These Christians living in Moslem territory were called *Mozárabes*. Those who were converted to Mohammedanism were termed *renegados,* though they preferred to call themselves *Muladíes*. The bishops of the Catholic church were appointed or deposed by the Moslem authorities, who also summoned the church councils. The lot of the Jews now improved enormously under the rule of their fellow Semites.

During the first forty years of Moslem occupation there were numerous quarrels, involving sanguinary fighting between rival parties among the conquerors, as there had been in the East between the Ommeyads and their finally successful rivals the Abbassides. One Ommeyad youth, Abd-er-Rahman, managed to escape, and after taking refuge in Africa succeeded in setting himself up as emir in Cordova. His rule extended from 755 to 788, and it was during his time that the great Mosque of Cordova was begun. The unconquered Christians, pushed into the northern mountain fastnesses, early began to try to regain their lost lands. The chieftain Pelayo won a small but sentimentally important victory at Covadonga in 718, thus beginning the reconquest, if that is a fair term to apply to a process which took seven hundred years and more. Pelayo, thought of as the founder of the Spanish monarchy, was king of Asturias. Navarre and Aragon gradually extended their borders, and the Moslems were driven out of Catalonia at about the beginning of the ninth century. The counts of Barcelona made themselves virtually independent. All was not harmony among the Christian kinglets either, and in their quarrels they did not hesitate to bring in Moslem aid. It took a long time for any real spirit of unity to develop in reconquered Spain, even when the southern border had been pushed to a line running roughly from about Coimbra, in Portugal, over to Toledo and thence northeast to the region around Pamplona.

Two important events took place in the later eighth century. One was the invasion of Spain by Charlemagne, who finally penetrated as far as Saragossa. When he was leaving through the pass of Roncesvalles (Roncevaux) his rear-guard was set upon by Basque mountaineers and Count Roland killed, a small historical basis for the great French epic, the *Song of Roland*. Another event was the discovery during the reign of Alfonso the Chaste (791-842) of the body of St. James the Greater, Spain's patron. The corpse is supposed to have been wafted in a stone coffin from Palestine across seas and mountains to Galicia, and was enshrined at Santiago de Compostela. The spot became a center of pilgrimages ranking next to Jerusalem and Rome, and the road leading to it, the "Way of St. James," was trod by countless thousands of foreigners, especially visitors from France. Santiago thus became an important center for the spread of French culture in the Peninsula.

The disorder in Moslem Spain did not cease with the advent of the first Abd-er-Rahman. The third ruler of Cordova of that name (912-961) was a really strong sovereign who deserved his assumed title of caliph. He not only brought rival Moslem factions under his control, but also pushed back the Christian kings in the North and even extended his sway over northern Africa. Agriculture, industry and trade flourished in his realm, and culture reached a high level. Abd-er-Rahman III's son Hakem II continued his father's strong policy, and devoted even more attention to intellectual activities. At the time of Hakem's death his son Hisham II was a minor, and the caliphate was ruled by a certain Mahomet, who had won the favor of Hakem's favorite wife. Mahomet was called Almansor ("Victorious through God's Aid") and won his title by gaining many victories over the northern Christians. His son Abdul-Malek continued his father's tradition, but the Almansor family fell in 1009, and with it the caliphate split. At one time in the eleventh century Moslem Spain was composed of no less than twenty-three separate little kingdoms, or *taifas,* of which Seville gradually became the most important. If the Christian kings had been more united, they might have driven the Moslems out. They did at least continue their general push southward, and the heads of the *taifas* sought the aid of the Almoravides, Moslem Puritans who had mastered northern Africa. Their stern and barbarous king Yusuf crossed the Mediterranean in 1086 and inflicted a crushing defeat on the army of Alfonso VI of Castile near Badajoz. Yusuf went back to Africa, but four years later returned and made himself master of all Moslem Spain except Saragossa, which was won by his successor.

Meanwhile, another fierce Moslem sect arose in Africa, the Almohades. In the century after Yusuf the Almoravides themselves became soft and sybaritic; the country was again split into *taifas* and was ripe for invasion. The Almohades fell upon the Peninsula in 1146 and in a quarter of a century had non-Christian Spain in their power. The Almohades were fierce and fanatical Berbers, and persecuted the Arabs and Jews as they did the Christians (Mozárabes). Their leader Yacub defeated Alfonso VIII of Castile in 1195, but the Christians had their revenge in the great battle of Las Navas de Tolosa (1212) in which the power of the Almohades was broken. The little Moslem states were conquered one by one, except Granada, which managed to maintain itself for two and a half centuries.

## PROSPERITY AND LEARNING

A recital of dynasties, invasions and battles in Moorish Spain is likely to be more informative than thrilling, but the accounts of Cordova, "the Bride of Andalusia," make fascinating reading. When London and Paris were smallish and filthy cities, Cordova stretched for ten miles along the banks of the smooth-flowing Guadalquivir and contained 200,000 houses, 600 mosques, 900 bath houses (!) and more than half a million inhabitants. Among its lovely palaces was Medinat-ez-Zahra, really a whole town built by Abd-er-Rahman III for his favorite wife. Perhaps allowance should be made for a certain oriental tendency toward exaggeration in the Moorish chroniclers, but they report that ten thousand men labored for forty years to build it. There were four thousand columns of marble or other ornamental stone, and fifteen thousand doors coated with iron or brass. The Hall of the Caliphs had a roof and walls of marble and gold, and one room contained a large basin of quicksilver, a present from the Greek emperor. At either side of the room were eight doors, set in ivory and ebony and adorned with precious stones. Nearly fourteen thousand male servants were in attendance, and the number of women, comprising the Caliph's harem and its servants, was 6,314. There were more than three thousand Slav pages and eunuchs.

Such wealth could come only from prosperous agriculture and commerce. It was accompanied by equally impressive cultural splendor. With the possible exception of Constantinople, Cordova was unquestionably in the tenth century the most civilized spot in Europe, at a time when the ancestors of most of us were physically and culturally unwashed. The library at Cordova, the greatest since that at Alexandria, is said to have contained four hundred thousand volumes, and was the delight of the scholarly Caliph Hakem II. The title catalogue alone comprised forty-four volumes. Schools were encouraged, and Hakem, in his efforts to diffuse culture, supported out of his privy purse twenty-seven free institutions of learning in Cordova. The University, with classes conducted in the great Mosque, attracted thousands of students not only from Spain but also from other parts of Europe. Hakem himself was a generous patron of men of learning, irrespective of their religion or country, displaying a tolerance that was later to be matched by Alfonso X of Castile.

The cities of Moslem Spain produced many men of high achievement, Arabic and Jewish scholars who were eminent in medicine, mathematics, astronomy, botany, history, jurisprudence, lexicography, grammar, geography and philosophy. This learning was not indigenous with the Arabs, but had its roots mainly in the ancient Greek culture, parts of which were thus developed and transmitted to the rest of Europe by the Moslems in Spain and Sicily. The earlier of these Spanish-Moslem scholars knew the Greek philosophers through the Byzantine Greeks. The Cordovan Aben-Masarra (883-931) influenced Avicebron and the Franciscan thinkers up to Duns Scotus. Aben-Hazam (994-1064), vizier of Cordova, is noted for a psychologically penetrating *Treatise on Love* (a subject in which the Arabs in general possessed some competence) and still more for his learned *Critical History of Religions*. His successors Avempace, Aben-Tofail and Averroes represent the Aristotelian philosophical current. The last mentioned is especially noteworthy. He was born in Cordova in 1126, studied medicine and law, enjoyed high political favor, was despoiled of his honors and banished, was restored to favor, and died in Morocco in 1198. His works are commentaries on Aristotle, whom he worshipped, or original treatises influenced by the great Greek. Averroes sought not only to interpret Aristotelianism, but also to reconcile science and religion. He accepted revelation, and taught that in case of conflict science should give way, an opinion shared by St. Thomas Aquinas. Averroes' commentaries were used throughout Europe in mediaeval schools, even though what was called Averroism, a very false interpretation of his doctrine, was regarded as blasphemous and was universally condemned. Another philosopher was the pantheistic mystic Mohidin Aben-Arabi (1164-1240), who influenced not only most of Islam but also Ramón Lull, the great Spanish philosopher of the thirteenth century, and Dante.

The pursuit of learning was paralleled by the development of literature and the arts, including compositions in verse. Arabic poetry is characterized by bold figures of speech, rich imagery and pomp of verbiage. Narrative poetry made little progress, but the lyric, especially the erotic, often imbued with lush sensuality, enjoyed great favor. The official language of Moslem territory was Arabic, and that was the language in which the more respected

forms of poetry were written. However, poetry sprang up in Andalusian *romance,* sometimes interspersed with Arabic, for the delight of the common people, in the market-place or on the streets.
The populace had no objection to crudity or to obscenity. A collection of such songs is to be found in the song-book of Aben-Cuz-
man.

Many of the artists and scholars in southern Spain were not Moslems or Christians, but Jews. One of the ministers of Abd-er-Rahman III was the Jewish physician Hasdai ben-Chaprut (945-970),
who encouraged the intellectual and artistic development of his coreligionists. The greatest of the Spanish Sephardic Jews was "the
St. Thomas Aquinas of Judaism," Moses ben-Maimon, better
known as Maimonides (1135-1204). The best known among the
scientific and philosophical works of this learned Cordovan is his
*Guide for Those Who Have Strayed* (*Moreh Nebukim*), composed
in Arabic but translated into Hebrew, Latin and various European
languages. It is in the main an effort to reconcile faith and reason,
and was utilized not only by Jews and Arabs but also by such
Christian philosophers as Albertus Magnus and St. Thomas
Aquinas himself.

## MOORISH ART AND MUSIC

The Spanish Arabs, not including the Berbers, loved to live surrounded by beauty in all its forms. They possessed a true artistic
sense, which displayed itself in design, in decoration rather than in
structure: witness the very word "arabesque." The modern world
is fortunate in possessing examples such as the Alhambra, the Ge-
neralife, the Alcázar of Seville, the Mosque of Cordova, and the
Giralda of Seville. The last, begun in the eleventh century to serve
as a minaret for the muezzin's call, though graceful and formerly
surmounted by a spire, has an appearance of solidity unusual in
Moorish structures. Any visitor to Spanish-Moorish buildings realizes, as he goes through patios refreshed with fountains or limpid
pools, through rooms whose walls are covered with lace-like trac-
eries of vividly colored plaster, beneath ceilings which suggest a

brilliant summer sky, through lush well-watered gardens, that the Spanish Moors were really gifted in adapting their buildings to a sophisticated and pleasurable mode of life in a sub-tropical climate. They felt, too, that God could be worshipped with sensuous beauty, and the Mosque of Cordova, with its thousand columns of granite and marble, of jasper and porphyry, its gorgeously ornamented walls, its lovely sanctuaries, its high minaret and its tranquil patio with lemon and orange trees, was reared to a God of loveliness and not to a stern and vengeful Jehovah. It is fascinating to speculate upon the emotions of a Jonathan Edwards if he had tried to preach there a sermon to and about *Sinners in the Hands of an Angry God*.

Although the Spanish Moslems took the Second Commandment literally, they did sometimes make sculptured representations of animals, as in the famous *Patio de los Leones* in the Alhambra. The little stone lions look neither happy nor lifelike. The Arabs did not develop the arts of painting and sculpture, but they were renowned throughout the world for their jewels and mosaics, for their work in ivory, enamel, silver and gold, their ceramics and their textiles. Their art as well as their architecture was mainly Byzantine in origin, but they improved on their models. Their method of incrusting iron with gold and silver (damascening) is still in use today in Spain. Moorish glass mosaics, like those in the Mihrab of the mosque at Cordova, are extraordinarily brilliant. Their glazed tiles (*azulejos*) in various colors possessed a lustre which has not been equalled, and were used, as imitations of them are still used, to decorate walls, well-heads, benches, etc. The glazing of pottery was really a fine art. Potters used an elaborate process of mixing copper, silver, sulphur, red ochre and vinegar. The mixture was applied over enamel, and a special firing for six hours was accomplished in an oven heated with dried rosemary twigs. The pottery, after burnishing, had a golden gleam which made it the most prized ceramic ware in Europe. The Valencians continued the tradition for a long time, until in the sixteenth century Italian pottery supplanted the Hispano-Moresque. Before then Italians called much Spanish pottery Majolica because it was carried to Italy in Majorcan boats.

It is said that at one time in Cordova there were 30,000 looms for silk-weaving, and in Seville even more. Both silks and woollens were often decorated with raised embroidery (*recamado*) of gold. Linen tapestries, woven mainly at Chinchilla, Valencia, Murcia and Granada, were greatly praised by contemporaries. A probable example of this work is the banner captured by the Christians at Las Navas de Tolosa, which is crimson, with raised gold embroidery and elaborate decorations of white, yellow, green and blue. It is preserved in the monastery of Las Huelgas, near Burgos. Gold adornment was also used on leather, for which the workers of Cordova were particularly famous.

The material artistic accomplishments of the Spanish Moors can still be seen and appreciated. Unfortunately their music cannot. Were they fond of music? Passionately. Here is the testimony of an eleventh century gentleman named Ahmed bin Muhammad Al-Yemeni:

"I was in Malaga, a Spanish city, in the year 406 of the Hegira (1015 A.D.) and was kept indoors for a long time by illness. Two friends, mindful of my delirium, cared for me tenderly. It was at night especially that I felt wakeful. All around my house there was an incessant jangle of singing, and of lutes, tambours and lyres, which disturbed me intensely and added to the restlessness and suffering caused by my illness. These toccatas and songs nailed themselves to my mind without hope of respite, so that I was filled with loathing for them, and would have liked to find a house away from all the noise. But this was difficult in Malaga, for the people are absolutely dominated by their passion for music. One night I awoke after dozing a little, and noticed that the tumult of odious voices and turbulent tunes had calmed down, leaving only a breath of sound, tranquil and lovely. I felt that my soul understood this music and could find repose in it, with none of the repugnance I had felt for the other. It was purely instrumental, without the human voice. Then it began increasing slowly in volume. I was drawn to it and disposed to listen, even when it reached the fullest possible strength. I found myself forgetting my misery in the emotional enjoyment, which almost caused me to imagine that the walls and floor were floating around me. And all this time there had been no sound of a human voice. I said to myself: 'For instrumental music, nothing could be more perfect. What kind of a voice will the musician have? How will it end?' Scarcely was the question asked before there came the sound of a woman's voice, clear and beautiful. I could not contain myself and got up, leaving my two companions sleeping. I opened the door of my room and followed the sound until I reached the part of the house whence I could overlook the neighbors. I saw a large garden with about twenty people in the center, seated in a row, with sweets, fruits and drinks before them. The girl who was singing sat apart from the others, and held her listeners spellbound. She sang and sang, and I, hidden above, could watch without being seen. As she sang a verse, I learned it, until I knew quite a number. Finally I withdrew to my room, thanking God, as though I had come out of a great trouble and were no longer ill or suffering. The next morning I got up, and went to see a friend, the Ulema of Cordova, who was living in Malaga, and told him what had happened. I recited the verses and described the house. He smilingly answered: 'That is the house of the minister so and so, and the slave girl comes from Bagdad, one of the best singers of Al-Mansur bin Abi Amir. She came into the possession of this minister after the death of Al-Mansur. The poems were written by the Spanish poet Muhammed bin Carloman.' " (Quoted from Julián Ribera, *La música de las cantigas,* translated and abridged by Eleanor Hague and Marion Leffingwell under the title *Music in Ancient Arabia and Spain,* Stanford University Press, 1929.)

Since with one unimpressive exception no Arab tune was recorded until the end of the eighteenth century, no one can say exactly how this music sounded, but there is abundant testimony to its popularity among Moors and Christians alike. From theoretical works like those of the great Al-Farabi (872-950) it is possible to learn something of the highly complicated rhythms and elaborate scales in vogue. The fundamental melodies seem to have been simple, the adornments quite elaborate, as in modern Spanish folk music. The octave was divided into seventeen notes, one-third tones,

giving absolutely perfect major thirds and sixths and minor sev-
enths. The scale was later of twenty-three quarter tones. Numerous
musical instruments were in use, including the lute, which the
Arabs introduced into Europe.

No amount of theoretical information quite explains the pleasure
of the gentleman in Malaga.

# V

## Christian Spain to 1252

### WAR AND CONQUEST

IF the civilization of the Moslem Spanish provinces seems splendid and brilliant, life in the little Christian states in the North, Asturias, León, Castile, Navarre, Aragon, Catalonia, seems dingy and squalid. However, by the middle of the thirteenth century, Castile had established its definite hegemony and prepared the way for the vigorous era of world-wide discovery and conquest that quickened the sixteenth century. Count Fernán González had made Castile independent of León and Asturias, and in the century after him Fernando I of Castile (1037-1065) became decidedly the most powerful of the Christian sovereigns of Spain. Fernando's son Alfonso VI (1065-1109) became king of Castile and León, extending his sway permanently over Toledo, and pushing on to Moorish Valencia. His reign included most of the career of the great Spanish national hero, Rodrigo Díaz de Bivar, better known as the Cid (ca. 1043-1099). The Cid was a vigorous servant of his sovereign, an excellent organizer, a truly great warrior and a loving husband and father. If he showed a stern fierceness, a lack of delicacy toward his enemies, and other vices likely to be encountered in primitive heroes, he also possessed virtues which have caused him to be celebrated from his own time to the present, in history, legend and song.

Alfonso granted territory in the north of what is now Portugal to his daughter Teresa's husband, Count Henry of Lorraine, thereby originating the Portuguese monarchy. Their son Alfonso Enriques was crowned king in 1145; in 1148 he captured Lisbon from the Moslems.

There was considerable strife in Castile in the first half of the twelfth century. Alfonso VIII (1158-1214) managed during his able reign to unite the Christians against the Moslems, and won the great victory of Las Navas de Tolosa in 1212. Alfonso's contingents included not only Castilians, Aragonese and Navarrese, but also French, German and even English warriors. Alfonso VIII's grandson Ferdinand III (1217-1252) was called Saint Ferdinand more for his victories over the enemies of the cross than for gentle piety. To the Christian dominions he added Cordova, Murcia and Seville before the middle of the century, and for the next two hundred and fifty years the Crescent waved over only a small and diminishing portion of the far south.

The three great military orders of Spain, so often mentioned in literature, those of Calatrava, Santiago and Alcántara, were founded in the twelfth century, and a fourth, Montesa, in 1317. The proud knights, *comendadores* and grand masters of these orders, which continued in existence through the time of Alfonso XIII, were a great force in the reconquest, and were much involved in the political activities of the kingdom.

Aragon, small at first, increased its dominions by inheritance, by the peaceful absorption of Navarre (1076) and by conquests of Moorish territory. In 1118 Alfonso I, the Battler, captured Saragossa, and pushed on as far as Murcia. Alfonso II inherited both Aragon and Catalonia, in addition to large territories in southern France. He cooperated with Alfonso VIII of Castile in victorious combats against the Moors.

In the fighting in the south of France during the Albigensian Crusades, Alfonso II's son Peter II was killed by Simon de Montfort. This death was not the only feature of these sanguinary crusades which affected Spain, for it was in connection with the Albigensian heresy that the Inquisition arose in southern France, and that institution was later to become famous below the Pyrenees. The same crusades brought into prominence a Spanish monk named Domingo de Guzmán, better known to us as St. Dominic, founder of the celebrated order which bears his name. St. Dominic vigorously censured Simon de Montfort for his cruelty.

Peter II was succeeded by the greatest monarch in Aragonese history, James I, the Conqueror (*Jaime el Conquistador*), a worthy compeer of Ferdinand III of Castile. When Jaime was a boy he had been a ward in the dangerous hands of Simon de Montfort, from whom he was taken by Pope Innocent III. Jaime was in full command of his kingdom by 1228, and he then began a career of foreign expansion which was to continue long after Aragon and Castile were united, and which bore significant political, economic and cultural results for all the Peninsula. In his desire to protect Mediterranean trade, Jaime conquered Mallorca in 1229, and the other Balearic islands in the ensuing six years. Valencia, conquered by the Cid in 1096 and held for three years after the hero's death, had fallen back into Moslem possession. Jaime rewon it in 1238. When he captured Murcia, he loyally kept his agreement to hand it over to Alfonso X of Castile: a hint at least of the final unity of Spain. Jaime was vigorous, highly sensual, and ferociously cruel (he had the tongue of the Bishop of Gerona cut out, then built and endowed a monastery to atone for his deed). At the same time he was deeply religious and unusually magnanimous. "He was a man, take him for all in all," and Aragon did not look upon his like again.

## THE MEDIAEVAL SOCIAL ORDER

The kings of Castile and Aragon did not accomplish their ends without the aid of their nobles, and the nobles lost none of the proud independence which they had shown since Visigothic days. In fact they not only fought each other, but at times challenged and resisted the royal prerogative. A new order also sprang up, the *caballeros,* who were plebeian in origin and at times took the side of the king against the hereditary noblemen. Later they tended to ally themselves with the rest of the nobility. The bishops and upper clergy were vigorous in furthering the interests of the church, and its position improved considerably.

Since Spain prospered materially, in agriculture, industry and trade, the free middle class became much more important, and the lot of the serfs was perceptibly bettered. The Jews had more ad-

"Castles in Spain."

*Gramstorff Bros.*

The Roman-built aqueduct of Segovia, still in use.

Alcántara Bridge, Toledo. Roman, Moorish and Spanish construction.

*Gramstorff Bros.*

The walled city of Avila de los Caballeros.

The Synagogue of Toledo, now called Santa María la Blanca.

A few of the thousand columns of the Mosque of Cordova.

The Moorish tower of the Giralda, by the cathedral in Seville.

The Court of the Myrtles, in the Alhambra of Granada.

The Court of the Lions, in the Alhambra.

The Hall of the Ambassadors, in the Alhambra.

Zuloaga: "Albarracín." A town
in the province of Teruel.

Dancing in the Gypsy section
of Granada.

vantages than at any other period of Spain's history, though their condition began to worsen by the beginning of the thirteenth century. The *Mozárabes* and *Mudéjares* (Moors living in Christian territory) got along very well indeed.

For centuries in Spain kings occasionally summoned councils of nobles and churchmen, but the people were not represented. The town representatives were admitted to a council in León in 1188, probably the first time in Europe that the towns were represented in such an assembly. These *Cortes* theoretically had no legislative power whatever, and the king was and continued to be the chief law-making authority. However, since the sovereign sought the advice of his Cortes and they exercised the right to decide how much money they would grant him, they often petitioned for and obtained desired legislation. The towns themselves had their own councils and officials, of whom the most important were the *alcaldes,* half mayors and half judges. In practise the towns were relatively independent of the king. Occasionally the towns would band together into brotherhoods (*hermandades*) and, like the nobles, might even wage war on their own account.

Justice was supposed to reside in the king, but the municipal *alcaldes* often assumed criminal as well as civil jurisdiction. Calderón's play *El Alcalde de Zalamea* well illustrates this tendency, and shows that the spirit of individual and municipal independence had by no means been suppressed in the latter sixteenth century. Forms of punishment in mediaeval Spain were no gentler than elsewhere in Europe: burning at the stake, burial alive, starvation, flogging, drowning, mutilation, or mere merciful hanging were in vogue. Torture and the "vulgar proofs," the ordeal by hot water, hot iron, and the wager of battle, were regularly used in the processes of "justice."

Although the Spanish Church grew in wealth and influence, it became slightly less national, for the Cluniac monks and a series of vigorous Popes caused the king to participate very little in ecclesiastical affairs. The monasteries and the Military Orders became independent of the bishops and were under the direct authority of the Pope or his legate. The Franciscans and the Dominicans worked mightily and successfully for the cause of religion.

Social customs were very different from ours of the present day. There were two sorts of marriage: *con bendición* (with the blessing of the church), and *a yuras,* a simple sort of contract. A third sort of union, *barraganía,* is supposed to have come into use through Mohammedan influence, and was recognized socially though not legally. Both parties were supposed to be single, but many married men thus extended their sphere of feminine influence, and so did some gentlemen in holy orders. The Church, obviously, frowned on the practice.

If the palaces of the kings and nobles in Christian Spain were rather barren affairs with no modern conveniences, it is easy to imagine how the mass of the people lived. Some houses had hearths and chimneys, and some even had glass panes in the windows, but most did not. Sanitary arrangements caused no worry at all, and diseases due to lack of sanitation were viewed as acts of God or the Devil. People usually slept on benches or on the dirt floor, though beds were beginning to come into use. Chairs were much less used than stools. Clothes were normally worn until they disintegrated, without being changed or washed. Effeminate garments such as nightgowns, male or female, were practically unknown, for people slept in all or part of their clothes or none. Since the climate was warm the greater part of the year and there was no such thing as refrigeration, meat was cooked with as many spices as possible to disguise putrescence. Meat was regarded as much more desirable than vegetables. It still is in Spain. Forks were unknown as yet, and individual plates little used.

The gallantry which we romantically attribute to the Middle Ages (a legacy from Sir Walter Scott?) was mainly a literary concept. There was real affection for wife and children and members of the household, of course, but woman's place was the home. Witness the proverb:

> La mujer casada,
> La pierna quebrada,
> Y en casa.

*A married woman's token*
*Is that her leg is broken,*
*And she stays at home.*

Although families tended to be large, the population of the country did not increase very rapidly. Man kept it down by wars and nature still more with plagues and diseases.

# VI

## From Alfonso X to Ferdinand and Isabella

### CIVIL DISSENSION (1252-1469)

FTER the time of Fernando III (1217-1252), the Moslems were no longer a serious threat to Christian Spain, and Spaniards had greater leisure to fight each other. Nobles fought one another, or the towns, or the king, with the higher churchmen occasionally entering the fray. The power of the sovereign was challenged, and might upon occasion yield to opposition, but the general tendency was decidedly toward an increase in the royal authority, a preparation for the highly centralized political system of Charles V and Philip II.

Fernando III's son was Alfonso X (1252-1284), whose nickname "El Sabio" means "The Learned" rather than "The Wise." It is customary to quote concerning him the dictum of the great historian Mariana: "Dumque coelum considerat observatque astra terram amisit," but the statement is hardly accurate. It is true that the king was interested in the sky and the stars, in science and in learning in general, but he did not neglect the more practical matters of earth. He was confronted with a difficult political situation and was not temperamentally fitted to cope with it. He won a few victories against the Moors, but unfortunately in one of the battles in 1275, his eldest son Alfonso de la Cerda was killed, creating rivalry with regard to the succession. Alfonso el Sabio lost much that he might have kept. He had an excellent claim to Gascony, which had come to the Spanish crown as the dowry of Eleanor of Aquitaine, wife of Alfonso VIII. Alfonso X, however, gave up all his claims when his sister married Prince Edward (I, of England and Aquitaine). Furthermore Alfonso was elected Holy Roman Emperor in 1257, but the opposition of several German princes and of the Pope, Alfonso's wars with the Moslems and with his own nobles, and the general lack of enthusiasm in Castile for the project combined to prevent him from ever going to Germany, and Rudolph of Hapsburg was finally chosen instead. Alfonso's nobles seized every pretext to combat their sovereign, and they were joined by the king's second son Sancho, who claimed the throne instead of allowing it to go, as Alfonso desired, to the son of the dead first son, Alfonso de la Cerda. The learned king was actually deposed in a Cortes held in 1282, and although he managed to win back some of the disaffected nobles, clergy and towns, he survived for only two years: a sad close for a reign which was culturally and artistically so brilliant.

Alfonso in his will disinherited Sancho, but the unfilial son was not the sort to let a scrap of paper stand in his way. He came to the throne as Sancho IV ("the Fierce"), but he too found his nobles hard to cope with. He put them down with an iron hand—at one time, for example, executing no less than four thousand partisans of his nephew. Civil strife continued after his death, for his son Fernando IV ("the Summoned") was only nine years old. Fortunately the lad's mother, María de Molina, one of the great women of Spanish history, by her moral authority and her political acumen managed to ally many nobles and towns with her son and to break up the plans made for invasion of Castile by Aragon, Granada, Portugal and France. The last two merely wished to do a little land-grabbing at the expense of a supposedly weak neighbor, a desire which springs eternal in the breasts of unscrupulous national leaders. Ferdinand, after displaying foul ingratitude toward his mother, who was a much better man than he, was killed in a minor campaign against the Moors, leaving as his heir a one-year-old boy.

This child, Alfonso XI, was most fortunate in his choice of grandmothers. María de Molina again came to the rescue and put down all insurrections of the turbulent nobles. Alfonso was declared of age at fourteen, and although he died before reaching forty, he established a reputation as one of the best kings that Spain ever had. His qualities were those needed in a rough age: vigor, single-mindedness, ruthlessness, and a diplomatic skill very close to craftiness. He did a great deal to increase the prestige of the crown, and managed to curb the power of the nobility without incurring too great enmity. He won the favor of the people by turning an attentive ear to their complaints and correcting abuses committed by his own representatives, by nobles or churchmen. It was therefore much easier for him to maintain the principle that legislation, as well as the interpretation of laws, was a function of the sovereign alone.

Alfonso XI's principal achievement was in political organization, but he was no mean soldier. In alliance with Aragon and Portugal he won an important victory over a coalition of Moors at El Salado, near Tarifa, in 1340. The Basque province of Alava was also added to the throne of Castile during this great king's reign.

Alfonso had only one legitimate son, Pedro el Cruel. He committed enough murders and other crimes richly to deserve his title of Peter the Cruel, though because he often championed the people against the nobles, popular tradition called him Peter the Justice-Dealer (*Pedro el Justiciero*). Perhaps his most endearing quality was his singular fidelity to his mistress, María de Padilla, a lady of excellent family, and the only person who seemed able to control her lover's vicious tendencies. Pedro's Portuguese minister Alburquerque persuaded him to contract a marriage with a French princess, Blanche of Bourbon, but Pedro endured the married estate only three days before flying back to the arms of María. The Pope disapproved, and insisted that Pedro return to his lawfully wedded wife, but Pedro found two bishops who were willing to declare the marriage void. Blanche was merely another victim of royal intrigue. Pedro later married Juana de Castro, but he stayed with her only one day, and then went back to María.

Pedro's nobles, usually joined by his illegitimate half-brothers, fought him at the rattle of a spear. Finally the oldest brother, Enrique (Henry) de Trastamara, won the support of the "White Companies," the Foreign Legion of those days, a band of adventurers led by the French Bertrand du Guesclin. Pope Innocent VI at Avignon offered Bertrand and his trained mob a large sum to leave France, and Enrique's ally, Pedro IV of Aragon, offered them an equal amount plus rights of pillage (except in Aragon) to come to Spain to fight Pedro. With the aid of these splendid ruffians Enrique won most of Castile. Pedro persuaded Edward III of England to help him, and Edward sent troops under the Black Prince, who defeated Enrique. The Cruel Monarch then engaged in such an orgy of ruthless promise-breaking and sadistic enemy-killing that the chivalrous Black Prince left in disgust. Enrique and Du Guesclin inflicted a crushing defeat upon Pedro at Montiel, even capturing the king in person, through trickery. The half-brothers fought in mortal combat, and Pedro was slain (1369).

In order to secure allies, Enrique had been forced to grant extraordinary privileges to the nobles, and he and his successors were plagued by them for many a long year. Moreover there was another claimant for Enrique's throne in the person of Costanza, illegitimate daughter of Pedro and María de Padilla, now the wife of John of Gaunt, Duke of Lancaster. Enrique was succeeded by his son Juan I (1379-1390). John of Gaunt appeared in Spain with an English army to claim the throne for his wife, but the matter was amicably settled by the marriage of Lancaster's daughter to Juan's son Enrique. Juan's reign was marked by a serious defeat of the Spaniards by the Portuguese at Aljubarrota in 1385.

Enrique III (1390-1406) was called "the Sickly" (*El Doliente*), but the epithet applied to his facial pallor and not to his disposition. He was very energetic, and managed to curb the power of his nobles, partly by securing the favor of the middle classes. He increased the royal power in the towns by sending *regidores,* usually learned lawyers, to act as magistrates instead of municipally elected officials. Enrique made his armies strong enough to inflict a crushing defeat on the Portuguese in 1398.

There were three cosmopolitan features about the reign of Enrique III. For one thing, he had married an English princess, Catherine of Lancaster. For another he sent an embassy to faraway Samarkand to confer with the great Tamerlane. Furthermore, two adventurers, Rubín de Bracamonte and Juan de Bethencourt, initiated the conquest of the Canary Islands (1402) and acknowledged them as a fief of Castile. Enrique was planning to conquer Granada when he unfortunately died at the age of twenty-seven.

Juan II (1406-1454), Enrique's son, was only two years old. The kingdom was fortunate in having as regent Juan's uncle Fernando, an excellent warrior and administrator, but Fernando left Castile to become king of Aragon in 1412. Juan II was an extremely weak king, and for most of his reign was under the sway of a powerful and energetic noble, Don Alvaro de Luna. Jealous rivals openly expressed their opposition to the royal favorite, often in the form of armed conflict. Luna was able to keep them down, but he was finally accused of witchcraft and Juan was persuaded to order Luna's execution in 1453. The king survived his favorite by only a year, ending a reign important for literature but politically disastrous.

## JUANA LA BELTRANEJA

Enrique IV is known as "Henry the Impotent" (*Enrique el Impotente*), and he seems to have deserved his nickname. According to investigations recently published by Dr. Gregorio Marañón, this unfortunate king was at best a eunuchoid type of creature, with a weak mind and a loathsome face and body. He first married Blanche of Navarre, and divorced her because they had no children. Next he married Juana of Portugal, and they too were childless for six years. Then the queen bore a daughter, officially named Juana, and popularly called "la Beltraneja." The queen had shown a marked fondness for a royal favorite named Beltrán de la Cueva, who openly boasted of being her lover. Since the king swore on different occasions, first that the child was, and then that she was not his daughter, the question of her paternity was and is difficult to decide. At all events, she was a desperately unlucky person, born to become the pawn of political intrigues.

The strife of the nobles under a king so weak and vacillating as Enrique brought the country close to anarchy. The question of the succession was important enough: who was to be the heir, Enrique's younger brother Alfonso, or his half-sister Isabel (Isabella the Catholic) or his supposed daughter Juana la Beltraneja? More vitally important was the question as to whether Castile was to be a strong monarchy or a loosely organized territory ruled over by quasi-independent and greatly over-privileged nobles and church-men. In July 1465, Enrique's opponents went so far as to uncrown him in effigy at Avila, in a very picturesque though politically de-pressing ceremony. They declared Alfonso king, but the poor boy died in 1468, very probably poisoned. Isabella was betrothed to the luckless Prince of Viana. After his death she rejected a host of suitors, including Richard III of England and the brother of Louis XI of France, and finally in 1469 married Ferdinand of Aragon. Enrique died in 1474, and Isabella, skilfully thwarting Louis XI and Affonso V of Portugal, who favored La Beltraneja, soon estab-lished herself as sovereign of Castile. La Beltraneja retired to a convent in Portugal, where she ended her unhappy days. Spain had at last achieved practical unity by the joining of Aragon and Castile, and was ready for internal progress and foreign expansion.

## CENTRALIZATION AND EXPANSION

In Ferdinand's kingdom of Aragon the victory of the monarchy over the anarchic nobles had been accomplished sooner, by the middle of the fourteenth century. Civil war continued after that date, but it was mainly caused by the conflict of the great city of Barcelona against the royal authority and by a few civil uprisings elsewhere. In general social progress was relatively greater than in Castile, but then the Aragonese populace had had farther to go, and the masses had been less free in the east than in the center of the Peninsula.

In the two centuries before Ferdinand, Aragon had pursued a policy of vigorous expansion. Pedro III (1276-1285) established his sovereignty over Mallorca and a part of Tunisia. A complicated and difficult struggle gave him Sicily, which, along with Sardinia, finally became a part of the kingdom of Aragon.

The early years of the fourteenth century witnessed a picturesque expedition illustrative of the eastern expansion of the Peninsula. At the suggestion of the king of Sicily, the roving captain Roger de Flor took his Catalan and other mercenaries to the aid of the tottering Roman emperor of Constantinople, Michael Palaeologus. Roger and his men were highly successful in combatting the Turks, and Roger himself achieved such position that he married the Princess of Bulgaria. Not long afterward he was murdered by jealous Byzantine nobles, but his men took most sanguinary vengeance. Finally they went to the aid of the Duke of Athens, and when he became recalcitrant, they deposed him. Thus was established the Catalan Duchy of Athens, which lasted for some sixty years after 1326. A stirring and popular drama, *Catalan Vengeance* (*Venganza catalana*), based on Roger's expedition and written by García Gutiérrez, was presented in Madrid in 1864.

A much more important, though less colorful, event was the conquest of the Kingdom of Naples by the Aragonese king Alfonso V (the Magnanimous, 1416-1458). By 1443 this vigorous warrior had won Naples and the south of Italy, and in his Italian capital set up a brilliant court. By force of arms, then, Spain had conquered much of Italy: in return Italy took her victor into camp with the irresistible force of her new and vigorous Renaissance culture.

Alfonso the Magnanimous left Naples to an illegitimate son, but Aragon, Sicily and Sardinia to his brother Juan II (1458-1479). Juan's reign was full of strife. When he died, old, blind and abandoned, a new era began for a Spain now for the first time united under the "Catholic Sovereigns," Ferdinand and Isabella.

The salient feature of Spain's political history up to the time of Ferdinand and Isabella was the struggle of the monarchs against their anarchic nobles, and of the towns against the large landowners or even against the king himself. The *Cortes,* or national assembly, an institution which grew up in Spain before it did in the rest of Europe, diminished in power with the growth of royal authority in the fifteenth century.

## THE SOCIAL AND ECONOMIC SYSTEM

In Castile there were three main classes, since the serfs had gradually been freed: nobles, bourgeois and free laborers. The nobles were growing poorer, because their wealth came mainly from the land, and the rise of free labor and of industry was a distinct disadvantage to them. The landed clergy were in the same case. The position of the laborers was much improved. The middle class, of traders and manufacturers, residing in the towns, grew much more prosperous. It was mainly from them that the lawyers came, and these *letrados,* as they were called, came to exert greater and greater influence in matters of government.

In the east of the Peninsula the upper classes continued to hold almost all the land, and the serfs, called *colonos* or *payeses,* were attached to the land until they redeemed themselves by a money payment, which extremely few were able to make. Serious uprisings of the *payeses* occurred, notably in the fifteenth century. The middle class developed only in Barcelona, Valencia and a few other towns which enjoyed royal charters of privilege (*fueros*). These *fueros,* showing remarkable respect for the rights of man, were zealously cherished by the inhabitants.

As the Christian conquests grew, a great many Mohammedans and Jews were included in Spanish territory, and many Jews who had been driven out of Moslem cities were welcomed in Castile. From the end of the fourteenth century onward, however, the difference in religion between Christians and non-Christians assumed larger importance and the lot of the Jews and the *Mudéjares* grew notably worse. The cause of their mistreatment was theoretically religious in origin, but it was economic as well, for most of the industry and commerce had fallen into Semitic hands, and Christian jealousy was to be expected. The final fate of the Jews and *Mudéjares* a little later was to be expulsion from the country. The Jews fared worse than the *Mudéjares,* and sanguinary pogroms occurred in Toledo, Cordova and Seville. It has been estimated, probably with some exaggeration, that the number of Jews killed in Spain in the years 1431-1447 was 150,000, and the number converted to Christianity 15,000. Even conversion was no guarantee of prosperity or popularity, for the "old Christians" sometimes looked askance at the new *conversos.*

The general level of prosperity during the later middle ages was not very high and the standard of living was depressingly low, despite progress in agriculture, mining, textile weaving, industry and commerce. Labor achieved a certain degree of organization. Fairs and markets were encouraged and frequently held, and foreign merchants visited Spain. Spanish traders went as far as England and Flanders. Bills of exchange came into general use.

The crown claimed ownership of the subsoil and the coastal waters, hence fishing and the mining of quicksilver, silver, lead and gold were a royal monopoly and an important source of income for the royal treasury.

Trade was hindered by the collection of customs dues, not only at the borders of the separate kingdoms, but also at the gates of practically every town. The system of weights, measures and coinage was irregular. Counterfeiting became a well-developed practice, even though the legal penalty was death by burning. Forms of contract, rates of interest, hours of labor and often even prices were subject to strict royal regulation.

The sheep-raisers banded themselves together into an extremely powerful corporation known as the *mesta,* which had its own magistrates and system of justice, and enjoyed many economic privileges. The industrial organizations known as *gremios* (guilds) were formed only partly for economic purposes. Their activities were more of a religious, social or philanthropic nature.

And who paid taxes into the royal coffers? People of the lower and middle class, because the clergy and the nobility were exempt. Such was generally the case in the rest of Europe.

## MEDIAEVAL SPANISH LEARNING

The two main cultural influences in mediaeval Spain were the French and Moorish, happily followed by the Italian in the fifteenth century. Castilians gradually established themselves as leaders in all realms, and it was later to be a fundamentally Castilian culture that was transmitted to Spanish America.

Although much of the energy of Christian Spain from the eighth through the fifteenth centuries was devoted to driving out the

Moslems, intellectual activities were not neglected. They were indulged in by the few and not the many, but the same was true in the rest of Europe. In Spain, as elsewhere, such education as existed was largely in the hands of the church. Unfortunately no great teachers like Abelard arose to gather important groups of pupils around them. Groups of scholars did exist in Toledo with the encouragement of Alfonso VI and Alfonso VII, but it remained for Alfonso VIII to give learning distinct official sanction.

The dates of the foundation of the great Spanish and European universities are somewhat nebulous, but it was about 1209 that Alfonso VIII established the "General Studies" at Palencia, later to be fused with the University of Salamanca, which dates from only slightly later, perhaps 1215. Around the middle of the century the Universities of Valencia, Seville and Valladolid were established. Salamanca was and continued to be the greatest of these, vying in popularity with the earlier Universities of Paris, Bologna and Oxford. The students and teachers together formed a sort of guild (*cofradía*), elected their own rector, or president, and enjoyed about the same legal privileges as the clergy. The professors read manuscript texts and commented upon them, and the students could borrow books from the university library to correct their notes. Such libraries, and those in the hands of monasteries and even of rich private individuals, were increasing in numbers. Examinations were given for the conferring of the degrees of bachelor and master. Some of the poorer aspirants to knowledge supported themselves by begging. Students were occasionally not well behaved, even turbulent in fact, and some apparently paid more attention to unorganized extra-curricular activities than to their studies. Some of the more serious became highly learned in medicine, theology or law. The course of study, the university organization, the mode of dress and many other features of the mediaeval Spanish university would startle us now, but the underlying realities were very much the same. Professors and students are very persistent types, and the seven thousand or so who made up the corporation of Salamanca in its heyday would be fairly recognizable now.

Primary education outside the Church did not really exist. Likely lads might find a friendly priest. The rich might hire tutors. Girls were not supposed to have formal instruction and precious few of them did. Ninety-odd per cent of the population had to get along without knowledge directly obtained from books. They managed somehow. When the renewed zeal for learning and the invention of printing came to Spaniards in the latter fifteenth century, they were ready to reap the benefit.

# VII

## Mediaeval Epic and Lyric Poetry

### EPIC POETRY

JUST when Spanish became a language fit for literary expression cannot be definitely stated. The first literary monuments date from the middle of the twelfth century, but they evidently presuppose a certain tradition. Latin had become the official language of Spain in 206 B.C., and in the nine hundred years before the coming of the African invaders the language spoken in the Peninsula had developed marked differences from that spoken in Gaul, Italy, and elsewhere. The comparatively little writing that was done was as close an approximation to classical Latin as the authors could muster, but that Latin was not the basis of everyday speech. The Roman soldiers who came to Spain spoke a language (*sermo vulgaris,* Vulgar Latin) which was quite different from the cultivated speech of such literary exquisites as Cicero and Caesar, Vergil and Horace, and even of Latin-Spaniards like the Senecas, Martial and Quintilian. This popular speech came to be called *romance,* and was for a long time thought of as something rather low as compared with Latin. *Romance,* called Low Romance and spoken throughout the Roman world from the sixth to the tenth centuries, which was to develop in the Peninsula into Spanish, Portuguese and Catalan, becomes more frequent in documents from the tenth century onward.

The first great manifestation of literary art in Spain is to be found in the epic, which existed perhaps as early as the tenth century. How did it arise? No one can offer definite proofs, for lack of documents. Scholars have discarded the nineteenth century theory that epics arose from brief songs (*cantilènes*) composed shortly after the events they commemorate and put together into a larger whole. A theory of Joseph Bédier, that the French epic originated in monasteries where relics of the hero were kept, or which were in some way associated with him, might apply to Spain also. The late Julián Ribera, Professor of Arabic in the University of Madrid, thought that an epic existed in Moslem Andalusia which spread to Castile, but his arguments have convinced few. The theory of French origin for the Spanish epic has more plausibility, but is hardly to be accepted as a full explanation. The greatest scholar of contemporary Spain, Don Ramón Menéndez Pidal, believes that the origin of the Spanish epic is Germanic. In other lands Germanic tribes sang of their heroes: the Scandinavians in their sagas, the Old High Germans in their *Hildebrandslied,* the Saxons in their *Beowulf.* So the Goths who came to Spain maintained their love of epic song, though they adopted the language of the conquered country.

Fascinating though theories of epic origins may be, they are much less interesting than the great Spanish *Poem of the Cid (Poema del Cid)* itself, the first surviving and most impressive example of the genre. It is divided into three cantos and contains about 3,700 lines. A few have been lost at the beginning. Each canto is divided into a number of *laisses* or stanzas of irregular length, and the lines show a considerable variation in length also. Most scholars think that the variation in number of syllables per line was due to the *juglar* or minstrel who composed the poem rather than to careless copyists. Assonance is used rather than full consonantal rhyme. Lines 17-20, for example, might sound thus in English:

> And citizens, men and women, all at the windows stayed.
> Tears came forth from their eyes, because they felt such pain,
> And with their tongues with one accord they all did say:
> Oh, God, how good a vassal, if his master were the same.

The plot of the *Cid* is relatively simple. Rodrigo (Ruy) Díaz de Bivar, banished by King Alfonso VI, gathers his retainers and fights his way eastward, winning signal victories over the Moors. He finally wins the great city of Valencia, summons his wife and daughters, and receives full pardon from his sovereign. His daughters are married to the proud but craven Infantes de Carrión, who, made the butt of jests at the Cid's Valencian court, start with their young wives back to Castile. In the oak forest of Corpes they strip and beat their wives in vengeance. The Cid demands and receives full satisfaction, the Infantes are ignominiously defeated by the Cid's champion, and his daughters are married to the Princes of Navarre and Aragon.

The landscape of Castile is austere, grave, sober, intense, severe, simple, and so is this, a characteristically Castilian poem. It is realistic, unaffected, and remarkably faithful to history, as we might expect from a work written hardly more than a generation after the death of the hero. Imaginary and supernatural elements are very few indeed, and in this regard the Spanish poem is conspicuously different from the French *Song of Roland* or the German *Song of the Nibelungs.*

The Cid is shown as the ideal mediaeval Spaniard, direct in purpose, unswerving in simple loyalty, brave and of untiring vigor, with a dignity which has for centuries been noted in his compatriots. In the poem there is no thought of romantic love or gallantry, but the Cid is presented as a man of strong family affections. When he is forced to part from his wife Doña Jimena and his two daughters, "they separate like tearing the fingernail from the flesh," and he "took his daughters in his arms and pressed them to his heart, for he loved them much." In other words, the epic hero is here no demigod, but a man of intense humanity. When crowds heard this poem recited by a minstrel in the market place, they must have felt a glow of sympathy to think that the Cid was a man like everyone, only greater, as they would like to be, and that he was confronted, just as they were, with the eternal problem of earning his daily bread.

The author of the *Cid* has a vision of reality which makes him akin to Velázquez, and a keen sense of the dramatic. He draws his landscape and his personages with few, simple and bold strokes, and achieves a true effect of primitive grandeur. His lines are rugged, dense, sure, and his poem stands like a hill rising from the Castilian plateau, stark, but with suggestions of invincible strength and permanence.

There must have been a score or more of other primitive epics which have not survived, and several of them have been partially recovered from prose chronicles into which they were later cast. Roderic, the Last of the Goths, had his saga; so did Fernán González, Sancho II, the Infantes de Lara (Salas), Sancho García and others, who had actually trod this earth. Bernardo del Carpio, however, who had his epic and appears in many later ballads, seems to have been a Spanish invention to match the French Roland.

These poems, recited to the accompaniment of musical instruments, represented history, biography, novel and poetry to popular audiences. They were the early mediaeval equivalent of reading, radio program and musical concert. The authors remained anonymous, fusing their spirit with that of the people. Since they were in the hands of minstrels, this whole group of compositions is said to belong to the *Mester de juglaría* (*Minstrelsy*), and had its heyday in the twelfth and thirteenth centuries.

Most of those who could write in the Middle Ages were connected with the church, and their poetic compositions are referred to as being included in the *Mester de Clerecía* (*Clerics' Mode*). The ecclesiastical authors were more learned than the minstrels and achieved a greater perfection of form. Since in the main their prime and very transparent purpose was to edify rather than to entertain, the modern reader of their poetic homilies is likely to be little amused. If he has cultivated a taste for literary pre-Raphaelitism, he will discern occasional flashes of beauty, as he might in the work of some early pyramid-builder or in an early Romanesque church.

The clerics who composed in this fashion used a highly monotonous stanza of four lines of fourteen syllables each, all with the same end-rhyme. It is called *Cuaderna vía* or "Fourfold Way."

A note may be inserted here to explain that Spaniards, to determine the number of syllables in a line or hemistich, count up to the final stressed syllable and then add one. This syllable following the stress may actually be present, it may be absent, or there may be two more. *Yo no sé, Todavía* and *En la víspera* would thus all count as four-syllable lines in Spanish verse.

The first Spanish poet whose name has been preserved was a worthy old lay-brother at the Benedictine Monastery of San Millán de la Cogolla: Gonzalo de Berceo. Born toward the end of the twelfth century, he lived a long and pious life, and left a legacy of some 13,000 lines of verse, mainly saints' lives, which he retells with naïve simplicity. He boasts that he writes with "counted syllables," often his chief merit, for his works are of interest mainly to the ardent mediaevalist. However, the modern reader may occasionally be relieved from boredom by sensing here and there a certain popular savor and a touch of lyric freshness. In fact, some contemporaries discover in him an "enchanting primitivism" and great delicacy of style. He has at least attracted more admirers in recent years than he had before.

Despite the term "Mester de Clerecía," not all poems in the "Four-fold Way" were on religious subjects. An example is the poem about Alexander the Great called *Libro de Alixandre,* written about the middle of the thirteenth century, perhaps by Juan Lorenzo Segura, in a dialect which shows strong admixture of Leonese elements. Whoever wrote it was a man of considerable learning, which he was not averse to showing off. Alexander the Great held great fascination for the Middle Ages, and the author of this lay shows familiarity with previous poems written about him, such as the Latin *Alexandreis* of Gautier de Chatillon, the *Roman d'Alexandre* of Alexandre de Paris and Lambert le Tors, and very possibly with Arabic sources. The poem is long, more than ten thousand lines, and tedious, except for the suggestiveness of many details and descriptions, such as the somewhat plateresque picture of Alexander's tent. The author likes to preach as well as to narrate and describe. He at least displays a certain cosmopolitan interest, and no one in his day minded anachronisms such as the singing of Te Deums in ancient Macedonia.

The contemporary *Libro de Apolonio* is very much shorter and more novelesque, and the story, based ultimately on some late Greek novel, was good enough to interest Gower (*Confessio Amantis*) and Shakespeare (*Pericles, Prince of Tyre*). It is a sort of primitive movie serial, full of long wanderings, lost children, shipwrecks, storms, pirates, abductions, sudden recognitions, all with a happy ending. The unknown author possesses narrative vigor and considerable poetic skill.

Both the *Libro de Alixandre* and the *Libro de Apolonio* were known to the author of the *Poema de Fernán González,* a three-thousand-line Castilian poem about a Castilian hero, which probably derived from an earlier heroic poem in the *Mester de Juglaría.* If the inspiration of the author, a monk from near Burgos, was languid, his patriotism was great. The manner of the poem is erudite, but the spirit is that of the primitive epic.

The heroic poems, or *Cantares de gesta,* degenerated in the late thirteenth and fourteenth centuries. Many, as has been suggested, were put into prose. The *cuaderna vía* continued to be used for narrative purposes, reaching its highest perfection in the work of Juan Ruiz. In shorter lines, there existed several representatives of the form known as the Debate, such as the *Elena y María,* in which two ladies argue as to the merits of their respective lovers, a cleric and a knight. Another example of irregular versification is the biography of St. Mary of Egypt (*Santa María Egipciaca*), a lady who sinned and sinned but repented.

The *Poema de Alfonso Onceno* narrates the history of Alfonso XI from 1312 onward. It is not written in the learned *cuaderna vía,* but on a basis of eight-syllable lines, henceforward to be the type in narrative poetry.

The *Poema de Yuçuf* is unusual because it is Arabic in source, and because it is written in Arabic characters though in the Spanish language, and in the *cuaderna vía.* Such works are said to belong to the *literatura aljamiada.* The story is that of Joseph up to the time when his father Jacob came to Egypt.

The epic is a typically Castilian product, and the lack of such poems in Portuguese and Catalan is noteworthy.

## EARLY LYRIC POETRY IN GALICIA AND PORTUGAL

In what part of the Peninsula was lyric poetry first heard? *¡Quién sabe!* It is known at least that the first of which written record survives is in the language of the west, Galician-Portuguese. And, it is more than likely that a primitive lyric existed there, as it did in Castile, for the Portuguese are supposed to be essentially sentimental and poetic. Moreover, even Castilian poets used Portuguese when they wrote lyric poetry, and some continued to do so even in the late fourteenth century. More than two thousand Galician-Portuguese songs are preserved in three old song-books or *Cancioneiros,* not rediscovered until the nineteenth century. There are three classes of songs. The *Cantigas de escarnho* are scurrilous and often obscene poems of satire and vilification. The *Cantigas de amado* are formal love songs supposed to be addressed by the lover to his lady. Decidedly the most appealing of the three groups are the *Cantigas de amigo,* in which a love-lorn lass laments the absence or faithlessness of her beloved. Some of this last class certainly go back to popular tradition, showing a characteristic structure, parallelistic stanzas repeating the same idea in different rhymes or assonance. Here is a sample:

> Ay frores, ay frores do verde pino,
> Si sabedes novas do meu amigo?
>  Ay Deus, e hu è?

> Ay frores, ay frores do verde ramo,
> Si sabedes novas do meu amado?
>  Ay Deus, e hu è?

> *Sweet flowers, sweet flowers upon the green tree,*
> *Oh, will you not say where my sweetheart can be?*
>  *Dear God, where is he?*

> *Sweet flowers, sweet flowers amid the tree's leaves,*
> *Know you aught of the lover for whom my heart grieves?*
>  *Dear God, where is he?*

While the oldest of these poems must be of popular origin, most of them were based upon Provençal and northern French models. The French troubadours, some of whom came to the Peninsula, exerted a very large influence on the poets of Catalonia, whose language was nearly the same as that of Provence, upon those of Galicia and Portugal, and later and more indirectly upon Castilian rhymesters.

The southern French troubadours were more perfect in form and substance, but the Portuguese are noteworthy for delicate expression of feeling. The Portuguese poets of these *Cancioneiros* were not only humble minstrels from the lower classes, but also members of the lower and upper nobility, including four kings. In any case their poetry was written for the castle and court, not for the market-place. It is not to be forgotten that instrumental and vocal music added to the charm of these poems, for they were all written to be sung. The dates commonly assigned to the Portuguese-Galician troubadour poetry are from 1085 to 1325. It was at its height in the reign of King Denis (1261-1325), no mean troubadour himself.

## EARLY LYRIC POETRY IN CASTILE

As most of the early epics of Spain were lost, so was its primitive lyric poetry. It existed in Castile none the less. Its favorite form was not parallelistic like that of Portugal, but was composed usually of a sort of chorus of two or more lines announcing the theme, commented upon in succeeding stanzas. The last line of each stanza had the same rhyme as the chorus, so when the minstrel sang such a song, his hearers knew after each stanza when to join in. This form, also used in other literatures, must have existed in the Peninsula from very early times, for we find it recorded in Moorish Andalusia in the eleventh century, and Professor Julián Ribera thought it arose there in the ninth. These popular songs were no doubt varied in subject matter, as sung by watchmen, mountain girls (*serranillas*), reapers, pilgrims, shepherds, and there were songs for special occasions such as Christmas (*villancicos*),

St. John's Day, May Day and many others. Many traces of them are to be found in later and more sophisticated poems.

The Castilian lyric poems which were actually preserved in writing and which were composed up to the middle of the fifteenth century, belong to the Troubadouresque school; that is, they are mainly in the style of the Provençal and Galician-Portuguese poets. The first preserved lyric in Castilian is called the *Razón de amor* (*Story of Love*), which clearly shows troubadour influence, and describes with considerable grace and freshness the meeting between a slim-waisted, black-eyed, red-lipped lady and her accomplished lover near a spring surrounded with sweet-smelling roses, lilies and violets. This poem, belonging to the early thirteenth century, is awkwardly connected with a *Debate Between Water and Wine*. A not very lyric watchman's song in Berceo's *Grief of the Virgin* (*Duelo de la Virgen*) may be a little earlier.

Surely there must have been many more songs in Castilian, but it was the fashion among sophisticated Castilians to write their lyric poems in Galician-Portuguese. The author who has far the largest number of poems attributed to him in the *Cancioneiros* was the royal troubadour, Alfonso X of Castile, and only one of his surviving songs was composed in Castilian.

# VIII

## The Learned King. The Early Novel and Drama

### ALFONSO EL SABIO AND MEDIAEVAL LEARNING

FRANCE and the rest of Europe lagged considerably behind Moslem Spain in cultural development, and Christian Spain was farther behind still. Perhaps too much of her energy went into fighting the Moors, as in the time of Fernando III. Yet it was in the reign of that monarch that the first Spanish prose developed, and real signs of intellectual activity began to be evident.

Toledo, recaptured by the Christians in 1085, became a center of studies for Christians, Moslems and Jews who had there taken refuge from the Almohade persecution. There translations were made of Jewish or Arabic works such as those of Averroes and Avicebron. The works were translated into Latin, and if their Latinity was not of the best, it did not prevent their spread to the rest of Europe. Spanish prose was mainly confined to moral and didactic works and had reached no artistic development. The early thirteenth century *Argument Between the Christian and the Jew* is the first, and very crude, Spanish debate between protagonists of two religions. In the time of Fernando III there were several prose catechisms and collections of apothegms of Oriental origin. History in the vulgar tongue was represented by dry chronicles. More sophisticated historians such as Lucas de Tuy and Jiménez de Rada wrote in Latin. Fernando III's son Alfonso X was the one who first dignified Spanish prose.

Alfonso the Learned (1252-1284) was a scholar who did not

succeed very well in practical affairs, but he was an amazingly active intellectual leader of his people, who has been called an "emperor of culture." He surrounded himself with men of learning, no matter what their religion or nationality, and his court was a sort of university, research institute, lawyers' convention, poets' retreat, conservatory and publishing house, encouraged and presided over by the beneficent genius of Alfonso himself.

No one knows precisely how much Alfonso participated personally in the numerous works which emanated from his brilliant court, but it is certain that he did direct, revise and follow the progress of his projects with eager interest. His poems probably hold most of his personal contribution. Alfonso composed more than four hundred songs, called *Cantigas de Santa María,* written, according to the prevailing fashion, not in Castilian but in Galician-Portuguese. They recount, often naïvely, miracles attributed to the Virgin or lyrical praises of the Queen of Heaven, and are all set to music. The verse forms are rich and varied, for Alfonso had at his command all the complicated metrical devices of the Galician-Portuguese school of troubadours. It is only occasionally that he rises above them to real lyric grace.

The scientific interests of the restless-minded king displayed themselves mainly in the study of astronomy. He even had a sort of observatory in Toledo. The value of the *Libros del saber de astronomía* and of the *Tablas alfonsíes* is now only archaeological, but what knowledge could Alfonso have had except of the cosmos according to Ptolemy? So Ptolemaic works were at his orders translated from Arabic and served as the basis for his *Astronomy,* which he revised and put into Castilian. The *Lapidario* was also based on Arabic sources, and explains the properties of precious stones. If many people believe now that opals are unlucky, small wonder that the Middle Ages connected stones with the signs of the zodiac and attributed to them all sorts of quaint and curious effects.

Alfonso would very probably have approved of college athletics and of contract bridge. For men he commends the outdoor games known to him, which strengthen the limbs and bring relaxation from the "cares and toils of life." For women, and for men who are shut in by weakness, sea voyages, imprisonment or rough weather, he recommends chess, dice and backgammon, and had a book composed about them, a mediaeval Hoyle, finished in Seville in 1283. It is said to mark a considerable advance over Arabic works on the subject.

Fernando III commanded his son to compile the laws of his realm, and Alfonso began his great compilation the year before he came to the throne. It is called simply the *Seven Parts* (*Siete Partidas*) from the number of its chapters, each of which begins with a letter of the name Alfonso. It is not concerned with numerology, however, and not merely with what we would call law, either, for it contains directions for the conduct of all classes of society in all walks of life. It is a code, but also a book of etiquette and a picturesque treatise on manners and customs. The legal part is based mainly on Justinian, the great Roman emperor and lawgiver.

Alfonso's contributions to science and law were important but it is the great historical works coming from his court that have given the Learned Monarch his right to the title of being "the father of Spanish prose." He may also be called the father of Spanish historiography, for his few predecessors are insignificant beside him. Alfonso's famous history of Spain is called simply the *Crónica general,* but is usually referred to as the *First General Chronicle* to distinguish it from its successors. Naturally no one could expect from the thirteenth century the scientific accuracy now demanded, but there is no question that Alfonso's compilers made a diligent study of sources and that Alfonso in revising their work sought and achieved amenity of style. His conception of history is not merely local, for he wishes to give the background of his country in the remote past, and so he goes back as far as the Flood, the wanderings of Japheth, the founding of Rome, the adventures of Hercules, Greek, Carthaginian and Roman domination of Spain, and Roman poets—Vergil, Ovid, Lucan—are as freely drawn upon as professional historians like Suetonius. And the history is not merely of Castile, but also of Portugal, Navarre and Aragon. Alfonso meant the "general" in his title. It is evident that the Spanish compilers felt great solidarity with the Goths, for the reigns of the Gothic kings are treated in detail. The first part of the *Crónica,* describing the loss of King Roderic, ends with a "Eulogy of Spain" and a "Lament for Spain" which have real poetic beauty. In the second part, composed somewhat later (1289), Spain's history is brought on down to the death of Alfonso's father, San Fernando, and it is to be noted that many Spanish epic poems were utilized as sources, for the poems were regarded as true. The whole marks a most extraordinary attempt at writing history. A later reworking, called the *Segunda crónica general* or *Crónica de 1344,* uses later forms of the early epics. The *Tercera crónica general* was the first to be printed, by Florián de Ocampo in 1541. It was from Ocampo's very uncritical edition that balladists and dramatists like Lope de Vega drew many a plot and episode.

Chronicles were also written of the reigns of Alfonso's successors, such as Sancho IV, Fernando IV, Alfonso XI, Pedro I, etc. Three by the stern old Chancellor of Castile, Don Pero López de Ayala (1332-1407), are noteworthy for their author's psychological penetration and incisive style. Fernán Pérez de Guzmán, who lived past the middle of the fifteenth century, is also conspicuous for his sharply etched portraits of contemporaries in his *Generaciones y semblanzas.* The work of Hernando del Pulgar, *Famous Men of Castile* (*Claros varones de Castilla*), 1486, is an excellent sort of *Who's Who* for the age just preceding Ferdinand and Isabella.

Alfonso performed a mighty service when he made Spanish prose a fit medium for literary expression. Although he encouraged particularly studies in science, law and history, his interest in prose fiction was also keen. The earliest stories to be written down in Spain were Oriental fables, supposed to teach some valuable moral lesson, and likely to be used by preachers for the edification of their flocks. The first collection of such stories was made by a converted Aragonese Jew, Petrus Alfonsi or Pedro Alfonso, who was baptized in 1106. The three dozen stories are in Latin, and are pretty clumsily told, but this collection, called *Disciplina clericalis,* grew quite popular in Europe, and the stories appear again and again.

Alfonso was directly responsible for the first Oriental book of fiction to appear in Spanish, the *Calila y Dimna,* translated from

Arabic at his order in 1251, just before he came to the throne. The stories had appeared first in Sanskrit. Then they were translated into Old Persian (sixth century), later into Arabic (about 750), and from Arabic into various languages besides Spanish. Calila and Dimna are lynxes and most but not all the stories are animal fables, connected rather loosely in a frame, and the virtues which they inculcate would seem to be shrewdness and craftiness rather than sheer goodness.

A much shorter and sprightlier collection of stories coming originally from Sanskrit is the *Sendebar,* or *Book of the Deceits and Wiles of Women* (*Libro de los engaños . . .*), a title given it in the translation made from Arabic in 1253 by order of Alfonso's brother Prince Fadrique. English readers are more likely to be familiar with a version coming through occidental intermediaries and known as the *Book of the Seven Sages.* The form in Spanish, however, is regarded as being closest to the lost original. The twenty-six lively stories are in a frame. A very wicked queen, infuriated, like Potiphar's wife, because the Prince, her stepson, rejects her generously proffered feminine charms, takes cruel vengeance by having him condemned to death. The king's Wise Men, casting the Prince's horoscope, learn that the Prince will certainly perish if within seven days he so much as opens his lips. They manage to postpone the execution by telling a story each day to the king to prove to him that no woman's word is to be trusted, and even though the stepmother counters with a story or two showing what shifty and untrustworthy creatures Wise Men are, the boy is reprieved each twenty-four hours. After seven days of this have passed, the Prince is able to speak and triumphantly proves his innocence. So the king has the queen stewed alive. It is too bad for the lovers of spicy yarns that the argument could not have gone on longer. No wonder the book has lived a couple of thousand years or so.

More edifying matters are discussed in a third Oriental contribution to Spanish prose fiction, the *Barlaam and Josaphat,* attributed to St. John of Damascus. Although Saints Barlaam and Josaphat are in the martyrology of both the Roman and Greek Catholic churches, their story is in reality a Christianization of the legend of Buddha. In addition to the main account of Josaphat's conversion by Barlaam, there are interpolated tales which have gained wide currency. One is the story of the three rings symbolic of the three religions, later used by Boccaccio, and the three caskets, which Shakespeare liked (*The Merchant of Venice*). Lope de Vega in 1618 made a dramatic version of *Barlaam y Josafá*.

Since Oriental stories often suited Christian ethical ideals, they were widely used in the pulpit and a number of such collections of *exempla* or apologues were made in Spain, as elsewhere. Their compilers were usually content to repeat each other, with a diligence which did more honor to their high moral purpose than to their art. One compiler, Clemente Sánchez de Vercial, managed to gather nearly five hundred stories into his *Libro de los ejemplos*.

The most gifted reteller of prose stories in the Spanish Middle Ages was a man of excellent literary ancestry: Prince Don Juan Manuel, nephew of Alfonso the Learned. He spent most of his life (1282-ca. 1349) at court or fighting, but he insisted that he had just as good a right to spend his leisure time writing as his compeers did to pass theirs rolling dice or engaging in other aristocratic pastimes. Don Juan Manuel was a serious and dignified Spaniard. He felt it his duty to improve his fellow man, but he was fairly tactful about it. His *Book of the Knight and the Squire* offers young aristocrats much information on astronomy, general science and theology, and on the ideal way of conducting themselves toward inferiors, equals and superiors. A longer *Libro de los estados* (*estados* might be called *walks of life*) owes much to *Barlaam and Josaphat*. Don Juan Manuel did his best to see that true copies of his works should be preserved, but some were nevertheless lost, such as his treatise on *engeños* (mechanical contraptions used in warfare), his book of poems and his book on knighthood. Surviving also are his book on hunting (*Libro de la caza*), his chronicles, a genealogy of his family and his *Libro infinido,* a sort of didactic pedagogical treatise.

While such works give Alfonso's nephew a place of honor among the large number of mediaeval writers who seek to instruct and to improve humanity, it is upon another book that his chief fame rests. His *El Conde Lucanor,* also called *El Libro de Patronio,* is a collection of fifty stories, held together in a very simple frame. Young Count Lucanor fifty times asks advice of his wise old counselor Patronio, who replies in each case with an appropriate tale. Most of the stories are of Oriental origin, and Don Juan Manuel could have read them in Arabic, which he knew. His principal virtue is not in his inventiveness or his flights of fancy. Originality, indeed, was far less esteemed in the Middle Ages than now, and Don Juan Manuel neither desired nor claimed to be producing something new. He was ever the teacher of good old truths, but he tells us in his foreword that he has wished to wrap up the wholesome moral lessons in a pleasant covering, just as liver pills are sugar-coated so that the liver will like them (Don Juan's own figure of speech). All moral lessons aside, for one can take them or leave them, Don Juan Manuel has a real style and a sense of art in the selection of his material. He was gifted with the ability of building up his stories, eliminating the superfluous and utilizing only the significant. There is never much embellishment, and no exuberance, but there has been enormous progress in story-writing since Petrus Alfonsi in the *Disciplina clericalis* put down in Latin his dry Oriental fables. It is noteworthy that Don Juan Manuel is not writing for preachers, but for the everyday man. He is interested in righteousness, but he does not fail to emphasize the need of shrewdness in ordinary life, and the real "lesson" of many of his tales is "Don't be duped." He has singularly little interest in love as a literary motif.

*El Conde Lucanor* appeared some thirteen years before Boccaccio's *Decameron.* The Spanish Prince would have no doubt been shocked at the Italian's insouciant levity, though he might have admired Boccaccio's rather Ciceronian style. Boccaccio is a delightful bad boy (he repented and grew very serious in time) with a great vital urge; Don Juan Manuel seems to have been born with a long gray beard, through which he can only occasionally smile amid the serious concerns of that serious thing called life. He has his moments, however, as when he is retelling the even then old story of the weavers who wove the magic cloth, or of the young man who tamed a wild woman ("una mujer muy fuerte y muy brava") he had just married, a fine preliminary sketch for *The Taming of the Shrew*. Probably the most artistic story of all is the admirable portrayal of the theme of ingratitude in *The Dean of Santiago and Don Illán of Toledo,* three centuries later made into an excellent play by Ruiz de Alarcón (*La prueba de las promesas*). Don Juan Manuel's thoughts were mediaeval and he does not suggest the Renaissance paganism of the greater Boccaccio, but he was the first Spanish story-teller with a distinctly personal style and literary craftsmanship. Spain had to wait until the time of Cervantes for stories as well told.

## THE MEDIAEVAL NOVEL OF CHIVALRY

Spanish literature up to 1300 did not show any very fervid imagination, but one literary form does, at least originally: the novel of chivalry, which was known in Spain in Don Juan Manuel's time and which continued to flourish luxuriantly for three hundred years, until Cervantes laughed away its absurdities at the beginning of the seventeenth century.

The romances of chivalry came to Spain by way of France, where large numbers of poems had been written with three general subjects: Charlemagne and his Peers, the worthies of antiquity, and the Arthurian heroes. For the future history of the novel, the Arthurian Cycle was the most important. First developed by Celtic bards, the material was taken over by courtly French poets like Chrestien de Troyes and woven into a fascinating web of love and adventure which captivated all Europe. The subject matter has not lost its vitality: witness the relatively recent *Tristram* by Edwin Arlington Robinson. In the thirteenth century the romances began to be turned into prose. Many of them were translated into Spanish, directly from French, or by way of Portuguese or Italian, and the fourteenth century saw them spread vigorously in the Peninsula. The translations were not works of art, but they were at least fertile in suggestions. Their popularity shows that literary taste, at least in the upper circles of society, was no longer satisfied with mere accounts of military prowess, of epic deeds, but demanded some of the refinements of gallantry, some connection between deeds of derring-do and the sweet passion of love. Castilians are supposed to be a stern and realistic people, but stern men are often hiding deeply emotional natures, and as far as the records go, they show that Arthurian and kindred stories were just as eagerly read by the sturdy Castilians as they were by the allegedly sentimental Portuguese or the volatile Andalusians. After all, few have not yielded at some time to the magic allure of Tristan and Iseut, of Launcelot and Guinevere.

The first independent and original full-length novel in Spain is *El Caballero Cifar,* a strange combination of saint's legend (St. Eustace in this case), of fictional material like that of the late Greek novels, of didactic preachments and of chivalric adventure, with a full supply of magical elements. It was composed around the year 1300. Even though its numerous sources are foreign, the unknown author manages to combine them into a fairly coherent whole, and, like his successors in the genre, manages somehow to infuse into all of it a distinctly Spanish spirit. One of his creations is the figure of the sly, earthy, practical and devoted squire, the Ribaldo, whose utterances and character hold a suggestion of Sancho Panza.

One of the most popular novels that the world has yet produced is called *Amadís de Gaula,* from the name of its doughty hero. It appeared in Spain some time during the first half of the fourteenth century, for it is mentioned by name before 1350, though unfortunately no early manuscripts of it survive. The sources are in general French Arthurian material, but it is not a translation. Much controversy has been indulged in as to whether it first appeared in the Peninsula in Portuguese or in Spanish, but the earliest form in which it survives is in the Spanish edition printed in 1508. Amadís is a peerless knight, loyal to his king and faithful to his lovely Oriana, in whose service he slays many a dragon and kills many a miscreant, and whom he finally joins in lawful marriage.

A success story with a happy ending. A true novel, because it combines plot and motive. A happy blending of two sure-fire elements, love and adventure. Whoever the author was, he obviously did his best to write well, both smoothly and picturesquely. The descriptions have considerable vividness.

The novel achieved its enormous vogue after the invention of printing, but it had been known in Spain for nearly two hundred years before it reached the press.

Almost contemporary with *Amadís* is a work of more than 1100 chapters, which traces the history of the Crusades up to 1271, the *Gran conquista de Ultramar,* based on various French sources, or perhaps on a translation of a French original now lost. To explain the genealogy of Godfrey de Bouillon there is presented among other legends that of Lohengrin, the Swan Knight, a theme which has not yet lost its charm.

## THE MEDIAEVAL DRAMA

Just one play remains to represent the drama in mediaeval Spain, and that not in complete form. It is an Epiphany play, the oldest surviving in any Romance tongue except the French *Jeu d'Adam,* and is entitled *Auto de los Reyes Magos.* The fragment preserved runs to about 150 lines and was composed toward the middle of the twelfth century. Gaspar, Melchor and Baltasar appear first separately and then together, discussing the strange star in the east. Deciding it must mean that the Messiah is born, they resolve to go and test the child, to see which of their gifts of gold, frankincense or myrrh he will choose. They inform Herod of the child's birth, and the fragment breaks off as Herod is consulting with his astrologers. The composition is written in rhyming lines of varying lengths, and possesses simple dignity, liveliness and a distinct popular tone.

The liturgical drama must have run in Spain the same course as elsewhere, being composed at first in Latin and then, in about the twelfth century, appearing in the vulgar tongue. We know that not only religious plays existed, but also secular ones, because there is a section in Alfonso the Learned's *Siete Partidas* encouraging priests to take part in plays concerning Christ's life, but forbidding them to take part in or allow in church satirical plays that might give rise to scandal. Unfortunately there is a blank space of about three centuries in the Spanish drama from which no plays at all survive.

# IX

## *Juan Ruiz. His* Book of Good Love. *Satire*

### THE ARCHPRIEST OF HITA

IF lovers of Spanish literature were told that a great holocaust of books was about to be made, but that one from the Middle Ages could be saved by their vote, that one book would pretty certainly be Juan Ruiz's *Book of Good Love.*

Juan Ruiz was a bull-necked, broad-shouldered, long-nosed, hairy fellow, with long ears, a thick chest and a deep voice, who loved wine, woman and song and somehow became a priest. He was an archpriest, even, of the little town of Hita, not far from Guadalajara. He was born in Alcalá de Henares, and spent most of his life in New Castile, thirteen years of it in jail in Toledo, where his archbishop put him for causes unknown. It did not break his spirit. His exact dates? Uncertain. He was born in the last part of the thirteenth century and died about the middle of the fourteenth. In other words, precious little is known about the details of his life, but a very great deal can be learned about him from his book, one of the most personal ever written and one of the most revealing.

### THE *BOOK OF GOOD LOVE*

Good love, Ruiz solemnly assures us, is the love of God, spiritual love, and his whole work is to lead men to that, so that they may avoid *amor mundano, loco amor,* which is very, very bad. He will give us examples of the latter, so that we may cease to do evil and cling to that which is good. He begins in pious fashion, with a verse invocation to the Lord to deliver him out of prison, and a sermon in prose, with appropriate quotations from the Bible and the church fathers. There follow two sincere and lovely little poems on the Joys of St. Mary. Then a fable. The whole composition is interspersed with fables, related with a verve and grace not to be matched until La Fontaine. Then the Archpriest tells us how he fell in love and sent a messenger to woo his lady. The messenger turned out to be a very aggressive John Alden to his Priscilla. Then he fell in love again:

(*Copla* 169, translated by E. K. Kane)
   A comely, sportive maid she was and amorous of mien,
   And when she walked her body swayed like rushes near a stream,
   Full beautiful, impetuous, cajoling, sly, serene,
   While in her eyes there slumbered love as in a fleeting dream.

But he had no luck with her. Don Amor appears to him, and is treated to a copious invective against love, with illustrative fables. Don Amor replies at length, with convincing examples and warnings, including a very lively French fabliau about Pitas Payas, a painter of Brittany. Lady Venus gives the Archpriest even more specific and efficacious directions, and when he falls in love with a sweet widow of Calatayud, his quest is successful. But no: this long and gaily narrated adventure did not happen to him, says our Archpriest, but to Lady Sloe and Don Canteloupe.

(*Copla* 909)
   And realize full well I spin my tale of Lady Sloe
   To teach a moral, not because it happened to me so.

We are likely to believe that if this particular episode was merely literary, at least Juan Ruiz had an excellent basis in personal reality for his imaginings. In the affair he introduces a deftly characterized go-between, Doña Urraca, who is a highly skilled professional at her trade, and who is able to bring great aid and consolation to distressed lovers.

The next love affair is unfortunate, and the Archpriest goes to take a sort of moral cure in the high, pure air of the mountains. The rigors of the high altitudes are lessened by gallant meetings with mountain girls, about whom Ruiz writes many delightful

songs, *serranillas*. The approach of Lent turns the Archpriest's
thoughts to higher things, and he composes a hymn to the Virgin
and two poems on the Passion of Christ. Then he describes with
great gusto a battle between Lord Flesh and Lady Lent. The latter
is triumphant for a season, but at last Lord Flesh and his hosts of
fowls, swine, cattle, deer and wild boars frighten off the ascetic
leader of fish, eels and oysters and Lady Lent flees through the Pass
of Roncevaux. On Easter, Lord Flesh and Lord Love become allied
emperors, and the glad populace, both lay and ecclesiastic, joyously
rushes out to greet them, while music pours from all sorts of instruments. The Archpriest is among those most rejoicing, and he
engages in several more gallant adventures. He pauses to meditate
upon death, which has snatched off his "loyal and true" go-between,
Doña Urraca, but he is consoled to think that she is sure of a place
in Paradise. The work ends with a strange hodge-podge: a dissertation upon arms at the disposition of the Christian for overcoming
the world, the flesh and the devil, a delightful dozen stanzas in
praise of little women, a characterization of the Archpriest's new
factotum, a lad named Don Weasel, and a statement (nine stanzas)
as to how the book is to be taken. It is a "long manual of great
holiness, a short breviary of sport and jest":

(*Copla* 1633)
   I've served you, merry gentlemen, although with little learning.
   And I have tried in jongleur's verse to please your every yearning:
   I ask but this, that in God's name, where'er you are sojourning,
   You'll say a prayer or two for me—'twill be my only earning.

One manuscript ends here, but another contains songs on the
Joys of Mary, on begging scholars, more praises of Mary, and finally
a *Song of the Priests of Talavera,* who complain bitterly because
Archbishop Don Gil de Albornoz has issued a strict order that no
priest shall have a mistress, "neither married nor single."

Such a summary outline of the merry Archpriest's seventeen
hundred stanzas can do nothing more than suggest their content,
and perhaps show the heterogeneous character of this mediaeval
miscellany. A very pleasant time can be enjoyed in tracing the

author's sources. Despite several protestations of ignorance on his part ("I am a very crude scholar," etc.), he knew a fair amount. His priestly vocation had familiarized him with the Bible and various books on canon law or of a devotional nature, which he rather proudly mentions. He did not have much knowledge of the works of classical antiquity, but Ovid's *Art of Love* was familiar to him. In the long episode of Don Melón and Doña Endrina, he is following and most artistically enlarging upon a pseudo-Ovidian play, *Pamphilus de amore,* the work of a mediaeval monk who was imitating the great master. When the Archpriest quotes Aristotle, Cato, Ptolemy and Hippocrates, he is citing second-hand material. Some sort of collection of fables, usually called *Isopetes,* he certainly knew. Of Arabic he knew at least something, perhaps much. He must have known French, since several of his sources could hardly have existed in Spanish, notably the description of the battle between Lord Flesh and Lady Lent, based on a *Bataille de Karesme et de Charnage.* It is possible that he knew Provençal poems directly, though more likely that they came to him through Galician-Portuguese. He mentions Tristan and Iseut, Flores and Blancaflor. His description of the tent of Don Amor is based on the *Libro de Alixandre.*

The restless Archpriest must have spent far more time outside his library than in it, but he had evidently read and heard a great deal of poetry and song. The narrative part of the *Book of Good Love* is written in *cuaderna vía,* which Ruiz is one of the last to use. To this monotonous form he gives amazing lightness and movement, so that one is only pleasantly lulled by the constant ding-dong of the four successive rhymes in each stanza. In the short songs inserted here and there Ruiz uses a highly varied assortment of metrical combinations, for he wanted his book to serve as a sort of manual for minstrels and poets. Many are in the form already mentioned as typical of the very early Castilian lyric. The *juglar* was meant to sing these poems, and the listeners could come in as they chose. The Archpriest himself informs us that he has composed a multitude of songs for dances and jigs, for Jewesses and

Mooresses, to go with instrumental accompaniment, for women who healed the sick with magic words, and:

(*Copla* 1514)

> I next made several blind men's songs for those who'd lost their sight,
> And songs for student roisterers who prowl about at night,
> And songs to grid from door to door for many a beggared wight;
> Ten folios full of mocking songs and others full of spite.

(All translations from Juan Ruiz are from E. K. Kane's sprightly version.)

It is most regrettable that these songs have been lost. Many of them would no doubt correspond in spirit and art to the modern limerick. The Archpriest also shows much interest in the musical instruments which should or should not be used to accompany them.

If the content of the *Book of Good Love* seems unduly disparate and heterogeneous, there is one definite unifying factor, the engaging and arresting personality of Juan Ruiz. He gives us his physical portrait (*Coplas,* 1485-89), but through the whole composition he displays even better his emotional and spiritual anatomy. He was possessed of the idea, not common in the Middle Ages, that his own personality, so interesting to him, would also interest his hearers, so he goes gaily ahead in the first person, and gives us the portrait of one of the world's most attractive sinners. His philosophy and theology are orthodox enough, and there is no reason to doubt his pious protestations or his sincerity in his more righteous moments, but he is born to sin as the sparks to fly upward. He repents with fervor in the morning, and sins again most joyously at night. His vitality is so great and his zest for life so ardent that he can never remember moral restraints very long. The sight of a pretty woman can distract him in a flash.

Juan Ruiz represents the conflict between the vital and the ascetic, and in him the vital triumphs, as it does in Boccaccio and Chaucer. Ecclesiastical moralists could jail him, but they could not quench his spirit or dull his verve, and he emerged from prison with an autobiography which gives him immortality when all his pious persecutors have been long forgotten. He has a perennial youth and freshness age cannot wither.

The *Libro de Buen Amor* is universal in its appeal, but also typically Spanish. It has a tremendous sense of movement, it is gay and rollicking, and it is highly democratic. It shows men as they are, and is written for all classes, the product of direct observation and not of cloistered meditation, brilliant but not carefully planned, fervent though not polished, quintessentially human.

## MEDIAEVAL SATIRE

If an antidote is needed for the boisterous insouciance of the Archpriest of Hita, it may be found in the works of the serious patrician, Don Pero López de Ayala, who lived a long life and found the fourteenth century world a pretty bad place in which to spend it. Born (1332), as he says in his *Chronicles,* in the reign of Alfonso XI, he lived through the times of Peter the Cruel, Henry II, John I, Henry III, and died (1407) a year after John II ascended the throne. He held high positions in the army, the navy and at court, and constantly displayed great vigor and intelligence, especially to his own profit. He was once captured by the Black Prince, Edward of England, and forced to pay a heavy ransom. When captured again, by the Portuguese, at Aljubarrota, in 1385, he was kept in an iron cage for more than a year, and his wife, his cousin, who was the Grand Master of Calatrava, and the kings of Spain and France thought enough of him to pay thirty thousand gold *doblas* for his release. He was ambassador to France, and rose to be Chancellor of Castile.

This soldier-scholar-poet-courtier found time for a large amount of literary composition during his busy life. He rendered into Spanish some of the works of Livy, Boethius, St. Isidore and St. Gregory, and the *Crónica troyana* of Guido delle Colonne, and made a partial translation of Boccaccio's *Fall of Princes:* an early evidence that foreign literary influence in Spain was beginning to be Italian rather than French. He wrote a good technical treatise on falconry, and noteworthy chronicles of the reigns of the four kings whom he served.

His greatest work is known as the *Rimado de Palacio*. It is a composition in *cuaderna vía* of very miscellaneous content, with interspersed poems in various meters. His verse is usually pedestrian, for he was no inspired poet. It is his satire that interests, his somewhat jaundiced picture of life in his time. His older contemporary Juan Ruiz could see ecclesiastical corruption and misbehavior, and many evidences of human depravity, but Ruiz was amused, and his mockery is gay. Ayala was depressed, and he speaks his bitter piece about all classes of society, from king to peasant. He is genuinely concerned about the state of the world, and embittered because he cannot do much to improve it. One cannot say that his pessimism was unjustified in the fourteenth century or that it would be misplaced now, but the world seems to waggle on somehow. At any rate, Ayala's voice said sternly just what he thought, with sturdy integrity, and in a mood of high moral dudgeon.

Another of the very last examples of the *Mester de clerecía* is the *Libro de la miseria del homne* (*The Wretched Estate of Mankind*). The subject is the same as that of Innocent III's *De contemptu mundi*. The author was apparently a monk of the fourteenth century.

Thoughts of the wretchedness of this life lead naturally to death. In France the *Dance of Death* theme, in which mighty Death summons all orders to come and join his macabre dance, was a fertile inspiration not only in literature but also in art, notably in Holbein. The Castilian *Danza de la muerte,* based on some French source, belongs to the early fifteenth century, and displays the same attitude of terror before man's inevitable end and the same thought of death as the great leveler, who seizes Pope and peasant, emperor and humble doorkeeper. In the composition there is no thought of serenity in the presence of death, which is viewed with a horror like that of Villon. The Spanish *Dance* has no great literary merits.

The satires of Ayala, of the *Miseria del homne* and the *Danza de la muerte* are general. Other satires are more particular, such as

the *Coplas del Provincial,* which satirized so bitterly the greatest
families of Castile in the reign of Henry IV that strenuous efforts
were made to suppress them. The *Coplas de Mingo Revulgo* form
an allegorical political satire of the same reign. The stanzas of the
poem called *¡Ay, Panadera!* poke fun at the cowardice of those
who fled from the field at the battle of Olmedo, calling them by
name.

Satire was not all in verse. The best satiric prose of the fifteenth
century is to be found in a book which has come to be called *El
corbacho (The Scourge),* by Alfonso Martínez, Archpriest of Talavera. He also wrote the lives of Saints Isidore and Ildefonso and an
*Atalaya de las crónicas,* but it is on the *Corbacho* that his fame rests.
The second of its four parts is (by men, at least) the most enjoyed.
It is a very sprightly satire on the foibles, affectations, vanities and
excesses of women, with much realistic detail, couched in racy and
popular language. The author's knowledge of the contents of a
fifteenth century lady's boudoir is extraordinary. He laments that
they contain all sorts of skin lotions, perfumes, breath-sweeteners,
bath-salts and every sort of adornment, but no books of prayer and
devotion. The ladies whom he describes must have been coquettish
and vain indeed. However, they made a delightful target for his
sharp-pointed pen, and in his style one can sense the germs of the
*Celestina* and the picaresque novel. He was influenced by the *Libro
de Buen Amor:* in fact it has been said of him that "he was as good
an archpriest in prose as he of Hita was in verse." Not quite that,
but he was a gifted satirist.

# X

## Fifteenth Century Poets. Ballads

### CANCIONERO DE BAENA

JOHN II who ruled in the first half of the fifteenth century (1406-1454) was a weak king, constantly under the domination of his powerful favorite Don Alvaro de Luna. His court was, however, a congenial spot for musicians and poets. In 1445 his secretary Alfonso de Baena offered him an anthology of contemporary and older poems in a volume, known as the *Cancionero de Baena,* which was far more gorgeous than its contents deserved. The number of poets represented is fifty-four, and the compositions nearly six hundred. It may be summarized in the oft-quoted and damning phrase, "muchas poesías, poca poesía." It contains courtly and not popular poetry, verse, rather, by representatives of the troubadouresque Castilian school, from the preceding century through Baena himself. One is Macías, who still wrote in Galician-Portuguese, and who stands in Spanish literature as the archetype of troubadours who died for love. His legend, so often repeated, is much more picturesque than his surviving poems. Another poet, Villasandino, shows some power of invective, but still more long-windedness. The older group of poets in the *Cancionero de Baena* were still imitating the Galician-Portuguese school, but the younger were beginning to show the influence of Italy. Of the latter the most important is Francisco Imperial, a Genoese goldsmith who lived in Seville. Imperial really understood Dante and wrote in imitation of him a *Decir de las Siete Virtudes.* Imperial's verse, at least because of its influence, was less sterile than that of nearly all the others whom Baena deemed worthy of a place in his anthology. All, with one exception.

71

That one was Juan de Mena (1411-1456). He was born in Cordova, and some have seen in him traits which would connect him with his fellow-townsmen the Senecas, Lucan and Góngora. He had studied in Italy, and became a Latin secretary to John II. His surviving prose is very bad, and so is much of his poetry. Not all. He had at least some new ideas, which foreshadow the Renaissance. For one thing, he insists that the vocabulary of poetry should be different from that of prose, and he borrows extensively from Latin and Italian to enrich the Spanish vocabulary. He also does violence to Spanish syntax, and it is evident that he is making of poetry a sort of Eleusinian mystery open only to sophisticated initiates. The difficulty of his poetry is increased by his numerous erudite references to classical mythology and history. He was highly esteemed in his own time and afterward, and exerted a considerable influence, but it is evident that his importance is due more to that than to his intrinsic merits. His most significant work is his *Laberinto de la Fortuna,* often called *Las trescientas* because there are 297 stanzas, a conscious imitation of the *Paradiso* of Dante. Mena's favorite poetic form was the *copla de arte mayor,* a stanza composed of eight twelve-syllable lines rhyming abbaacca, which enjoyed a vogue of more than a century, though it is only a trifle less monotonous in unskilful hands than the *cuaderna vía.*

## THE MARQUIS OF SANTILLANA

The best poet of the century was not included in Baena's anthology at all. He was a magnificent gentleman named Don Iñigo López de Mendoza, Marqués de Santillana, Conde del Real de Manzanares, Señor de Hita y Buitrago, etc., and his achievements are greater even than his titles. He was heavily involved in political and military affairs, but found time for much study and writing. If most of his compositions reflect the same inspiration as that of his contemporaries, some of them, at least, show him as much more modern because of his more extensive following of Italian models.

The Marquis of Santillana was a highly conscious artist, familiar

with much of the art which had preceded his. A letter and prologue (*Prohemio*), which he sent with a copy of his poems to Don
Pedro of Portugal, is the first document of literary history and
criticism in Spanish. Santillana's definition of poetry is of interest.
It is "an artificial creation of useful things, covered or veiled with
a very pretty covering, composed, marked out and scanned according to a definite count, weight and measure." Utility and beauty of
form, then, are insisted upon, as well as creative power. He divides
past poetry into three classes: the sublime, the poetry of the ancients;
the moderately good (*"mediocre"*), the work of those of his own
times and not long before; and the base, poems made by ballad-
mongers and song-peddlers, "in which people of base and servile
condition take delight." Despite this aristocratic scorn on the part
of Santillana, his poems which are most esteemed today are based
on popular forms. He was unfamiliar with the popular epic of
France and Spain, and did not know the Provençal poets directly,
but he knew the northern French and the Galician-Portuguese
schools. Among his contemporaries and close predecessors, he quite
rightly held the Italians in the highest esteem. He was also familiar
with Catalan poetry, and praised Mosén Jordí de Sant Jordí and
Ausías March. Fortunately Santillana's library, including a magnificent copy of the *Roman de la Rose,* is preserved almost intact.

The Marquis wrote comparatively little in prose, aside from his
*Proemio e carta.* Of great interest, however, is his collection of
popular proverbs, which he calls *Proverbs That Old Women Quote
by the Fireside* (*Refranes que dicen las viejas tras el fuego*). It is
the first such collection to be made in any vulgar tongue, and suggests the rich proverbial lore of Spain which Sancho Panza was
later to draw on so freely.

Most of Santillana's poems are in the allegorical Dantesque style.
His *Comedieta de Ponza,* in *arte mayor* stanzas, is a description of
the naval battle in which Alfonso V of Aragon and his two brothers
were defeated and captured; it is supplied with a wealth of mythological and pedantic trappings. Boccaccio is brought into the poem
to utter consolation to the distressed wives involved, and Dame
Fortune to prophesy their smiling future. The poem also contains

an imitation of the *Beatus ille,* the first imitation of Horace in Spanish. The Marquis' dialogue of *Bías contra Fortuna* is a long-ish poetic dissertation on the vanity-of-vanities theme. The *Doctrinal de privados* (*Manual for Favorites*) is a satire against Don Alvaro de Luna (after his death), whom Santillana opposed. The *Proverbios de gloriosa doctrina,* a longish work in which the author ransacks Solomon, Socrates, Plato, Aristotle and others for didactic purposes, was written especially for John II's son Henry III.

The preceding works display the Marquis as a poet of culture and dignity, but his charm and grace are far more evident in his *Canciones y decires* and his ten *serranillas.* We have seen that Santillana professed a fine scorn for popular compositions, but he was not above taking them and stylizing them with a very true delicacy and keen poetic sensibility. Probably he considered them trifles, but to any modern taste they are far superior to his longer and more ambitious compositions, more universal in their appeal and more perfect in execution. In general they follow the tradition of the Galician-Portuguese school, though they are all in Castilian; the verse-forms are uncomplicated and the lines short. One of the most delightful is the sentimental little *Canción* which begins:

> Si tu deseas a mi
> Yo non lo se;
> pero yo deseo a ti
> en buena fe.

Another which appears in practically all anthologies is the Marquis' *villancico* for his three daughters, based on four popular refrains.

Santillana is, rightly, most celebrated for his *serranillas.* Some of them have *vaqueras* (cow-girls) rather than mountain lasses as their heroines, and are more akin to the French *pastourelles.* The robust Archpriest of Hita makes his *serranillas* highly realistic or even grotesque, for aristocratic delicacy was not his forte. The Marquis poetizes them, endows them with subtle allure, gives them charms according to his graceful fancy, and infuses his poems with his own refined sensuality. The best-known of the *serranillas* is

*La vaquera de la Finojosa.* The Marquis, having lost his way in rough country, is overwhelmed with the vaquera's gracious beauty, which he wishes he had never seen, but not really, for he says to her:

> . . . Donosa,
> ¿dónde es la vaquera
> de la Finojosa?

She is quick-witted as well as beautiful, and she replies (if we may change her profession from *vaquera* to *pastora*):

> The shepherdess laughed
> And said: "Be at rest;
> I sense all too well
> What you would request.
> Finojosa's shepherdess
> Does not desire
> And does not intend
> To yield to love's fire."

In other *serranillas* the rustic encounter is described as less unfortunate. Santillana's graceful stylizing of rural themes was later to be matched by Lope de Vega.

The Marquis has another claim to preeminence in Spanish literature: he was the first to write sonnets in Castilian. His forty-two efforts he frankly calls *Sonetos fechos al itálico modo,* and they are at best none too successful imitations of Petrarch. The form proved uncongenial, and it remained for Boscán and Garcilaso to naturalize it in the next century.

## VILLENA AND MANRIQUE

One of Santillana's poems was *On the Decease of Don Enrique de Villena.* The latter gentleman (1384-1434), of royal ancestry on both sides, displayed a strange mixture of learning and superstition. His political ambitions rapidly went up in smoke, and he retired to devote himself to the pleasures of alchemy, literature, gastronomy and love. Even in his own day he was thought of as a magician, black variety, who had made a pact with the Devil, and he so appears in literary works down through the nineteenth century.

Only fragments are preserved of Villena's *Arte de trovar,* enough to show that it is based on the work of Provençal theorists. A treatise on astrology has been attributed to him, and he wrote a dissertation on how to avoid the effects of the Evil Eye, in whose baleful power he believed. His treatise on leprosy and his *Labors of Hercules* have only minor interest. At the request of the Marquis of Santillana he made a translation, the first in Spanish, of Dante's *Divine Comedy.* He also made a translation of Vergil's *Aeneid,* the first in any vulgar tongue. It is unfortunately marred by its swollen and labored style. Probably his most enjoyable work is a sort of cook book, the *Tratado del arte de cortar del cuchillo,* or *Arte cisoria (Art of Carving).* Some of the dishes he describes must have been amazing concoctions, and perhaps helped to bring about his early death.

In his credulousness Villena belongs to an age which we superciliously like to consider very dark. In his interest in Italy and the classics, he foreshadows the Renaissance. His penchant for the grosser pleasures of life might belong to any age.

Some of the poets who came after Santillana and Mena were less modern than they, less subject to the new Italian influence. They were fairly numerous: the best of those of the sad reign of Henry IV were Juan Álvarez Gato and the two Manriques. The first was a smooth versifier, perhaps at his best in festive pieces, though some might prefer his religious poems. Gómez Manrique (1412?-1490?) was a very active warrior, politician and courtier. His governorship of Toledo was signalized by two achievements: he rebuilt the famous bridge (de Alcántara) and by the force of his oratory he kept the city from going over to the Portuguese. With a hundred lances, he escorted Ferdinand of Aragon on the way to marry Isabella. He had little regard for his hundred poems, which were preserved by chance, but which would rank just after those of his uncle and of Mena. He is also important in the history of the drama for his nativity play, in which Princess Isabella and her ladies took part, for dramatic *Lamentaciones* for Holy Week, and for two

*Gramstorff Bros.*

The Visagra Gate, Toledo. Combination of Moorish and Christian styles.

*Hispanic Society of America*

Knocker, about 1500. Mixed style.

Typical Hispano-Moresque plate. Late 15th Century.

*Hispanic Society of America.*

St. Francis. High-relief embroidery of the sixteenth century.

*Hispanic Society of America*

St. Francis. Figure in wood, by Alonso Cano (1601-1667), sculptor and painter.

*Culver Service*

Looking down toward the lovely cathedral of Burgos.

San Juan de Los Reyes, in Toledo. Late Gothic.

The somber grill-shaped Escorial. Renaissance Classic. Architect, Juan de Herrera.

*Culver Service.*

R. Balaco: "Columbus Before Ferdinand and Isabella."

F. Pradilla: "Juana La Loca." She carried about with her the corpse of her husband, Philip the Handsome.

*Culver Service*

L. F. Usabal: Portrayal of the Conquistador,
Hernán Cortés.

The Conquistador Pizarro before Emperor Charles V.

Antonio Moro (Antonis Mor van Dashorst): "Philip II."

secular masques (*momos*) to be played for birthday celebrations.

Gómez Manrique was the nephew of one excellent poet, the Marquis of Santillana, and the uncle of another, Jorge Manrique. The last named died in 1478, before reaching forty, from wounds received defending the cause of Isabella. Most of his poems are rather conventional, but one is an exception. The famous *Coplas* on the death of his father (Don Rodrigo Manrique, Grand Master of Santiago) are deservedly in most anthologies. The theme is one of the most worn in all literature: the transitoriness of human life and the inevitability of death. Not much new about that, and it is not novelty that gives Manrique's flowing verses their perennial appeal. It is his dignity, his grace of expression, his perfection of form, his transformation of his own grief into the sorrow of humanity in the presence of man's inevitable fate, into a reflection of the vanity of past splendor. Manrique's poem, like Villon's haunting *Ballade des dames du temps jadis,* has been translated into many languages. Longfellow's version is particularly happy:

> Our lives are rivers, gliding free
> To that unfathomed, boundless sea,
>     The silent grave!
> Thither all earthly pomp and boast
> Roll, to be swallowed up and lost
>     In one dark wave.

> Tell me, the charms that lovers seek
> In the clear eye and blushing cheek,
>     The hues that play
> O'er rosy lip and brow of snow,
> When hoary age approaches slow,
>     Ah, where are they?

> Where are the high-born dames, and where
> Their gay attire, and jewelled hair
>     And odors sweet?
> Where are the gentle knights, that came
> To kneel, and breathe love's ardent flame
>     Low at their feet?

Where is the song of Troubadour?
Where are the lute and gay tambour
    They loved of yore?
Where is the mazy dance of old,
The flowing robes, inwrought with gold,
    The dancers wore?

O World! So few the years we live,
Would that the life which thou dost give
    Were life indeed!
Alas! thy sorrows fall so fast,
Our happiest hour is when at last
    The soul is freed.

After a eulogy of his father, Manrique ends:

As thus the dying warrior prayed,
Without one gathering mist or shade
    Upon his mind;
Encircled by his family,
Watched by affection's gentle eye
    So soft and kind;

His soul to Him who gave it rose;
God lead it to its long repose,
    Its glorious rest!
And, though the warrior's sun has set,
Its light shall linger round us yet,
    Bright, radiant, blest.

## THE BALLAD

Santillana and Mena mark a stage of transition from the Middle
Ages to the Renaissance, and the ballad may be said to do likewise.
Distinctly mediaeval in origin, it was popular with poets of the
sixteenth century and afterward, and the subjects of ballads were
frequently used for drama or novel, not only in Spain but elsewhere,
on into the twentieth century.

The word *romance,* at first meaning simply the vulgar tongue,

Spanish, came to be applied specifically to this one form of composition, the ballad. It is composed on the basis of groups of eight
syllables. The octosyllabic form seems particularly suited to the
genius of the language and has been more popular than others for
about five hundred years. A few ballads are in *romance menor,* on
a six-syllable basis, as used later by Góngora and many others.

Here is a sample of an old ballad. It refers to the murder of
King Sancho while he was besieging Zamora, a city held by his
sister Urraca. In Spanish it begins thus:

> Rey don Sancho, rey don Sancho
> No digas que no te aviso
> Que de dentro de Zamora
> Un traidor ha salido . . .

An English translation of the whole short ballad:

> King don Sancho, King don Sancho,
> I warn thee, warn thee well,
> That from Zamora's city
> Hath come a traitor fell.
> His name Vellido Dolfos
> Dolfos Vellido's son.
> Ere now he wrought four treasons
> With this five will be done.
> If traitor was the father
> The son is traitor more.
> In don Sancho's camp they're crying
> Don Sancho's wounded sore.
> Vellido Dolfos killed him,
> Great treason hath he done.
> And after this foul murder
> Through a postern gate he's run.
> And through the streets of Zamora
> He shouted as he stepped:
> It was high time, Urraca,
> That promises be kept.

Another favorite is the *Ballad of Count Arnaldos:*

Oh, who could have such fortune
　　On the sea so far away
As once had Count Arnaldos
　　On the morn of St. John's Day.
He was hunting on that morning,
　　With a falcon on his hand;
When he saw a small ship coming,
　　Coming to the land.
Its sails they were all silken,
　　And its rigging lace, but strong,
And the captain on the foredeck
　　Was singing such a song
That it made the sea all quiet,
　　And it lulled the wind to sleep,
And it lured the silver fishes
　　To swim up from the deep.
It drew the birds from Heaven
　　To rest upon the mast.
Then up spoke Count Arnaldos,
　　Then up he spoke at last:
"For God's sweet sake, oh, Captain,
　　A boon I crave of thee;
For I never heard such singing
　　On land or on the sea,
Oh, teach me that strange chantey!"
　　Then the Captain said, said he:
"I do not sing that chantey
　　Save to him who goes with me."

The original uses assonance, as early Spanish ballads do, not full rhyme.

The vexed question of the origin of the ballad in Spanish has been much discussed. It may well be that ballads arose out of longer epic poems, that they were fragments detached because they were particularly striking and remained quite easily in the memory. Once the genre was started, it was easy for poets to add compositions in general imitation of models and on all sorts of subjects. The early ballads are anonymous, but a word of caution may be appropriate with regard to the term "popular" applied to them. It does not mean that they sprang spontaneously from some group of people, from a singing chorus. They must have been consciously composed, but it is true that they became modified according to the tastes of their hearers as they were handed down by word of mouth from generation to generation.

Nobody can say exactly how old the oldest Spanish ballad may be. None in its surviving form is older than the fifteenth century, but it is by no means impossible that some were composed before that. "Old ballad" means one composed in the fifteenth century or before. The *romances viejos* are likely to be short, on Spanish epic themes, often presupposing in the hearer a knowledge of the life of the hero or the event involved. The *romances fronterizos* (*Frontier Ballads*) commemorate events in the border warfare between Christians and Moors, and are also old and short. The oldest of them is probably *Cercada tiene a Baeza,* referring to a siege in the year 1368 and perhaps composed not long afterward. The *romances juglarescos* (*Minstrel Ballads*) may be said to represent the last poetic development of the epic. They are longer, more personal, more romantic, and most of them concern Charlemagne and his paladins. The *romances eruditos* were composed by learned gentlemen after 1550, and were usually uninspired and prolix rehashings of chronicle material. They resembled the *juglarescos* in the use of full rhyme instead of assonance. *Romances artísticos* are those composed by sophisticated poets from the late fifteenth through the seventeenth century: Cervantes, Góngora, Quevedo, Lope de Vega and many others, whose ballads compose one of the most delightful parts of their reportory. *Romances vulgares,* the sort sung by street singers, are likely to celebrate the achievements of highwaymen, bandits and similar worthies, or to rhyme some recent event or scandal. They were composed from 1600 on to the present, for popular consumption. They are about on a par with *The Wreck of the Old Ninety-Seven* or *The Death of Floyd Collins,* or *Casey Jones.*

Broadsides containing ballads began to be published very soon after the invention of printing. The first printed collection was the

Antwerp *Cancionero de romances,* before 1550, enlarged in 1550 and running through many editions. The *Silva de varios romances,* three parts, 1550-51, also enjoyed several printings. These anonymous collections were soon followed by those of authors who included mainly their own compositions, largely *romances eruditos.* The large *Romancero general* went through three editions by 1604, with a second part in 1605. Then numerous collections on special subjects appeared: the Cid, the Twelve Peers of Charlemagne, etc. Scientific interest in Spanish ballads began in Germany in the nineteenth century. In Spain, Agustín Durán, beginning in 1828, published in his *Romancero general* no less than 1,900 ballads.

# XI

## *The Era of the Cathedrals*

### ARCHITECTURE

THE most impressive monuments of the Middle Ages are their cathedrals, extraordinary witnesses to the artistic sense and power of cooperative effort in a period which we complacently regard as far inferior to our own. The earlier churches of Spain were Romanesque: relatively low, with round arches and thick walls, a style which reaches its culmination in the great cathedral of St. James at Compostela and which is contemporary with St. Sernin at Toulouse. Since the Moors were in the south of Spain, this Romanesque architecture is to be found in the north. It was often inspired by French models. The inspiration for Spanish Gothic, beginning in the early thirteenth century, also came from France. Witness the origins of the great cathedral of Burgos, an early and exquisite example of Gothic architecture in Spain. Queen Berenguela sent Bishop Mauricio to the court of Henry II of Germany to ask the hand of his daughter Beatrice of Swabia for her son Fernando III. The Bishop spent six months on his mission, and as he traveled saw several cathedrals in process of construction. He was particularly impressed by Notre-Dame in Paris. Hence when the Cathedral of Burgos was begun in 1221 (work continued on it for three hundred years), the general style was French Gothic, with the typical emphasis on the vertical: high pointed arches, flying buttresses and heaven-seeking spires. By now the stone of which it was built has assumed a golden color, and to view it at sunset across the Arlanza is to behold a sort of fairy vision. León, regarded by many as the most beautiful Gothic cathedral in Spain, is almost entirely a product of the thirteenth century. The cathedral of Seville, built around an old mosque, is the largest Catholic Gothic church in Christendom. It is impressive from without, but its interior, much better lighted than most Spanish cathedrals, gives an especial impression of space and majesty. Spain has not often adopted foreign innovations wholeheartedly, and most of her remaining cathedrals are composites of many elements, native and foreign.

It is true that the mediaeval cathedrals are monuments to religious fervor, but they are likewise witnesses to cooperative civic enterprise. Their uses were primarily but not wholly religious, for they also served as meeting-places, town halls, theatres and libraries. They gave opportunity for expression not only to the architect, but also to the sculptor, the woodcarver, the maker of stained glass, the artificer in gold, ivory and jewels, the painter, and, by no means least, the skilled ironworker. It seems that Spaniards, with characteristic obstinacy, took pleasure in seizing a resistant medium like iron and twisting it into the delicate shapes of their fancy, and fortunately for us their work seems imperishable. They lifted a craft into the realm of high art.

All European architecture in the Middle Ages is likely to be thought of as either Romanesque or Gothic, but in Spain there existed a combination of one of these with something Oriental. In short, *Mudéjar* art. The *Mudéjares* were the Moslems whom the Christians conquered at various times and places and who were allowed to keep their own religion. When the *Mudéjares* built, they showed a fondness for decorative archways, for exposed brick and glazed tile for ornamentation, for the horseshoe arch, though other elements in their structures might be European. Excellent examples may be seen in Toledo, in the synagogues, in the Puerta del Sol and the old Bisagra gate, in the church of San Lorenzo in Sahagún and elsewhere. The numerous carved and painted ceilings (*artesonados*) to be found all over Spain are admirable samples of *Mudéjar* art. Its influence is also to be found in bookbindings and miniatures.

## SCULPTURE AND PAINTING

Sculpture was regarded as an accessory to architecture and developed along with it. The subjects were mainly the Virgin Mary, saints and apostles. In the eleventh and twelfth centuries Spaniards did remarkable sculptures not only in stone but also in ivory. In the next two centuries Spanish sculpture was second only to the French, and notable examples can be seen in the cathedrals of Burgos, León, Toledo and Pamplona. The figures grew more lifelike and less conventional. By the fifteenth century statues of deep beauty and considerable originality appeared in Spanish churches and monasteries. Two of the greatest sculptors were Gil de Siloé and Diego de la Cruz. The beautiful little Carthusian monastery (La Cartuja de Miraflores) outside Burgos has fine examples of their work in the richly adorned High Altar and the statues of King Juan II and his queen, Isabel of Portugal, gilded, it is said, with the first gold brought from America. Gil de Siloé's recumbent figures of the same king and queen in the mausoleum at Miraflores have a Renaissance glow and smoothness plus a real Spanish gravity and serenity. The artists worked under the patronage of Queen Isabella the Catholic.

Painting did not develop early in Spain. The earliest paintings, altar-pieces and murals of the twelfth and thirteenth centuries, are of religious subjects, but show an emphasis on the artists' personal observation. From the thirteenth to the sixteenth centuries Spain was a melting pot of various influences in painting, and many artists from abroad came and worked in the Peninsula: Sienese, Florentine, French, Flemish. Spanish artists studied and worked abroad, especially in Italy. The tender, human and plausible art of Giotto (1276-1336) was particularly influential.

In the reign of Juan II, in 1428, the Fleming Jan van Eyck visited Spain, and his influence lasted for a century or more. His miniature-like richness, his precise realism and his shiny finish in execution were widely copied, as by Luis de Morales (1509-1586), called the "Divine." Morales' subjects were always religious and he achieved considerable emotional effect.

The spirit of Italian painters like Giotto and Fra Angelico was sunny, happy, but their Spanish followers were different. There is nothing joyous, for example, in the able painting of Raphael's disciple Luis de Vargas (1502-1568), who is said to have scourged himself frequently and to have kept an open coffin by his bed, in which he lay to remind himself of inevitable death. Not all Spanish painters were so lugubrious, but they did not acquire in the Renaissance the sensuous pagan tone of, say, a Titian or a Giorgione.

## MUSIC

Spanish art has left its records, but the annals of music are far more tenuous. Mediaeval Spanish music is a fascinating subject. It would be delightful to know just how a troubadour at the court of Alfonso the Learned or a group of pilgrims on the way to Santiago de Compostela or a gang of merry students played and sang their songs, but precise knowledge is lacking. It is quite true that some early Spanish music has been deciphered, but musicologists do not agree that the deciphering is accurate.

It is at least true that both religious and secular music flourished vigorously in Christian Spain. Plain song was fully developed by the thirteenth century, and church music followed in general the same development as in France. The chants in the rite of the Mozárabes, the Christians in Moorish Spain, were officially suppressed in 1076, but they persisted after that, even though the Roman rite, with Gregorian music, was accepted practically everywhere.

How much influence did Arabic, Moorish-Andalusian music exert? A very ticklish question, about which scholars differ even more than on the general question of Oriental influences in the Peninsula. Certainly the Arabs had a superior culture, they were gifted musical theorists and performers, and they were constantly thrown into contact with Spaniards of all conditions for nearly eight hundred years. Could Spaniards fail to take something from them? The late Professor Julián Ribera, in *La música de las cantigas,* claims that the Moors used the diatonic scale and a complete system of harmony, which spread to Castile by the thirteenth century. He has found few to agree with him fully. In his enthusiasm for all things Moorish he suggests that this Moorish musical influence was dominant, all-important not only in Spain but also in France, among the Troubadours, for example. Mr. J. B. Trend, an English music critic, is much more cautious. He says in *The Music of Spanish History,* Oxford, 1926: "It is difficult to say to what extent Spanish music was influenced by the music of the Arabs, for the Arabs had no fixed musical notation. . . . The Moorish contribution to Spanish music, then, is the Mudéjar style—that is, a manner of performance rather than a type of musical construction; and this Oriental manner of performance has always been exaggerated, and is still being exaggerated, by gipsy performers." To the untutored listener's ear, there is decidedly something Oriental, at least un-European, about simple melodies heavily adorned, with distinctive rhythms, generally within the compass of a sixth, and performed with zest and intensity. If the music is not Moorish in origin, it is at least different, far from commonplace, and highly stirring.

# XII

## *From the Catholic Sovereigns to Philip II*

### THE UNIFICATION OF SPAIN

THE unknown author of the *Poem of the Cid* had some idea of Hispanic unity, a concept which kept growing throughout the Middle Ages. No one single region alone could have developed into the great world power that was Spain in the time of Charles V and Philip II. The reign of Ferdinand and Isabella was a period of preparation upon which Charles V built up a great empire in Europe and the Americas. In the days of the Philips Spain fell from her high estate.

The union of Castile and Aragon in the persons of Ferdinand and Isabella did not mean immediate political union of the two kingdoms, but the foundations were laid. Separate laws and customs continued to be in vogue, as strong traces of them remain until now, but it was inevitable that a common policy should be adopted. The first step was to bring order to the realm: in other words to put down arrogant nobles and to centralize the royal authority, which was hardly more than nominal in the anarchical times of Enrique IV. Nobles who resisted had cause to regret it, for they were vigorously and sternly put down. Many were executed, their castles razed and their revenues diverted to the crown, particularly in Galicia and Andalusia. In a few years the pacification was complete. The middle classes were easier to deal with, for they were royalist already and stood to profit from a strong orderly government. The towns were made to depend more and more on the central authority. The sovereigns made it clear that they intended to rule without interference. The Cortes were summoned very infrequently. In Aragon they met seldom, and in Castile only nine times in the years 1475-1503. From 1482 to 1498, vitally important years for Spain, the Castilian Cortes were not summoned once.

The chief authority in governmental matters in Castile was the *Consejo Real,* formerly composed of the upper nobility and high-ranking churchmen. In 1480 the *letrados* (lawyers recruited from the middle classes) became a majority of the body. Nobles could attend, but were deprived of a vote, and later they were excluded altogether. The Council thus became subservient to the will of the sovereign. Other councils were formed for special matters: for the Inquisition, for the Americas (*Consejo de Indias*) and for the Military Orders, and still others in Aragon. A host of officials were needed to enforce the orders of the councils, and a complicated bureaucracy thus came into existence.

The chief court of justice was the Royal Chancellery, under which were several regional courts called *audiencias.* Isabella made a strenuous effort to purify the administration of justice and to prevent ecclesiastical courts from interfering with the royal juris-diction. Ferdinand acted similarly in Aragon.

For their schemes Ferdinand and Isabella realized that they needed a better army and more money, and to both matters they devoted serious attention. The collection of stamp taxes (docu-mentary taxes), customs duties and the *alcabala* or sales tax was regularized and made more efficient, and the proceeds from the sale of the *Bula de la Cruzada* (indulgences sold supposedly for prose-cuting the war against the infidel) became a permanent part of the royal income. As a consequence the revenues in 1504 were about thirty times what they had been in 1474. To take any money or any gold, silver or copper out of the country was strictly forbidden.

The army was increased in size, and one man in twelve between the ages of twenty and forty was made liable for military service. The seigneurial levies were gradually done away with and the fighting units made uniform in size: 500 men under each captain and twelve such *capitanías* or 6,000 men under each colonel. Some of the infantry had guns (arquebuses), and each brigade had 64 pieces of artillery, which used balls of stone. Each *coronelía* (6,000 infantry) had 600 horse attached. The navy was also increased and reorganized.

## EXPULSION OF MOORS AND JEWS

With the country pacified, the next obvious step was the conquest of Granada. A new war against the Moslem had broken out in 1481. Ferdinand, aided by a few victories and much more by the use of lying and treachery, in which arts he was as gifted as modern politicians and dictators, managed after ten years to reach the plain of Granada and to lay siege to the city itself. It was bravely defended by Boabdil, but hunger forced him to surrender, on January 2, 1492, seven hundred and eighty-one years after the incursion of Tarik. The Crescent no longer waved over a foot of Spanish territory. According to the terms of surrender, the Moslems were not to be disturbed in Granada or elsewhere, and could freely practise their religion. It was not very long before this treaty was nullified by the Spaniards, and a royal decree was issued in 1502, stating that all Moslems (Mudéjares) must either accept Christianity or leave the country. The decree was urged by many men of high position, including Cardinal Cisneros, Archbishop of Toledo. Most of them elected to remain, and were called Moriscos. Since their new religion was accepted under duress, they were often suspected of lack of orthodoxy and were persecuted as Spanish religious intolerance grew.

After 1492, then, Ferdinand and Isabella were in possession of all the Iberian Peninsula except Portugal and Navarre. Portugal was not to be joined to Spain until 1580, but in 1512 Ferdinand took advantage of an opportunity and overran Navarre. The Pope sanctioned the conquest of the part lying south of the Pyrenees, and it was permanently added to the Spanish dominion.

It is pretty certain that to Spaniards of the time of Ferdinand and Isabella the important event of the year 1492 was the conquest of Granada. They probably did not pay much attention to an obstinate visionary named Cristóbal Colón, whom we are pleased to call

Christopher Columbus. He could not get attention elsewhere in Europe, either, but the Spanish sovereigns, while not exactly bursting with enthusiasm, at least made it possible for him to fit out three rather diminutive boats with which he made strange history. The sovereigns were also careful to make an agreement with him as to the legal conditions of any possible benefits from the voyage of exploration and for the organization of any lands which he might occupy. So America was discovered and organized and the foundation laid for the largest colonial empire that the world had yet seen.

The American colonies, known as *Indias,* were given the form of government in vogue in the mother country. A council, the *Consejo Supremo de Indias,* was formed to take charge of the new lands. Governors were appointed by the crown (Columbus was the first and not very successful one), and the Exchequer was represented by the proper number of high and low officials to collect taxes. The legal and ecclesiastical systems followed those of Spain. Queen Isabella made one startling innovation: she declared the natives to be free in the eyes of the law. The general European attitude toward savage peoples was that they had no rights and were natural objects of slavery. In theory Isabella's legislation was unprecedentedly liberal. Unfortunately practices arose which were in contravention of her idealistic provisions, and human greed often led to cruel abuse of helpless natives. At the worst, however, the Indians in Hispanic America survived in far greater numbers than in the supposedly more civilized nations such as the United States and Canada.

Another event of some importance took place in Spain in 1492 in addition to the conquest of Granada and the discovery of America: the expulsion of the Jews. Of the piety of Queen Isabella there can be no doubt, and we may grant that she was motivated mainly by a desire for the purification of the faith. The Jews, naturally enough, had resisted conversion, although some had become sincere Christians, and they were a hindrance to the establishment of one exclusive religion. Many of them were also rich and envied, cordially hated by a large section of the Christian population. At any rate, a royal decree was promulgated on March 31, 1492, requiring all Jews to accept conversion or suffer expulsion within four months. The decree applied to both Aragon and Castile, and Navarre and Portugal soon followed suit. Some Jews accepted baptism, but those forced into exile were far more numerous, and have been said to number as many as two million, probably a great exaggeration. Conservative estimates put the number of exiles at 165,000, converted 50,000, lives lost in the carrying out of the decree 20,000. The exiles scattered widely, and groups of their descendants, still practising the Sephardic rite and still speaking Spanish, are to be found in Turkey, Greece and the Balkans, with a fair-sized colony in New York.

## THE SPANISH INQUISITION

There can be no doubt that by the time of the Catholic Sovereigns belief in one form of religion had come to be viewed as a necessary component of national unity. The days when Alfonso the Learned could impartially gather Christian, Moorish and Jewish scholars and artists at his court had long passed. The faith of Spaniards was intense, and it was to be képt pure. It seemed to the Catholic Sovereigns logical and desirable to request the Pope to set in motion an organization that would secure more perfect unity in Church and nation, and free them from dissident elements. On November 1, 1478, Pope Sixtus IV issued a bull authorizing Ferdinand and Isabella to set up the Inquisition. The judges were to be carefully selected men known for their wisdom and virtue, more than forty years old, masters, or doctors of theology, who were to investigate heresy. No one could be convicted without the testimony of two witnesses. A thirty or forty days' period of grace was always offered, during which the unorthodox could repent and be reconciled with the Church. The accused was presumed guilty until he cleared himself, and he did not know who his accusers were, but he could give a list of his enemies and their testimony was disregarded. It is sometimes forgotten that the Inquisition had nothing to do with infidels, that is, with Jews and Moors, but only with professing Roman Catholics. After 1492 the problem of the infidels did not exist anyway, for the last of the Moors were driven out and the Jews expelled.

The number of converted Jews in Spain was large, and there were many rich and powerful, holding high positions in the State or in the Catholic clergy itself. The sincerity of their faith was questioned, and they were suspected of Judaism. The *Catholic Encyclopedia,* article on *Torquemada,* says flatly that Spain was full of *Marranos* (a word used by the populace for converted Jews, which may be connected with Hebrew words meaning "Accursed," but which in plain Spanish means "Swine") and that these Marranos "endeavored to Judaize all Spain, and that the Catholic faith was in great danger from them." Those statements represent an extreme view. It is undeniable that some converts were insincere and that they continued Jewish or Mohammedan practices. They were therefore heretical.

Inquisitions, even accompanied by imprisonment, torture and agonizing death, were nothing new in the world in the late fifteenth century. A recent writer, Mr. William T. Walsh, in *Characters of the Inquisition,* New York, 1940, suggests that the first real inquisitor was Moses. When the Israelites, with the connivance and aid of Aaron, bowed down to the Golden Calf, Moses forced the people to drink the ground-up idol and ordered the Levites to set upon the idolaters. About three thousand were slain (Exodus XXXII, 28). Moses caused even more bloodshed when the incorrigible Israelites consorted with Moabitish women and worshipped Baal-peor. In other words he made stern efforts to stamp out heresy.

A more Christian spirit prevailed in the first three centuries of our era, when the Church sought to avoid bloodshed ("Ecclesia abhorret a sanguine"). The idea, as championed by St. Augustine and other Fathers, is summed up in the words of Lactantius (died 325): "If you attempt to defend religion with bloodshed and torture, what you accomplish is not defence but desecration and insult." Exclusion from the Christian communion was regarded as sufficient punishment for the unfaithful. The principle did not prevail, and the harrying and burning of heretics began. The persecutions were accomplished oftener and more cruelly by an irate populace or by an over-zealous sovereign, such as Frederick II of Sicily, than by the Church, which tried to proceed slowly, fairly and leniently.

The Inquisition as a formal organization in the Middle Ages was established by Pope Gregory IX, who ruled 1227-1241, with the appointment of special permanent judges who were to cooperate with the bishops in the suppression of heresy. The Inquisitors were members of the newly founded Orders of Dominicans and Franciscans, and their activities were conducted mainly in the south of France, against the Albigensians. The organization was also set up in Aragon in 1232. One of the most famous mediaeval inquisitors was a Spaniard of Tarragona, Nicolás Eymeric, who spent forty-six years in his stern efforts to ferret out heresy and left to posterity a *Manual for Inquisitors,* the *Directorium Inquisitorum.* The total number of heretics burned as a result of his investigations is not known.

There was nothing startlingly novel about Ferdinand and Isabella's Inquisition. It was new because it was totally independent of the bishops, was more under the control of the sovereigns and was more strictly organized. The proceeds from estates confiscated from those condemned by the Inquisition were supposed to revert to the crown. This feature must have greatly pleased Ferdinand, who was in constant need of money to pay for his wars. It led to the suspicion that some men were haled before the Inquisition because their estates were coveted.

The first Inquisitors appointed by Ferdinand and Isabella were two fierce Dominicans who set to work in Seville, holding their first *auto de fe* in 1480. They proceeded cruelly and were guilty of abuses, and Pope Sixtus IV found complaints against them all too well justified. He threatened to remove them. The real organizer of the Spanish Inquisition was the Queen's confessor, a Dominican named Tomás de Torquemada. He was personally unambitious, able, devout, fearless, zealous, stern and inflexible, a servant of the God of Justice rather than the God of Mercy. He made the Inquisition a vigorous instrument, in the main efficiently administered. His very efficiency in his unlovely duties caused him to be abominated by many, and his name is still mentioned with horror in many places, especially by Protestants and Jews. "Fierce Dominican bigot," "man . . . of unbounded arrogance under a cloak of humility," who "thirsted for the blood of heretics" (M. A. S. Hume, *The Spanish People*): these and worse terms have been applied to him. Mr. Walsh, ardent Catholic apologist, says: "To the Spanish Catholics, almost to a man, he [Torquemada] was a gentle student who had left the cloister to perform a disagreeable but necessary task, in a spirit of justice tempered with mercy. . . . To some he was more than that; he was a saint. . . . People began to pray at his tomb. He has not, however, been canonized." Quite true, he has not.

It is very difficult to determine the number of heretics who were burned at the stake during Torquemada's term of office. Juan Antonio Llorente (1756-1823), a renegade ex-Secretary General of the Inquisition, in his *Histoire Critique de l'Inquisition,* says that some 8,000 were burned and 100,000 given other forms of punishment. Llorente is not trustworthy, and his figures should probably be divided by four. Say 2,000 burned. The Inquisition also proceeded against the dead, and corpses of heretics were disinterred and burned. Those who managed to escape could be and were burned in effigy, and their property confiscated. A distinction should be made: the Inquisition itself never burned anybody. The convicted were turned over to the Civil Arm for punishment. Since, however, the civil authorities could be and sometimes were excommunicated if they failed to carry out the directions of the Inquisition, the distinction is a fine one. Torture was used not as punishment, but to extract information. The practice was by no means peculiar to the Inquisition, for civil courts had constantly used it all over Europe. Inquisitional torture was not supposed to endanger life or limb. As late as the eighteenth century one abbess, Mother Agueda de Luna, died after torture, but that was a rare occurrence. She had confessed to having five children by a corrupt follower of Molinos, Father Juan de la Vega, who was imprisoned for life.

It is beyond doubt that the severities of the Spanish Inquisition have been exaggeratedly reported by those hostile to Spain or to Roman Catholicism. It is equally true that Spain and the Catholic Church have suffered in reputation on account of it. It lasted a long time in Spain and in Spanish America, for it was not finally abolished until 1820.

## TERRITORIAL EXPANSION

Ferdinand and Isabella had cemented political and religious unity in the Peninsula. To Ferdinand's ambitious spirit, however, that was not enough. He planned to make Spain a great world power and he had every reason to think that he had succeeded by the time he reached old age. He was an out and out imperialist, and he strove by every means in his power to extend the Spanish dominions and to thwart France and the Holy Roman Empire. England was not yet very important, and there were no other rivals in sight. Portugal had a glorious history of discovery and colonization, and after Columbus' first voyage it was evident that Spanish and Portuguese claims would conflict. The matter was settled by the Line of Demarcation established by Pope Alexander VI, a Spaniard of the Valencian family of Borja (Borgia), and later amplified by the treaty of Tordesillas in 1494. Conflict arose in Africa, however, and the final result was that Spain remained in possession of the Canary Islands, Bugia, Algiers and Tripoli.

The expansion of Spain in Europe was at the expense of France. In 1493 Charles VIII agreed with Ferdinand to cede the Catalan regions of Cerdagne and the Roussillon, in return for Ferdinand's promise to aid no enemy of the French except the Pope, to form no matrimonial alliances between members of the Spanish royal family and those of England, Austria and Naples. Ferdinand was never known to keep a promise inconvenient to him, and he and his queen planned to marry their children to the best political advantage. A series of unfortunate deaths brought alliances with Portugal to nothing, and projected marriages in Navarre were refused. Henry VIII of England married Catherine, and their scandalous divorce precipitated the break between the English Church and the Papacy. One marriage had most important results, that of Princess Juana to Philip the Handsome, son of Maximilian of Austria.

Charles VIII of France had hoped to keep Ferdinand bottled up at home while he himself pushed France's claims to the kingdom of Naples. The Spanish king, however, also wished to keep France from expanding and to widen his own dominions. Negotiation and war were both indulged in, with varying fortunes and with various alliances, secret treaties, truces and renewed hostilities. The result was that the gifted Spanish general, Gonzalo de Córdoba, known as the "Great Captain," won a series of successes which gave Spain possession of the Kingdom of Naples in 1504.

That year also marked the death of Queen Isabella. In her will she left her daughter Juana as her heir. Juana, known to history as "Juana la Loca" (the Mad), was inordinately jealous, though not without some cause, of her handsome Hapsburg husband, Philip I, and was mentally unbalanced despite lucid intervals. Philip was ambitious, and took over the rule of Castile, while Ferdinand withdrew to Naples. However, Philip died in 1506, and Ferdinand was summoned back to be regent. He busied himself with intrigues to curb the power of Louis XII of France, whose troops were finally driven out of Italy. Moreover Isabella's former confessor, now the Archbishop of Toledo, Cardinal Jiménez de Cisneros, at his own expense fitted out an expedition to fight in northern Africa, with considerable success. The capital of Río de Oro (Spanish Western Sahara) still bears the name Villa Cisneros. That was only a small tribute to a great man.

The policy of Ferdinand, however questionable his methods according to high moral standards, had thus brought Spain to a position of great importance in European affairs. He was a truly great "Aggrandizer," and no more unscrupulous than many of his contemporaries and ours. When he died in 1516 Spain was ready to become the most powerful nation on earth if another leader appeared. He did, in the person of the Catholic Sovereigns' grandson, Charles of Ghent.

## THE REIGN OF CHARLES I

Charles' mother Juana was still alive, but incapable of ruling, and her sixteen-year-old son was called from the Low Countries to be King of Aragon and Navarre and regent of Castile. Cardinal Cisneros was in charge in the interim. Charles demanded to be proclaimed King of Castile, a request to which Cisneros acceded despite the opposition of the Cortes, and in 1517 the young sovereign reached Spain, surrounded by a large group of Flemish courtiers, who were heartily disliked by Spaniards. He dismissed Cisneros without even granting him an interview.

The reign of Charles I of Spain involves the history of all Europe. From his mother Juana and his grandfather Ferdinand he inherited Castile, Aragon, Navarre, Cerdagne and the Roussillon, Sardinia, Sicily, Naples, the Spanish possessions in Africa and America; from his father Philip I he had considerable territory in northern and eastern France, Flanders, Luxembourg and the Low Countries. He was furthermore the heir of Maximilian, and a most likely candidate as Emperor of the Holy Roman Empire. He was actually elected to that position after the death of Maximilian in 1519, and as Emperor Charles V ruled one of the most extensive empires known to history. That is, he tried to rule it, but it was loosely bound together, held infinite possibilities of dissension, and its different portions had very different aims and interests. Moreover, it was in Charles' time that Protestantism arose to make matters more difficult. In all probability, it would have been much better for Spain if circumstances had allowed her to concentrate upon her own national interests. As it turned out, she wasted an enormous amount of blood and wealth trying to cope with the problems of the rest of Europe, which did not intrinsically concern her. Charles regarded himself, for example, as the champion of Catholicism, which he labored mightily to impose on all his dominions. The Protestants were too stubborn, and he was unsuccessful. Francis I of France was also his constant rival, and the two were at war most of the time. Both accepted aid from the Protestant German princes when it suited them, and Francis even allied himself with the Turks. In general, Charles was successful in his wars with Francis. In fact, the French king was thoroughly beaten at the battle of Pavia in 1525, captured and imprisoned in Madrid. This was the occasion, by the way, when Francis wrote to his mother the too oft-quoted words, "Madame, all is lost save honor." It may be remarked that to Francis and to many of his contemporaries honor did not involve keeping one's plighted word. About the only tangible result of the French and Spanish wars in Italy was that Charles gained possession of Milan. Fighting in northern Africa was a practical necessity, for the Barbary pirates, supported by the Turks, not only attacked Spanish ships but even struck the Spanish coast and made forays inland. The pirate Barbarossa, a Greek renegade, became so powerful that he controlled the kingdoms of Algiers and Tunis. He was made an admiral in the Turkish navy, and from Tunis threatened Spanish Italy. Charles personally conducted an expedition against him in 1535, and Barbarossa was dethroned. The success was only temporary, however, and a Spanish expedition against Algiers in 1541 entirely failed. The African Moslems and the Turks continued to bedevil the Spaniards in the Mediterranean throughout the sixteenth century. Spanish troops met the Turks on land also, for Spaniards were among those helping to hold back the Crescent in Hungary.

Although these wars seemed to bring a temporary advantage, they were terribly expensive, and often victories could not be followed up for lack of funds. Spain herself certainly profited very little by them. Fortunately the economic losses which war entailed were counterbalanced by profits from another source, America. The time of Charles I was the era of conquest and organization across the Atlantic, the time of intrepid adventurers and *Conquistadores* like Cortés, Pizarro, Núñez de Balboa and a great many others. European wars and American adventure consumed no small amount of Spanish man power, but at least America sent Spain abundant gold and silver, and the mother country enjoyed with her new colonies a very extensive and profitable trade. The ports used were Seville and Cadiz, and all shipping was in the hands of Spaniards.

On the whole, Spain was enjoying a period of considerable prosperity. Manufacturing was encouraged, though unfortunately at the expense of agriculture. Plain dirt farming was suffering from the encouragement given to sheep-growers and their powerful organization known as the *Mesta*. Much land was devoted to grazing which might more profitably have been used for growing crops. All forms of economic activity were hedged about with strict and numerous regulations, the purpose of which was to facilitate manufacture and trade within the country. The result, however, was to make production difficult. With more and more men going to the wars, to the colonies or into the Church, agriculture, industrial production and trade gradually but surely declined and by the end of the reign of Charles I Spain's apparent political splendor rested on an insecure foundation. By the end of the century the number of sheep, for example, dropped from seven to two million. The number of looms in Seville, reported in the earlier days of Charles I at fifteen or sixteen thousand (perhaps an exaggeration), declined to four hundred. Toledo had lost most of her silk weaving by 1558. Spain's failure, in spite of great efforts, to establish a sound basis of economic prosperity, foreshadowed her inevitable disappearance as a great world power. Perhaps Spaniards, instead of rushing forth to high and exciting adventure, should have stayed at home and made money. ¿Quién sabe? They had energy enough, Heaven knows. No doubt they lacked the prosaic virtue of prudence.

palities when she was travelling in the Low Countries. The nobility followed the royal example, and even if the attitude smacked strongly of dilettantism, at least the general level of culture rose greatly. This background of culture was a necessary foundation for the great artistic works which were to appear in the sixteenth and seventeenth centuries.

## ANTONIO DE NEBRIJA

The most brilliant scholar of the time of the Catholic Sovereigns was Antonio de Nebrija (Lebrija) (c. 1441-1522). He began his studies at Salamanca, but at the age of nineteen went to Italy for ten fruitful years. He returned to spread in Spain the humanistic knowledge which he had so eagerly obtained. Nebrija taught at his Alma Mater, until Cardinal Cisneros took him to Alcalá, where he continued to teach until his death. Nebrija was in charge of the Latin and Greek texts of the Complutensian polyglot Bible, but that great effort by no means consumed all his energies. One of his earliest works was a Latin grammar (*Introductiones Latinae*), afterwards translated into Spanish. The Latin-Spanish and Spanish-Latin dictionaries which Nebrija prepared were decidedly the best of their day. In 1492 he wrote the first grammar ever composed of any modern language, the *Gramática sobre la lengua castellana*. In addition, he left works on theology, law, archeology, pedagogy, and rhetoric and composed elegant Latin poems. His career also included marriage and seven children.

Posterity has not contradicted Nebrija's own high estimate of his achievements. He was the greatest of the Spanish humanists, but by no means the only one. He and his fellows, many of whom studied in Italy, did much more to spread the new knowledge in Spain than did Italian scholars who taught in the Peninsula (Peter Martyr, Lucius Marinaeus, the Geraldini brothers), though the contribution of these foreigners was important.

## THE RENAISSANCE INFLUENCE IN LITERATURE

Naturally a change in the spirit and style of Spanish artistic manifestations accompanied and paralleled the transformation of intellectual life in the later fifteenth century. The change was gradual, however, for Spain has always been a relatively conservative country. Italian influence had begun to make itself felt before the middle of the fifteenth century; witness Santillana, Mena, Imperial, but the tone of Spanish literature continued to be much the same. By the sixteenth century a greater difference is observable, and there are new elements in literary art which are specifically characteristic of the Renaissance. They are new, but this is a point worth stressing: Spanish literature, no matter what influences bore upon it, retained a distinct flavor. In a word, it remained very Spanish. The Renaissance modified and enriched it, but did not change the essence.

Another kindred point which deserves emphasis is the continuity of Spanish literature, the persistence of themes and forms. In sixteenth century French literature the break with the past was sharp, in Spain it was not. Take the Spanish ballad, for example. Ballads were popular in the fifteenth century, and they continued to be popular in the sixteenth and seventeenth. They are still written today, in the same traditional *romance* meter. The subjects of the old ballads were used frequently by the dramatists of the Golden Age: witness the famous Cid plays of Guillén de Castro. Spain was proud of her past and never broke with it.

The fusion of the traditional and the new is excellently illustrated in Spain's second greatest novel, the *Celestina*.

## THE NOVEL

Seven years after America was discovered, Granada captured and the Jews driven from Spain or forced to accept conversion, there appeared in Burgos, with no author's name, a work in dramatic form in sixteen acts, called the *Comedia de Calisto y Melibea*. It was certainly the work of Fernando de Rojas, a converted Jew, and a lawyer who was at one time *alcalde mayor* of Talavera, near Toledo, for in 1525 Rojas' father-in-law, aged seventy, was tried by the Inquisition for Judaism, and his testimony includes the statement that his daughter Leonor Alvarez was the wife of the "Bachiller Fernando de Rojas, who composed *Melibea*."

In 1501 another edition of the *Comedia* appears in Seville. It contains a "letter from the author to a friend of his," stating that the author found the first act, and, admiring it, spent fifteen days' vacation adding to it, an act a day. It is not absolutely certain that the letter is really by the author, and at any rate practically all agree that the sixteen acts are all the work of one author, Fernando de Rojas. Some acrostic verses in this and subsequent editions declare Rojas to be the author.

In 1502, in Seville, there appeared another edition, with five new acts inserted, beginning in Act 14, and called a *Tragicomedia de Calisto y Melibea*. The question of authorship of these five interpolated acts is still vexed, although most critics would agree that their insertion was esthetically unfortunate.

The book is commonly referred to as *La Celestina,* from the name of the principal character. While it is usually thought of as a novel, it is unquestionably dramatic in its structure, though not prepared for presentation on the stage. Here is what happens:

Calisto, a handsome and rich young man of excellent family, follows his falcon into a garden, where he sees a peerlessly beautiful blonde maiden named Melibea. Stricken immediately with love, he declares his passion to her and she rebukes and curtly dismisses him. His tirades of despair are heard by his crafty servant Sempronio, who suggests that he have recourse to "a bearded old hag who is called Celestina, a witch, astute, wise in every sort of wickedness" who can "provoke hard rocks to sensuality if she has a mind to it." Calisto, mad with love, will accept any means to win Melibea. Celestina finally secures an interview between the two, in which Melibea promises that Calisto may come to her through her garden the next night. Calisto's servants go to Celestina to claim their share of the reward. She refuses them and they murder her and are executed. The next night Melibea and Calisto are united in a love which is carnal but infinitely poetic. (In the twenty-one act version, this intimacy is prolonged for a month.) Calisto, leaving his lady's chamber by a rope ladder, slips and falls to his death. Melibea, since life is now meaningless to her, hurls herself from a high tower. The drama ends with an invective against love by Melibea's father Pleberio. "Oh, love, love! . . . Who gave thee such great power? . . . Men have given thee a sweet name; thy deeds are bitter. . . . Oh, my daughter, dashed to bits! . . . Why hast thou left me sorrowing? Why hast thou left me sad and alone in *hac lachrymarum valle?*"

The reader too may be left in a "vale of tears," but he is esthetically enriched.

The literary significance of the *Celestina* is in its masterly fusion of idealism and realism. On one side is the aristocratic world of Calisto and Melibea and the overwhelming passion which moves them. Theirs is a love quintessentially pure in that it comes into being without extrinsic causes, because it exists in and for itself, like that of Romeo and Juliet, and the lovers are oblivious of all but themselves, devoted to one another, ardent yet tender, concentrated upon their passion, free from all thoughts of material advantage. Opposed to this world stands Celestina, ex-prostitute and madame, possessed of vast experience and many unsavoury skills, who is quite incapable of disinterested love, but she has seen impetuous and inexperienced couples before, and knows how to use their love for her own selfish ends. Surely her chief sin is greed, and it is selfishness that brings about her death, as it makes murderers of Calisto's servants. The book shows plebeian and aristocratic attitudes at the same time, exerting their effect upon one another, and not presented separately. Sadly enough, it is Celestina who is in control, and her attitude prevails until she overreaches herself. Perhaps love, presented as a mystic, irresistible and tragic force, is the real culprit: a blind Cupid whose random arrows inflame and slay.

The *Celestina* shows a Renaissance concentration on the human and not the divine; its world is homocentric. Some of Calisto's statements are even heretical, for example, that he is far happier in Melibea's love than all the saints in Paradise; that God is good not in essence but because he has endowed Melibea with such perfect human beauty. The heroine's suicide is a crime, of course.

The best-delineated character is Celestina herself. She is shrewd, wily, an uncompromising realist, with a vast knowledge of the ways of men, untiring energy, and a sense of humor; dynamic and vital. The *Celestina* is a masterpiece of literary portraiture, and in motion rather than static.

The minor characters are excellently drawn, too: the crafty servants Parmeno and Sempronio, whose amours parallel on a lower plane the love of Calisto and Melibea; the sensual *enamoradas* Elicia and Areusa; the rough braggart Centurio, and many another.

The style of Rojas, with his Classical-Renaissance background, is exuberant, overflowing, even turbulent. The language of the aristocratic characters is high-flown, filled with mythological references. The speech of Celestina and her cohorts is much pithier, racy, colloquial, with a true popular savour.

The *Celestina* was probably written in the early 1490's. So was a novel called *The Prison of Love* (*La Cárcel de Amor*) by Diego de San Pedro, which Menéndez y Pelayo has aptly called the *Werther's Leiden* of its day. It belongs to a class called the sentimental novel, in which love is the principal theme and is specifically discussed. It is all very sad; the hero Leriano, rejected by the lovely Laureola, takes to his bed and at last commits suicide by tearing up the letters she had written him in happier days and swallowing them. If today we are not amused by the elaborate allegory and sickly sentimentality of this little book, we may at least remember that it is a preliminary attempt to study the psychology of love. Its popularity is attested by more than two dozen editions in Spanish, and it was translated into more than twenty languages.

Juan de Flores (late fifteenth century) in *Grimalte y Gradissa* wrote a continuation of the highly sentimental *Fiammetta* of Boccaccio. Flores brings Fiammetta to a sad death through despair, and there were many readers to bemoan her fate. Flores also wrote a *Historia de Grisel y Mirabella,* which had great success, and exerted influence in Spain, Italy (Ariosto's *Orlando Furioso*), France, and England (Fletcher, *Women Pleased*).

An anonymous *Cuestión de Amor* (1513) debates this question: which of two lovers is more unfortunate, one whose beloved is dead, or one who serves a cruel fair one hopelessly? The gentlemen are Spanish, but the action takes place in Naples, and the novel gives a picturesque account of festivities and the mode of life at the Spanish court in the warm Italian city. It is in mixed prose and verse, and the characters were real people: the cardinal of Bruges is Cardinal Borgia, Belisena is the noted Bona Sforza, etc. In the *Cuestión de Amor* the action is more vigorous and the sentimentality less cloying than in San Pedro and Flores.

Spaniards of the early sixteenth century who read these outpourings of languorous emotion were also reading a more virile sort of novel, the *Amadís de Gaula,* which in some form or other their ancestors might have perused about two centuries before. It was the 1508 redaction of Garci-Rodríguez de Montalvo, however, that gained real popularity. He added a book of his own invention narrating the heroic deeds of Amadis' son Esplandián. The Amadis series finally included two dozen books. One author, Juan Díaz, killed off Amadis, but another brought him back to life to witness the achievements of his sons, grandsons, and great-grandsons. Another series of chivalric novels narrated the deeds of Palmerin, and many were written about other heroes. A novel of chivalry quite different in tone was actually the first to be printed, in Valencian, in 1490. It was called *Tirant lo Blanch* and the author was Johannot Martorell. Cervantes praised it because in it knights ate and drank and died in their beds and made wills before their death. In other words, it was more realistic, even to the point of obscenity, and it contains the germ of the burlesquing of the chivalric novel itself.

These novels are not highly esteemed today, and few indeed read them for sheer pleasure, though many certainly read worse literature. Their exaggerations, their absurdities, their lack of real characters are all too evident. It is not hard to understand, however, that the adventures of Amadis seemed to the sixteenth century

Spaniards hardly less fantastic than the exploits of a Cortés, a Pizarro, a Balboa. The simple fact is that the books were most widely read, and translated into numerous languages. Francis I of France is said to have read *Amadís* while he was Charles V's prisoner in Madrid, and to have ordered Herberay des Essarts to put it into French. It was Englished by Thomas Paynel in 1568.

After all, why should not these novels have been popular? They were sure fire: lots of adventure, lots of love, a thrill on every page, big strong brave men doing mighty deeds to win sweet lovely feminine creatures in holy wedlock; men who displayed an admirable loyalty to their natural overlords and to the women they loved. They are vigorous in tone and optimistic in tendency. They may not reflect the actual practices of sixteenth century society, but they are a significant portrayal of an ideal. Spain too was energetic and confident; and the popularity of the novels of chivalry waned as Spain's efforts became evidently unsuccessful. Philip II died, a magnificent failure, in 1598, and the last original novel of chivalry appeared in 1602, three years before Cervantes published his deathless satire.

## RENAISSANCE DRAMA

It is too bad that Spain's mediaeval drama is lost, except for the twelfth century *Auto de los reyes magos*. No basis of comparison exists for the drama of the Renaissance, which therefore seems to arise suddenly and without precedent. It is understandable that the title of "father of the Spanish drama" should be conferred on a man who came relatively late. He was Juan del Encina (1468-1529). At least a little is known of his life. He studied at the University of Salamanca, where he evidently developed a talent for music. He entered into the household of the Duke of Alba, in whose palace some sort of dramatic spectacles were shown. Encina supplied them with music. About 1498 he failed to win appointment as singer in the Cathedral of Salamanca. Going to Rome he had better fortune, becoming a member of the Choir in Pope Leo X's chapel. In 1509 he was named Archdeacon of Malaga, though he had never been ordained. He was back in Rome in 1512. The Cathedral Chapter of

Malaga insisted that he come back, and take full vows as a priest, but he evidently preferred life in Rome. As he approached fifty years of age, he began to repent of his frivolous life. Appointed Prior in the Cathedral of Leon, he was ordained priest and went on a pilgrimage to Jerusalem, saying his first mass on Mt. Zion. He seems to have resided in Leon until he died about 1529.

Fortunately many of his musical compositions are preserved, and sixty-eight have been published. Most of his literary works appeared in his *Cancionero,* Salamanca, 1496, which begins with an *Arte de la poesía castellana:* the theories of the troubadours modified by the Renaissance. He includes adaptations in Spanish of Vergil's *Eclogues.* The original poems included in the *Cancionero* are partly in the Dantesque-allegorical school, and decidedly heavy, but the sacred and profane *villancicos,* little poems in popular form, with short lines, are fresh, light, delicate, charmingly imaginative.

Encina's importance is in the history of the drama. His plays are very far from perfection, and their art is rudimentary, but at least Encina has the honor of secularizing the drama in Spain. His *autos,* such as the not-too-amusing *The Beating (Auto del repelón),* have at least suggestions of real comedy, and the accompaniment of song suggests the later *zarzuela* or musical comedy. Encina lived at a time of transition, and he is a combination of native mediaeval and Italian Renaissance attitudes. His *Eglogas* are influenced by Vergil, but are more dramatic. Some continued a tradition of religious plays connected with Christmas, Good Friday, and Easter. His *Egloga de Fileno,* influenced by the Italian Tebaldeo, ends in suicide (cf. *La Cárcel de Amor*). The comedy on the theme of love called *Plácida y Victoriano* has some excellent maxims on jealousy. *Cristino y Febea* has a pleasant subject: a hermit who is lured from solitude when love shows him a beautiful nymph. These plays show a marked advance over any drama preceding them, even though his plays were for the palace and not for the people.

In the history of the Spanish theater, the *Celestina* cannot be forgotten. After all, it is a drama, though not of proportions for the stage. It inspired several plays and exerted considerable influence on the later drama and novel.

The *Celestina* may have suggested, for example, one of the plays of Bartolomé de Torres Naharro (died c. 1531). He had a more exciting life than Encina, and he wrote better plays. He was born near the Portuguese border, and seems to have become a soldier. Suffering shipwreck, he was captured and held prisoner by Algerian pirates. Ransomed, he became a priest and spent much time in Rome and Naples, where he enjoyed the patronage of Pope Leo X and other high personages. It is thought he died about 1531.

Torres Naharro published his *Propalladia* (*"The First Fruits of My Muse"*) in 1517, in Naples. It contains poems, all but two of the author's plays, and the first essay on dramatic theory by a Spaniard. The principles are classsical. A sharp distinction, lost in later Spanish dramatic practice, is made between tragedy and comedy, and comedy is "nothing but an ingenious artifice of noteworthy and finally happy events." Comedies may be a *noticia,* more realistic, or a *fantasía,* more imaginary, though they should "have the color of truth." Decorum should be observed, for it is "like the helm of a ship." The number of characters should be from six to twelve.

Torres' verses, in traditional rather than Italianate verse forms (he has three sonnets, but they are in Italian), are not remarkable, but in the drama his place is important. His allegorical-pastoral *Comedia Trofea* was shown before Leo X in 1502, when a Portuguese embassy brought presents from India sent by King Manuel of Portugal.

The author's gifts for realism and satire are far better shown in plays such as the *Comedia Tinellaria* (*tinella* means "kitchen") which attacks corruption in the household of a cardinal. Incidentally his familiars and servants speak a confusing medley of Latin, French, Italian, Valencian, and Castilian. The *Comedia Soldadera* is another genre picture, this time of military life in Italy. These are *comedias a noticia,* and Torres does not hesitate to satirize corruption in State and Church. As examples of the *comedia a fantasía* the *Comedia Jacinta* and the *Comedia Himenea* may be mentioned. This last is of considerable interest as a suggestion of the cloak and sword play, in which the honor theme is involved. Torres' dramatic art is still imperfect, and his characters lack human warmth, but he is an important forerunner of the great playwrights who are to follow.

Greater poetic gifts were granted to Gil Vicente, who was born somewhere in Portugal, about 1470, and who has been called the Portuguese Plautus. About him very little is known, except that he was a frequenter of royal courts, that he was a musician, poet, actor, and author, and that he had two children who published his works. It is not quite certain whether the goldsmith named Gil Vicente was the same person.

Gil Vicente lived when the literary frontiers between Spain and Portugal were frequently crossed. Of his forty-three works, twelve are in Portuguese, eleven in Spanish, and twenty a combination of the two. He lived at a time, too, when Erasmus of Rotterdam (1467-1536) was setting an example of criticizing sham, hypocrisy, and malpractice on the part of the clergy. Erasmus did not attack the fundamental dogma of the Catholic Church, of which he remained a member until his death, and he and Luther became violent enemies. Yet Erasmus' satire was sharp and biting, and his influence on his contemporaries tremendous. His works were not put on the Index until after his death.

It is not surprising that Gil Vicente and many another author should reflect the critical attitude of Erasmus. The Portuguese dramatist was only one of those whose criticism foreshadowed the coming reform in the church.

The savorer of dramatic literature is more concerned with the plays of Gil Vicente than with his satirical attitude. In 1502 Vicente presented in the Royal Palace in Lisbon, to celebrate the birth of the prince who afterwards became João III, "the first thing played in Portugal," as he said. The "things," on this occasion, were little more than monologues, with courtiers disguised as shepherds, and show the influence of Encina's *Eclogues*. Vicente may quite properly be called the father of the Portuguese drama, even if his first play was in Castilian. He soon developed beyond Encina, and his dramatic compositions are of a considerable variety. His *autos,* such as "The Four Seasons," "The Sybil Cassandra," show a mixture of Biblical elements with Pagan mythology, along with traditional popular songs. In "The Four Seasons," for example, the angels surround the Infant Jesus, and sing to him this old Spanish carol:

> The rose blooms in the garden
> And there I fain would go
> To see the little nightingale
> Who sings so sweet below.

Then Jupiter invites the four seasons to visit the newborn babe, and David recites fragments of the Psalms.

The mediaeval theme of the "Dance of Death," imbued with delicate Renaissance features, appears in Vicente's trilogy of the *Barques,* which take all classes of society to Hell, Purgatory, or Glory. The satire of the various classes is keen, particularly in the *Barca de la Gloria* in Castilian, and popes, cardinals, archbishops and prelates are not neglected. The *auto* ends happily, for Christ appears and takes the poor sinners to glory.

Less intense in theme are two strictly chivalresque plays, *Don Duardos* (1525) and *Amadís de Gaula* (1533), both based on novels of chivalry. Vicente also has the honor of composing the first comedy of magic (*Comedia de Rubena,* 1521), a form of drama which was destined to enjoy great popularity up into the nineteenth century.

The *farsas* of Gil Vicente present a noteworthy gallery of popular types, often with great comic force: the pedantic and pompous doctor (*Farsa dos físicos*) anticipating Molière; the old man who makes love to young women (*O velho da horta*); the prideful hidalgo who has lots of pages but starves his servants; Negroes, gypsies, procuresses, gallants, husbands and wives.

If Vicente's verse is sometimes careless and limps slightly, he is none the less a true poet, and his delicate elaborations of popular motifs and forms have been excelled only by Lope de Vega. His lyricism is a fundamental part of his work, even more evident in his plays than in his separate poems. While he writes of the people, he writes for aristocratic audiences.

Other plays survive in Spain in the early sixteenth century, though few by known authors and none quite up to Gil Vicente's standard. One collection of them contains ninety-six pieces, *autos* (one-act plays), on Biblical themes or saints' lives and allegorical plays called *farsas*. They are mainly of value for theatrical history. The next great name is that of Lope de Rueda (1510?-1565), a Sevillian goldbeater turned playwright, actor, manager, and barnstormer. Encina and Vicente wrote and played for the aristocracy, Rueda for everyone. He was the first Spanish dramatist who brought the theater to the people.

Not that the people had never seen plays before, for it is recorded that Italian companies of strolling players were in Spain by 1535, and Rueda clearly shows the influence of Italy, notably in his five full-length comedies. Four are written in prose, a habit soon lost, and one in verse. In addition he wrote three pastoral colloquies, one in verse, a dialogue on the *Invention of Breeches,* in verse, probably two *autos,* Biblical in subject, and ten *pasos* or curtain-raisers. It is the last that have given Rueda his reputation, and established a tradition in Spain which has lasted to the present day. They are one-act pieces, dramatizing simple episodes, with sprightly characterizations of popular types, real *vis comica,* natural dialogue and language interspersed with proverbs, adequate to the mouths of its users. *The Olives* (*Las aceitunas*), a neat version of the theme of counting chickens before they are hatched, has been called the best play of the sixteenth century.

Cervantes in the preface to his own "Eight Plays" speaks of having seen the great Lope de Rueda play, describes his stage of planks on trestles, the orchestra composed of one old guitarist, and the sheepskin costumes, contained in a bag, for pastoral plays. But observe that Cervantes calls him great, and affirms that he took the drama out of its swaddling clothes, and Lope de Vega said, "*Comedias* are no older than Rueda."

Juan de la Cueva, of Seville, flourished in the second half of the sixteenth century. He was not a man of great culture, but he is of importance in the history of the Spanish theater. After spending three years (1574-77) in Mexico, he returned and showed his first play in his native city in 1579. In all, fourteen of his dramas survive, which show some vigor and brilliance, but are very imperfectly put together. Some of his plays are based on Ovid, Vergil, Livy, but he prided himself also on using "la ingeniosa fábula de España"; i.e., themes from Spanish history and legend, such as the Seven Princes of Lara, the Siege of Zamora, Bernardo del Carpio. His *El Infamador* used to be considered a forerunner of the long line of Don Juan plays, but it is not. The hero Leucino is no Don Juan, but a braggart and a liar, who is finally executed for false swearing and attempted rape. Cueva reduced the number of acts of plays from five to four. Before he died, the great Lope de Vega, possessing all Cueva's virtues and many more, had seized the monarchy of the Spanish stage.

There were many other dramatists before Lope de Vega. For example, Rey de Artieda (1549-1613) has one surviving play (*Los Amantes,* 1584) based on the famous legend of the Lovers of Teruel. Cristóbal de Virués wrote melodramas filled with terrible happenings, and his chief characters die at the end of Act V. These authors sought to establish the tragedy in Spain, as did the great Cervantes. Their work was incomplete, imperfect, and they do no more than suggest the genius of Lope and his compeers.

## LYRIC POETRY

The reign of Charles V was glorious for its conquests, but they were lost. Not so with the productions of certain lyric poets, for they still live with an ever fresh appeal.

The Italian influence came in with the Marquis of Santillana, who even wrote sonnets, but it remained for two poets of the early sixteenth century to acclimatize the Italian forms: Boscán and Garcilaso de la Vega. As in the case of Wyatt and Surrey, they were both noblemen, firm friends, one older than the other, and their poems were not collected until after both were dead.

Juan Boscán Almogáver, of an aristocratic Barcelonese family, was a courtier of Charles V. Once in the year 1526 while the court was in Granada, Boscán had a memorable conversation with the accomplished humanist and Venetian ambassador, Andrea Navagero.

The Italian urged the Spaniard to try writing poetry in the newer meters in vogue in Italy, which he considered quite superior to the Spanish. Boscán did. He began to use the eleven-syllable line, which has been employed by Spanish poets ever since, in the sonnet, or in other forms. He introduced the Italian octave, tried the *terza rima,* the *canzone* (*canción*) and the *silva,* a combination of eleven- and seven-syllable lines, with rhymes here and there. It must be confessed that Boscán was not a really gifted poet, and he did not achieve even technical mastery over the new forms, but he was a true innovator and his new measures were greatly to enrich Spanish poetry.

To the taste of many, Boscán's verse is surpassed by his prose, as displayed in the translation which was printed in 1547 of that most delightful of all books of etiquette, Castiglione's *Book of the Courtier.* Castiglione had been ambassador in Spain, and died there. Boscán must have been a kindred spirit, for his free translation is smooth and adequate. Boscán died in 1542.

Boscán said that he would not have persevered in his poetic attempts but for the encouragement of his younger friend. Garcilaso de la Vega seems almost too good to be true, for the gods had refused him nothing—except the woman he loved. He was of the upper nobility by birth and breeding, and a man of excellent culture, familiar with Greek, Latin, French, Italian. He could handle a sword or lute with grace, was said to be the handsomest man of his time, was constantly in love, and died young serving his emperor in the war in Southern France. It is granted to few men to exemplify so perfectly the ideals of an age.

Garcilaso was born about 1501; most of his life was spent at court, on campaigns in the wars between Charles V and Francis I, or on diplomatic missions. He was married in his early thirties to a noble and rich lady named Doña Elena de Zúñiga, whom he never mentions in his poems. His real passion was for a Portuguese lady-in-waiting in the royal household, Doña Isabel Freyre, who scorned him as she had scorned Portugal's foremost lyric poet of the time, Sa de Miranda. Doña Isabel married Don Antonio de Fonseca in 1529, and died in childbirth about four years later. Her death inspired one of the most poignant sonnets in the Spanish language. Garcilaso was mortally wounded near Fréjus, September 26, 1536.

Garcilaso's poems are not large in bulk, and were published along with Boscán's works by the latter's widow in 1543, in Barcelona. Only about forty-five hundred lines in all; a good refutation of the idea that Spanish literature consists of a series of brilliant improvisations. Garcilaso had a strict literary conscience, and although he was no professional man of letters, he had the true artist's longing for perfection, and his compositions remained as models for succeeding poets.

The cultural and artistic background of Garcilaso is typical of the Renaissance. He has not only read the classics and the Italians, he has also assimilated them and made them his own. His sources can be traced, and have been, but he has imbued all his poems with his own originality, his distinctly personal interpretation. His poetic world is peopled with nymphs and shepherdesses, his rivers and forests are half real and half Arcadian, but his feelings are real, his emotional life intense, and his mode of expression is delicately stylized. He is never obvious, he does not wear his heart on his sleeve, but is always truly aristocratic, sophisticated, elegant. His characteristic tone is one of gentle melancholy, which he does not express directly in the first person singular, but in lovely formal cadences which can be interpreted by those who care to penetrate them.

Garcilaso's longest compositions are his three eclogues, constituting more than half of his total production. The most moving is the first, in which the shepherds Salicio and Nemoroso, both representing aspects of Garcilaso's feeling, bemoan the death of the shepherdess Elisa (Isabel Freyre): one of Spain's most beautiful threnodies. The two elegies, one on the death of the brother of the great Duke of Alba, and the other to Boscán, are less deep in sentiment, but most happy in form. The one *epístola,* addressed to Boscán, is Garcilaso's only attempt at blank verse, a form which has never gained much popularity in Spain. Of the five *Canciones,* the third, written while Garcilaso was in exile on an island in the Danube, is particularly graceful, and breathes a true love of nature. The fifth

*Canción* is an admirable imitation of the style of Horace. It is a charming trifle, written to the author's friend Mario Galeota to help him with his suit for the daughter of the Duke of Somma. The strange form, taken by Garcilaso from Bernardo Tasso, is still known in Spanish as the *lira,* from the first line *"Si de mi baja lira . . ."* It is a five-line stanza, of seven- and eleven-syllable lines, rhyming ababb, and afterwards enjoyed great popularity.

Garcilaso's thirty-eight sonnets are superior to Boscán's, for the younger man possessed both deeper inspiration and greater virtuosity. It was he who established the vogue of the sonnet in Spain. The most noteworthy poem in this form is the tenth, written on the occasion of the death of the same Isabel Freyre: "Those gentle charms, discovered to my hurt . . ." Perhaps sonnet XXV, fully as deeply felt, refers to the same sad event. XXVIII is a charming expression of the "gather ye rosebuds" theme. Petrarch is Garcilaso's model, but the sonnets are not mere imitations.

Garcilaso has been called the faultless poet, just as he was, by Renaissance standards, very close to being the perfect courtier. His taste was impeccable, his gift for delicate expression seldom excelled. His main theme is love, his chief mood one of melancholy. Romantic fire and passion are not to be found in his works, but his obvious restraint suggests an even greater depth of feeling. Along with his infinite refinement there is a sense of dignity, of gravity, even, which so often distinguishes Castilians. Remember, too, that his poems are composed in practically flawless form, and you can understand the esteem in which he was held by his own age and until now. He was the Ronsard of his country and age.

The innovations of Boscán and Garcilaso did not pass unchallenged. The chief opposition came from a worldly cleric, Cristóbal de Castillejo (1490?-1550), who served as secretary to Ferdinand, King of Bohemia and Hungary, and brother of Charles V. Castillejo was always hard-up since Ferdinand was stingy, but he turned down a bishopric because it would not bring in enough money. His gallant adventures were not in harmony with his cloth.

Yet Castillejo was a man of real poetic gifts. His moral and devotional poems are not noteworthy, but his satires and his love poems, directed to various ladies, possess real wit and charm. He stoutly championed the traditional meters of Spain, and wrote a sprightly satire "Against Those Who Abandon the Castilian Meters and Follow the Italian." Since Castillejo spent most of his life out of Spain and since most of his poems were not published until 1573, his campaign in favor of the native tradition had no great effect. The great Spanish poets of the Golden Age do indeed continue to use the older Spanish verse forms, but they make frequent and free use also of the newer measures imported from Italy.

# XIV

## Spain's Glory and Decline. Philosophers. Mystics

---

IT would be easy to make a symbol of the great Charles, whom the historian, Karl Branli, unhesitatingly calls the best sovereign of his time, just as Spain was unquestionably the greatest world power for a fairly long period. Charles, though gifted with physical vigor and spiritual energy, grew tired and gave up the reins of government. In 1556 he abdicated and retired to the monastery of Yuste. In the same way Spain, expending tremendous vitality, reached a summit of power and brilliance, and then her energy seemed to flag, and she sank back into a near lethargy.

Charles would no doubt have preferred to leave all his dominions to his son Philip, but it was clear that the Germans would not tolerate Spanish control, and the crown of the Holy Roman Empire went to Charles' brother, Ferdinand. Since Philip's first wife (and first cousin) María of Portugal had died, Charles had sought alliance with England by marrying Philip to Mary (1553), but the marriage disappointed his hopes by remaining childless. The Spanish prince left England in 1555.

### THE REIGN OF PHILIP II

Philip II, carefully trained for the throne by his gifted father, was a truly Spanish king who spent a long and extremely industrious life in the service of his country and his religion. Called "The Demon of the South" by his enemies, he was esteemed by the countrymen for whom he labored so mightily. In his own hands he not only concentrated the important affairs of the kingdom, but even minor details. Unwilling, because he distrusted others, to delegate authority, and suffering from an ingrained tendency to hesitate, he often let the affairs of the kingdom go while he toiled laboriously over details better left to subordinates.

Philip was constantly at war. First he fought with Pope Paul IV over his Italian possessions, and the Pope, though he excommunicated Philip, and allied himself with the French and even with the Sultan of Turkey, was defeated. Against the French Philip won an important victory at St. Quentin, but failed to follow it up by marching on Paris. After a treaty was signed in 1559, Philip hoped to seal peace by marrying Henry II's eldest daughter Elizabeth. Peace, however, was not to be had, and the wars with France continued off and on throughout his reign. Philip's generals and the celebrated Spanish soldiery won many victories, but because of diversions elsewhere, or lack of funds, or indecision, proper advantage was not taken of them. Philip was fairly well satisfied when Henry IV of France accepted Catholicism, for he hoped that France as a Catholic nation would not oppose his purposes.

The Jews had been expelled from Spain in 1492, but another group of people remained as objects of suspicion: the Moriscos, descendants of the Moors who had stayed in Southern Spain after the fall of Granada. Though they were an industrious lot, the sincerity of their conversion was doubted, and the populace and many of the clergy viewed them with distrust. Vexatious restrictions were imposed on them: they could not talk Arabic or use Arabic names or dress, they were forbidden the use of arms and even the taking of baths, regarded as an outlandish heathen custom. In 1567 an even harsher edict was directed against them, and they were finally goaded into a revolt which lasted four years. They were defeated by Philip's illegitimate half-brother, the dashing Don Juan of Austria, and surviving Moriscos were sent to other parts of Spain.

The Moriscos had been aided by African Moslems and even Turks. African pirates continued to make depredations on the Spanish coast, and the Turks were alarmingly strong. Against them Philip fought with considerable success. In 1564 he forced the Turks to raise the siege of Malta, and seven years later Christian (mainly Spanish) forces under Don Juan of Austria fought and won the great naval battle of Lepanto. One of the Spaniards wounded was an obscure doctor's son, Miguel de Cervantes. The naval power of the Turks in the Mediterranean was broken. It was a glorious victory, but the rest of Europe profited rather more than Spain. Again the victory was not followed up, though Don Juan was anxious to pursue his advantage, even to capture Constantinople, and set himself up as ruler of a new Byzantine Empire. Don Juan did indeed go so far as to capture Tunis, but Philip withdrew support, and the Spaniards had to retire.

If Mohammedans gave Philip some trouble, Protestants gave him much more, and his difficulties with his subjects in Flanders were a constant source of expense. His troops were fighting there during practically his entire reign, and the war caused an enormous drain on the Spanish treasury. The Flemings objected to being governed by foreigners, they disliked Philip's policy of centralization, and they were enraged at the severe measures taken to suppress heresy. The early leaders of the uprising in the Low Countries were Catholic, but in time the struggle assumed the character of a Protestant revolt. The Duke of Alba, sent by Philip to quell it, has left a name in history for cruel severity. His successor, Requesens, followed a more moderate policy. Don Juan of Austria took a hand (his troops mutinied) and Alexander Farnese was rather more successful. Spanish troops could win victories in the field, but afterward they were likely to be needed elsewhere, or money and supplies gave out and the troops supported themselves by plunder. The outcome was that the Protestant Netherlands practically won their independence, though Spain would not acknowledge it. For Spain the result was that she had spent badly needed men and resources to no good end.

In one of Philip's endeavors he was attended with complete success, at little expense and without bloodshed. King Sebastian of Portugal, Philip's nephew, embarked on a madcap expedition in the north of Africa in the summer of 1578. Sebastian lost his life in the battle of Alcazar-Kivir, and he had no heir. Philip quickly grasped his opportunity and claimed the Portuguese throne. His mother was a Portuguese princess, as was his first wife. The claims of others were weaker, and Philip had the advantage of military force, and with promises of a certain amount of autonomy to his new subjects he was crowned King of Portugal. Philip's fourth wife Anne of Austria died at Badajoz while he was on the way to his new dominion. Letters from the king written then to his two daughters are filled with grief and affection, and show a side of his character quite different from that of the stern and cruel monarch usually presented to readers of history. However, Philip never seemed amiable to Englishmen, Frenchmen, Turks, or Portuguese. If he had been wise enough, perhaps complete Peninsular unity might have been made permanent. There were important geographic, historical, economic, and racial reasons for it. Perhaps the cleavage had already become too profound. At any rate, Portugal broke away after sixty years.

Philip, once the husband of Mary Tudor, had never given up the idea of becoming King of England. In the early fifteen-eighties much was against him. His first son Charles (Don Carlos) who seemed to inherit a taint of insanity, had to be confined, and died at the age of twenty-three; Philip's fourth wife also died. The King was in trouble in Flanders, and France had grown much stronger. Naples was in rebellion, and the Pope and the Spanish bishops had defied the Spanish sovereign.

In spite of all this, Philip began to make preparations for an expedition against England. Philip claimed the English throne through descent from John of Gaunt. The Spanish ambassador was in close touch with Mary, Queen of Scots, who was finally persuaded to disinherit her son James (June, 1586) in favor of Philip. The anger of the Spanish nation was sufficiently inflamed by the depredations of bold captains like Drake and Hawkins, who captured so many galleons on the Spanish Main. The plan of invasion was grandiose: one hundred and fifty great ships, capital ships, as we might say, plus six hundred smaller vessels, were to take a force of thirty thousand sailors, seventy thousand soldiers, and sixteen hundred horses. Some of the troops were to be ferried over from Flanders. The plan had to be modified considerably. The difficulties in raising the necessary money were enormous. Philip worked like a slave, but he had poverty, inefficiency and corruption to contend with. The expedition was supposed to be ready in 1587, but it was not. Drake upset Spanish plans by his gallant dash at Cadiz in that same year. He burned the ships in the harbor and caused further delay, which in time caused more expense. Bad weather made it hard to concentrate ships. Santa Cruz, a fine sailor who was to lead the expedition, was reproached by Philip, and died, it is said, of a broken heart. He was replaced by the Duke of Medina Sidonia, old and incompetent, who begged Philip to call off the whole affair. Farnese in Flanders advised against it, because he knew it would succeed only if conditions were ideal. Philip went doggedly on, trusting Spanish valor, which was indisputable, and the righteousness of his cause, which was far more debatable.

Consequently about one hundred and thirty ships and twenty-five thousand men sighted the Lizard on Sunday, July 30, 1588. The rest of the story is familiar history. Half the ships and less than half the men returned to Spain, beaten by battle and storm, unhappy survivors of their nation's greatest defeat since 711. It is easy enough to see now that Philip's policies were mistaken, disastrous, but it is hard not to admire his sturdy and tireless efforts in the pursuit of what he considered to be the ideal for his country and his religion. His last days continued to be troubled; he was the victim of cruel physical suffering, which he bore with characteristic fortitude until death delivered him in 1598.

## THE DECLINE OF PROSPERITY

Philip's reign had been filled with splendid failures. He was not blind, but perhaps neither he nor any of his subjects realized how bankrupt the nation had become. Agriculture and industry had suffered greatly after the expulsion of the Moriscos. Manufacturing was robbed of incentive by oppressive taxation. Fishing had suffered because boats were commandeered for war. The population was diminished by war, disease, and colonization in the New World.

For large sections of the population, Spain must have been a pretty unhappy country to live in.

The period following that of the great Philip was one of accelerating decline and decay, relieved only by literary and artistic splendor. Philip III, as his father realized, was a weak, extravagant, and pleasure-loving young man, likely to be governed by favorites. He was, mainly by the Duke of Lerma. He could have concentrated his energies, if he had had any, for Flanders had been left to his sister Isabel (it reverted to Spain once more in the time of Philip IV), and Portugal was calm. However, a new expedition was planned against England, and a storm dispersed the fifty ships which were to take part in it. The Spanish effort to support Tyrone's rebellion in Ireland came to nothing. Philip spent funds which he could not spare in helping his sister Isabel in the Low Countries against the Dutch Protestants. One extremely capable Spanish general and statesman developed, Ambrosio Spínola. He was usually victorious, even though he often had to use his own personal funds. When the Dutch asked for a truce, he saw the advantages of a cessation of fighting, and in 1609 the truce was signed for twelve years. One feature of the war had been that the Dutch, developing their maritime power, began to seize Portuguese colonies.

In 1618 the Thirty Years War broke out, and in 1620 Spain entered it on the side of the Emperor Ferdinand, for family reasons and to carry out the traditional policy of aiding the Catholic cause. For Spain the war lasted until 1659. Spínola carried all before him, but the final result was misery and disaster for Spain.

Philip III's reign (1598-1621) was also marked by petty wars in Italy and great trouble with North African and Turkish pirates, whose activities with regard to Spain were paralleled by English and Dutch depredations.

It was in Philip III's reign that the Moriscos, numbering perhaps half a million, were finally expelled, first from Valencia (1609) and then from the entire country. The Moriscos were industrious and had contributed much to the economic life of Spain. So the third

Philip when he died in 1621 left his country much poorer than he found it.

Philip IV, weaker son of a weak father, was destined to occupy the throne for a long time, from 1621 until 1665, and to see his land grow poorer and still poorer. Philip IV's royal favorite was the Count-Duke of Olivares, whose disagreeable face is familiar to all who have seen Velázquez's portrait. The long-jawed and weak countenance of Philip IV by the same artist is equally familiar. The truce with the Dutch expired in 1621, and Olivares resumed hostilities, against Spínola's advice. The Spaniards won no particular advantages by land fighting, and suffered from the successful sea raids made by the Dutch. Spain continued in the Thirty Years War, and Spanish infantry seemed likely to turn the tide in favor of the Catholics. France was nominally Catholic, and practically ruled by Cardinal Richelieu, but she was more intent on the development of her own power than anything else, and in 1635 entered the war on the side of the Protestant princes. Spanish troops continued to win victories which were, as usual, nullified by lack of funds to push the advantages. In 1643, however, French troops under Condé defeated the Spaniards at Rocroi, the first time in two hundred years that Spanish infantry had been defeated when conditions were anywhere near equal. The moral effect on Spain's enemies was tremendously encouraging, and henceforth Spanish defeats followed thick and fast. The Peace of Westphalia formally recognized Dutch independence and the rights of the Dutch to the Portuguese Colonies which they had seized in the East Indies, and which they still held. The Catholic Netherlands remained Spanish. Fighting between Spain and France continued until 1659, when according to the terms of the peace Spain gave up Cerdagne and the Roussillon, her Burgundian possessions, a large part of the Catholic Netherlands, and Sardinia. The Spanish princess, María Teresa, was married to Louis XIV. Their grandson, as it turned out, was later to begin a new dynasty in Spain.

Meanwhile there had been much trouble in Catalonia, then as now a proud and restless portion of the Spanish Commonwealth. The Catalans felt that Olivares was interfering with their ancient liberties, their *fueros,* and they objected to excessive taxes and to having soldiers quartered on them. Catalonia finally broke into open revolt, and in 1640 actually formed a republic under the protection of France, who had carefully fomented discontent in Spain. The King of France was acknowledged as ruler in 1641, but the Catalans found the French were as hard masters as the Castilians. The disorder caused the dismissal of Olivares in 1643. Although Philip formally reconfirmed Catalan charters in 1653, the war dragged on for six years until, in the peace of 1659 with France, Catalonia was acknowledged as a part of Spain.

Olivares was mainly responsible for trouble in another quarter. Portugal had been well treated by Philip II, and even under his successor's minister, Lerma, conditions remained fairly satisfactory. What Olivares sought, however, was an amalgamation of the two countries, with equal burdens imposed on each. In 1635 he began to tax Portugal much more heavily. A rebellion broke out at Evora in 1637, and though it was suppressed, the whole country rose in 1640, at the time of the Catalan revolt, and the Duke of Braganza was proclaimed King as João IV. The war, prosecuted half-heartedly by Spain, dragged on for twenty years, and in 1668 Portugal's independence was formally recognized and there was no more hope of complete Peninsular unity.

Philip IV's son Baltasar Carlos (also painted by Velázquez) died in childhood. His heir was a poor little epileptic, aged four, known as Charles the Bewitched (Carlos II el Hechizado), the son of Philip's second wife, Mariana of Austria, who happened to be also Philip's niece. The unfortunate boy was expected to die, but he lived to "rule" until 1700. Since it was early seen that he could have no issue, his whole reign was involved with plots for the succession. There were three parties, one favoring the French, one the Austrians, and a third desiring Don Juan of Austria, a gallant general, son of Philip IV and the famous actress María Calderón. Don Juan died in 1679. Louis XIV fought several wars with Spain, in which other nations, even Sweden, became involved. The main result was French seizure of Spanish possessions in the Netherlands. Charles II favored the Austrian party, for his mother and second wife were Austrian, but Louis XIV was too strong. Charles wavered long, but finally made a will leaving his kingdom to Philip of Anjou, Louis' grandson, with the proviso that Spain and France should never be united under one king. The House of Austria thus came to an ignominious end, and Bourbons were to occupy the throne until 1931.

Politically the dominance of the House of Hapsburg in Spain was characterized by a high degree of centralization of authority in the hands of the royal personage, or his favorite, and a consequent bureaucratic organization. With modern means of communication, Philip II might have ruled his dominions as autocratically as any modern dictator. The Cortes lost vastly in power, for they were summoned only to grant taxes, and they regularly complied with royal requests. In 1665 the subsidy-granting privilege was given exclusively to the towns, and the Castilian Cortes did not meet at all in the reign of Charles II. The Cortes of Aragon, Catalonia, Valencia, and Navarre always met independently, and were much more ready to present grievances and regularly were loath to vote taxes. The towns throughout the kingdom lost most of their autonomy, and the royal hand was much heavier on them than throughout the Middle Ages. The King exerted his control mainly through the Royal Council with various subdivisions.

## WAR AND WASTE

The all too numerous wars in which Spain engaged were desperately expensive, so that existing taxes had to be increased and new ones added. By the time of Philip IV, it has been calculated that one third of the income of the nobility and one eighth of the value of all the usual articles of food went directly to the state, plus a tax of fourteen per cent on all sales. Thoroughly reliable calculations are lacking because of the confused financial history of the period, but it has been estimated that Spain's taxes under Philip III amounted to twenty-four million ducats, three hundred and sixty million dollars, of which perhaps not more than half constituted net national income. The national debt at one time amounted to a billion and a half dollars. The income of the royal family in the time of Ferdinand and Isabella amounted to about two hundred and fifty thousand dollars a year; in the time of Charles V to two million, two hundred and fifty thousand, and for Philip IV about twenty million. Of course there were extraordinary occasions such as royal marriages which called for extra expenditures. When Philip III went to San Sebastian in 1615 to get married, there were sixty-five hundred persons in his train, besides an escort of four thousand Guipuzcoans; there were seventeen hundred and fifty mules with silver bells, twenty-seven hundred and fifty saddle mules, and the requisite number of carriages, royal coaches, and litters. One of the masquerades given by Olivares to the visiting Prince of Wales, later Charles I, is said to have cost five million dollars. But wars were even more expensive: six hundred million spent in Flanders from 1598 to 1609, and other wars cost even more.

It must be remembered, too, that sixteenth and seventeenth century armies were relatively small, ordinarily twenty to forty thousand men. Moreover, the population of Spain was not large, somewhat less than seven million in the mid-sixteenth century, and less than six million at the end of the seventeenth. It has been estimated that a fifth of the population was in the church—priests, monks, nuns—and so contributing nothing in a military or economic sense.

Much of Spain's debt was owed to foreigners—Flemish, German, and especially Genoese bankers, who ordinarily charged fifteen to thirty per cent per annum and were likely to charge thirty-three and a third per cent for renewing a note, unpaid by a Spanish king. No doubt the bankers considered the risk very great, and they were right.

Not only were armies small, but they were likely to consist largely of mercenaries. The Spanish armies were badly administered, honey-combed with graft, and often unpaid. Armies in Europe were generally accompanied by ladies who had a special liking for military life. No statistics are available on the matter, but one author reports that Charles V's expedition to Tunis had room for four thousand *enamoradas*.

Firearms had come into general use, but troops so armed were considered as auxiliaries. The main Spanish troops were pikemen; see Velázquez's celebrated *Surrender of Breda* (*Las Lanzas*). Cannon had considerably improved, and were much used later in the seventeenth century.

Strangely enough, Spain had no official navy. Ships were purchased or rented from Spaniards or foreigners, and merchant ships were pressed into service, with unfortunate effects on commerce. Very few were built by the state. Spain was at a disadvantage on the seas as soon as England, France, and Holland developed national navies. In the sixteenth century Spanish ships were manned by volunteers, but in the seventeenth century fishermen were pressed into compulsory service. Most of the galleys had three banks of oars, like the Roman triremes, and were manned by criminals and slaves. Cannon were the main armament, but Spanish tactics depended mainly on getting in at close range and boarding enemy ships. The longer range of the English guns used against the Spanish Armada was a decisive factor in the British victory in 1588, and the lighter and faster English ships were much easier to maneuver than the ponderous Spanish galleons.

## THE ROLE OF THE CHURCH

It would be hard to exaggerate the importance of the Church and religion in Spain under the House of Austria. Tolerance was not one of the virtues of the times, among Catholics or Protestants. The spirit of Luther and Calvin was perhaps not very different from that of Torquemada. Protestantism did not make any real headway in Spain, though criticism of abuses in the Church was never lacking, and Erasmus, who was a secretary of Charles V, exerted more influence than was suspected. Spain took a prominent part in the Counter-Reformation and her role in the Council of Trent (1545-1563) was an important one. Spaniards were active in preparing reforms and in carrying them out. The Inquisition did its work efficiently, and another organization arose with great propagandist zeal in the maintenance and spread of Catholicism: the Jesuit Order. St. Ignatius of Loyola was a man of extraordinary energy, a *conquistador* of religion. After a wild youth in the army, he was wounded defending Pamplona against the French in 1521, and spent his convalescence reading religious books. He made a pilgrimage to Jerusalem and studied theology at Barcelona, Alcalá, Salamanca, and Paris. In Spain the Inquisition made him stop street preaching, but in Rome he was more successful. He and his friends called themselves the "Company of Jesus" and in 1539 organized themselves into a military order, which in 1540 was approved by the Pope. Loyola became the first general. They vowed implicit obedience to their superiors, especially to the Pope, and always interested themselves particularly in education. They were able to exercise an especially strong influence because they did not gather in monasteries but lived among the people. The older orders, the Augustinians, Franciscans, as well as many of the regular clergy, were opposed to the Jesuits, and Philip II at first objected to them. They had, however, the support of the Pope, and Philip came to see that they were a great help in the religious unification of his dominions. The Inquisition even imprisoned the Jesuit Provincial (Commander) in Spain, but the Pope took the Jesuits' side, and they prospered exceedingly, because they combined superior attainments with vigorous prosecution of their ideals. They were also important, along with the other orders, in spreading Catholicism in Spanish and Portuguese colonial possessions, which have remained predominantly Roman Catholic. Loyola himself died in 1556 and was canonized in 1609.

Spain was a deeply religious nation, but it cannot be said that morality, public or private, was perfect. Far from it, but the religious ideal was dominant, and touched all phases of life to a greater extent than now. High devotion and saintliness as well as corruption and bigotry were to be found in the Church. It is the custom now to object to the participation of any church as such in secular affairs: in the seventeenth century and before such participation was considered natural. The Spanish sovereigns saw to it that they exerted in their own persons considerable power over the Spanish Church, and even so devout a king as Philip II fought his spiritual overlord, the Pope, for claiming authority to which Philip objected. By the time of Charles II, there were fewer signs of religious fervor, though the Church as an organization continued to be relatively rich and powerful.

## THE SOCIAL AND ECONOMIC ORDER

Social conditions from the time of Charles I (V) to Charles II showed little that was novel. The line of cleavage between the upper nobility, who flocked to court, and the lower classes became more marked, and the nobles gained a reputation for pomp and pride that has clung to them until now. Yet there has always existed in Spain a democratic tendency: witness the popular play of Rojas Zorrilla (1607-1648) called *None Beneath the King,* which implies that even if the King can do no wrong (and other plays, such as *The Star of Seville,* challenge that theory), below the King all others are equal. Yet the number of noble titles increased greatly, by royal grant or what amounted to outright purchase. In 1541 there were only three hundred thousand taxpayers in the country, and of them more than one hundred thousand were *hidalgos.* Even before Charles V the nobles had lost much of their political power, but they still occupied most of the positions of prominence.

The most noteworthy social change took place not in Spain, but in the Colonies, in which millions of Indians were converted to Christianity and their mode of life profoundly modified. Objections were raised to enslaving the natives, but the institution of slavery was accepted. In Spain most of the slaves were Moslem prisoners and Negroes. They were allowed to earn something for themselves, and might eventually purchase their freedom.

The Jews and Moriscos disappeared from the Spanish scene, but a new though small class appeared about the middle of the fifteenth century: the Gypsies. They were restless, and some of them were accused of being light-fingered; a law of 1499 required them to settle down in towns and ply honest trades on pain of enslavement or expulsion. Similar ordinances were enacted in the eighteenth century, but the Gypsies remained very much as they had been. Cervantes probably sums up popular opinion of them in his *La Gitanilla*. Numbers of them still live in various Spanish cities, such as those who dwell in pleasant whitewashed and electrically lighted caves in Granada. They are delighted to trade horses, or tell fortunes, or perform rather lurid dances, for a consideration. They have supplied Spain with some excellent guitarists, dancers, and bull-fighters.

The guilds continued to flourish, but began to decline toward the end of the seventeenth century. They became rather more specialized, and a skilled worker in gold considered himself much above a water-carrier or muleteer. Their exclusiveness—and the general decay of all Spain—finally ruined them.

The general standard of living was unquestionably lower than it is today in Spain, but how much lower no one can say. The wealth that came from the Americas was rather illusory. Much of it went to pay war expenses or to pay for foreign goods, and did not improve the economic condition of the people at large. Hunger and misery undoubtedly increased as the House of Austria went on its downward way. The number of unemployed grew. Since there was no such thing as unemployment relief and social security legislation, suffering was undoubtedly great. The average standard of living must have been low.

Historians are wont to comment on the immoralities prevalent in Spain under the Hapsburgs. Yes, conditions were bad, and morals lax. They usually are, if one looks around. Philip IV had thirty-two illegitimate children, and his royal example must have been followed by his people. Statistics are lacking.

Dueling continued despite strict laws against it, and writers of the times deplore a large assortment of crimes. (In 1938 the Federal Bureau of Investigation reported one million, four hundred and thirty-three thousand, eight hundred and twelve major crimes in the United States.) Spanish university students, not having the outlets of football, dances, and other extracurricular activities, devised their own, which were far less orderly than those of the present day. Student carousings, town-and-gown clashes and other riots were frequent.

Many members of the lower orders who had no work supported themselves by begging and theft. (In the United States in 1938, in one hundred and seventy-one cities with a total population of about twenty-one million, thefts amounted to twenty-eight and a half million dollars.) A luminous description of one thieves' organization in Seville is given by Cervantes in *Rinconete y Cortadillo,* and the Picaresque Novel gives a vivid description of Spanish life on the outer margins. The thievings of high and petty officials were probably more serious.

Public amusements were likely to be unrefined. Jousts and tournaments went out of fashion in the sixteenth century and bull-fighting gained in popularity. Equestrian contests with *cañas* (reed spears) were frequently indulged in. Strolling players toured the country. The first permanent theater was established in Madrid in 1579, and in the larger capitals drama became a passion, with playwrights composing a phenomenal number and variety of plays. Men occupied most of the theater, and the "groundlings," called in Spain *mosqueteros,* "musketeers," were often lamentably rowdy. Women sat in a balcony concealed by a grill which had a separate entrance. Actors and actresses were not highly esteemed members of society, and stage dancers were particularly condemned by stern moralists.

## PHILOSOPHERS AND SCHOLARS

Considerable strides had been made in higher and lower education, but the percentage of illiteracy was very high. By the end of the seventeenth century the Spanish universities had sadly decayed. The number of students at Salamanca, for example, dropped from seven thousand five hundred to about two thousand in the year 1700. In order to keep out unorthodox ideas, Philip II had forbidden Spanish students to study at any foreign centers except Coimbra, Bologna, and Rome.

Spanish thought could not fail to be affected by the currents of the Renaissance. Spain has never been remarkable in the development of systematic thought, though the number of her philosophers has not been so small as many foreigners have imagined; perhaps because it has been particularly hard for Spaniards to dissociate thought from the other activities of the whole man, *el hombre de carne y hueso,* as Unamuno says. It has been claimed, as by Salvador de Madariaga in *Englishmen, Frenchmen, Spaniards,* that the Spaniard is essentially a creature of feeling: hence the splendid outpouring of lyric genius at practically all periods, and the vigor of Spanish activity in the pursuit of some ideal, a religious one for example, which could be felt and not merely apprehended with the mind. Nevertheless in Luis Vives (1492-1540), Valencia produced a noteworthy philosopher whose influence was felt in his own country and in Bruges, Louvain, and London, where he taught. He, as well as other pre-Cartesian philosophers, adopted doubt as the first principle of thought, and he inspired Bacon, Descartes, and the Scotch school. He was a friend of Sir Thomas More and of Erasmus; the former revised the English translation of Vives' book on the education of women. Vives was vastly interested in culture, and his views were remarkably modern. In his *De tradendis disciplinis* he says, "We [scholars] must transfer our solicitude to the people. Having acquired our knowledge, we must turn it to usefulness, and employ it for the common good."

There were other philosophers just after Vives who made a valuable contribution to thought. They remained orthodox, but one heterodox might be mentioned, the Aragonese Michael Servetus (Miguel Servet), a doctor who discovered the circulation of the blood before Harvey, and a theologian whose views on the Trinity were regarded as unholy. He jumped from the frying pan of the Spanish Inquisition into the fire of John Calvin of Geneva, who had him burned at the stake in 1553. The wood was damp, and the torture was prolonged. Servetus had pleaded with Calvin to have his sentence changed to decapitation, but Calvin was firm in this service of God.

Humanistic studies continued, and the sixteenth and seventeenth centuries produced many noted scholars. They were men; but the mantle of Queen Isabella's teacher and maid of honor, Beatriz

Galindo, *La Latina,* fell in the sixteenth century on Luisa Sigea de Velasco (d. 1560) who was celebrated for a rare combination of erudition, poetic ability, in Latin, and physical beauty. Pedro Simón Abril (c. 1530-c. 1595) translated Aristotle, some of Plato, and several Latin works, and wrote grammars of Latin and Greek. Juan de Vergara translated more of Aristotle. Hernán Núñez (1478-1553), *el Comendador Griego,* edited or translated many classic texts. These humanists are merely a few among the best.

Interest in the collection of proverbs continued. Gonzalo de Correas (died 1631) made a *Vocabulario de refranes y frases proverbiales.* The well-known French teacher of Spanish, César Oudin, made a collection of Spanish proverbs translated into French (Paris, 1605) and there were other collections. The best dictionary of the seventeenth century is by Sebastián de Covarrubias: *Tesoro de la lengua castellana o española* (1611, second enlarged edition 1673).

Historical studies were also pursued. The history of Spain best known in the Golden Age was Florián de Ocampo's version (1541) of Alfonso X's *Crónica general,* which was largely drawn on by dramatists and balladists. The best-known historian was the Jesuit Juan de Mariana (1535-1624) whose *Historia de rebus Hispaniae libri XXX,* later translated into Spanish by the author, was highly successful. Mariana admits fabulous material, though sceptical as to saints' legends, but he has a sense of proportion and unity, and considerable dramatic feeling. There were many more specialized histories and personal accounts of adventures. The letters of Christopher Columbus, whom Madariaga has sought to prove a Galician Jew, are of interest. More vivid are the *Cartas y relaciones,* of 1523-25 of the great conquistador Hernán Cortés, to Charles V, which were later translated into Latin, French, and Italian. Cortés was a tough soldier, but he had studied at Salamanca. An amazing amount of miscellaneous information about the New World is given by Gonzalo Fernández de Oviedo (1478-1557) in his *Historia General y natural de las Indias,* only the first part of which was published in Toledo, 1526 (second and third parts 1851-55). The much better educated priest Bartolomé de las Casas (1470-1566) wrote a history of America, and a short *Account of the Destruction of America,* in which he almost frantically sought to prove that the natives of America, endowed by nature with all virtues, had been corrupted, brutalized, and most cruelly treated by their Spanish conquerors. Although Las Casas was violently contradicted by many contemporaries, his books gave foreigners their centuries-old idea of Spanish cruelty in the colonies. Cabeza de Vaca's *Naufragios* (*Shipwrecks*), 1542, give a vivid description of that explorer's adventures in and around the southwestern United States.

Garcilaso de la Vega (*el Inca,* 1540-1615) was related to the poet of that name, and to Ataualfa, the last of the Incas. His works give a picturesque account of Hernando de Soto and of Inca characters and legends (*La Florida del Inca,* 1605, and the *Comentarios reales,* 1609-1617).

In science, Spain's contributions were noteworthy. Geographical and geodetical knowledge was vastly expanded. Plans were made for a Panama canal. The special maritime compass invented in 1525 by Felipe Guillén greatly aided navigation. The Gregorian calendar was corrected by Pedro Chacón and others. Great advances were made in naval construction, ocean currents and instruments of navigation were investigated and map-making much improved. Human anatomy was studied by others besides Servetus. Hospitals for epidemics were established, as in Seville, in the early seventeenth century. Daza de Valdés studied the human eye, and invented spectacles, such as those afterwards worn by Cervantes and Quevedo. Impressive studies were produced in zoology, history, and pharmacology, attendant upon the discovery of the New World. Dr. Francisco Hernández, who organized an expedition in 1570, alone catalogued, described, and painted more than fourteen thousand different plants of America, in fifteen volumes. The knowledge of botany was thus tremendously extended. The plants included the potato, which acquired much more than scientific interest in Europe. Much was added to the knowledge of metallurgy and mining.

Great impetus was given to the development of international and colonial law, especially through the work of Francisco Suárez and

Francisco de Vitoria, to whom Grotius acknowledged his indebtedness. Martínez de la Mata anticipated Adam Smith in claiming that labor was the only true source of wealth. Vives and others thought that land should be owned by society in general; that property should be taken from its owners and redistributed for actual use. Needless to say, this theory was not put into practice.

In the realm of Spanish thought, theology was the study most cultivated, and theologians were numerous. It seems useless to give a catalogue of names, no matter how important religious speculation was at the time. The annals of literature contain the names of an extraordinary number of men and women who were in religion, and many secular authors wrote works bearing on it. Mystic and ascetic writers won fame far beyond the confines of Spain.

## MYSTICS

One of the most remarkable women of the sixteenth century was Teresa de Cepeda y Ahumada (1515-1582), better known as Santa Teresa. She was born to a noble family in the old Castilian town of Avila. When she was about seven years old she planned to leave home with her brother to seek martyrdom. The novels of chivalry fired her imagination, and she even began to write one. At the age of nineteen she took vows in the Carmelite convent of Avila. Her spiritual life was intense and she had many visions, but her activity was also external, and she was extraordinarily energetic in the reformation of the Carmelite order. In all she founded seventeen convents. She incurred many enmities. The Papal Nuncio, Monsignor Sega, opposed to the Barefoot Carmelites, once confined her in Toledo, calling her a "restless and gadding woman." He might have added that she was an excellent seamstress, chess-player and horsewoman, and pretty withal. She was even haled before the Inquisition, but was set free. Her sanctity was triumphantly recognized after her death, for she was beatified in 1614 and canonized six years later.

St. Teresa, at the behest of her confessors, wrote an autobiography, the *Libro de su Vida* (Salamanca, 1588), which she preferred to call *The Book of God's Mercies*. It is much more an account of her inner life, her spiritual crises, her religious ecstasies, than an account of her doings. Her prose is simple, direct, glowing, and her autobiography has often been compared to the *Confessions of St. Augustine*. More facts of her external life will be found in the book which tells of the convents she founded, the *Libro de las fundaciones*. It is interspersed with lively anecdotes and shrewd counsels to her nuns.

The most significant work of St. Teresa was *The Inner Citadel, or The Mansions of the Soul* (*El Castillo interior, Las moradas,* 1588). The seven mansions or apartments are the seven degrees of prayer by which we enter into our own spirits, into that "tiny inmost heaven in which the soul finds its Creator." The book is one of the world's most spontaneous and sincere mystic raptures, whose beauty is perceptible to saint and sinner alike.

The four hundred and nine letters of St. Teresa which survive are vivid, natural, colloquial, even racy, and show admirably her combination of practical sense and religious devotion.

St. Teresa also wrote poems, simply for the enjoyment of her nuns. They are written in short traditional meters, and are fervent expressions of her faith, her mystic longing.

St. Teresa was of noble birth. A younger Carmelite whom she met in 1568 and converted to her reform was the son of a weaver: Juan de Yepes y Alvarez (1542-1591), later revered as St. John of the Cross (San Juan de la Cruz). Born in the same province as St. Teresa, he entered the hospital of Medina del Campo as a nurse, and took his final vows as a Carmelite in that city in 1564. He too founded many houses of his Order, and held high positions in it.

The works of St. John of the Cross were not published until long after his death. The first which he wrote was the *Spiritual Canticle,* a dialogue in forty strophes between the Soul and its Bridegroom, Christ, with forty chapters of prose commentary. In this, as in his other works, St. John was inspired by the lovely poetry of the *Song of Solomon* (*The Canticles*). In *The Ascent of Mt. Carmel* (*Subida del Monte Carmelo*) and *The Dark Night of the Soul* (*Noche oscura del alma*) the theme is the progress of the soul from the black night of the senses, under the guidance of faith, until it reaches the mystic ideal of direct and complete union with Christ. The saint's *Living Flame of Love* (*Llama de amor viva*) describes the workings of the Holy Spirit, which is the Flame, upon the Soul, now at one with God. In all cases St. John exposes his mystic doctrine first in the form of verse and then in prose to explain and expand it. His subtle prose and his complicated exposition are hard for the uninitiated, but no one can miss the intense rhapsodic beauty of the verse, sublime in thought, lovely in expression. St. John of the Cross was one of the great mystic poets of all time. He expresses in words the ecstatic aspirations which El Greco put upon canvas.

The Dominican Fray Luis de Granada (1504-1588), who wrote voluminously in Spanish and Latin, was widely known and popular, and his Ciceronian style was greatly admired. His *Guide for Sinners* (1556) was particularly celebrated.

Fray Luis de León (1527-1591) was an Augustinian and Professor of theology at Salamanca. He never considered himself primarily a poet, for among his contemporaries he was especially known for his Latin religious works, *De Fide, De Spe, De Caritate, De Creatione Rerum, De Incarnatione,* etc., which few read today. There were greater theologians and scholars in Spain, such as Benito Arias Montano, but no greater poets. His poetry merits separate treatment.

# Arcadians and Realists of the Sixteenth Century

## THE RENAISSANCE LYRIC

POETS like Garcilaso, playwrights like Encina and Vicente, prose writers like Fernando de Rojas, added enormously to the cultural progress of the Peninsula, both by their own solid achievements and by the new directions which they gave to Spanish and Portuguese literary art. Spanish tradition has had many elements of permanence, of continuity, but the Italian Renaissance came as an external force to revivify the Spanish spirit, to provide the enlivening force which created a period of splendor known as the Golden Age. It might be said roughly to include the period of the last three Spanish Philips, from about the middle of the sixteenth century to the latter part of the seventeenth: the ages of Camoens in Portugal, and in Spain of Cervantes, of Lope de Vega, El Greco, Velázquez, and a host of only slightly less-endowed geniuses.

The example of Boscán and Garcilaso was of great effect upon succeeding poets. They may be divided into the Italianizers and the traditionalists, though such a division is rather arbitrary. The situation was this: succeeding poets in general utilized the new Italian verse forms and poetic modes introduced by Boscán and Garcilaso; but they also used the older traditional ones, such as the ballad, the *redondilla* (four eight-syllable lines, rhyming abba) and other stanza forms.

One of those who followed Garcilaso closely was a nobleman, soldier, and graceful poet of Valladolid, named Hernando de

Acuña (1520-1580?). He is particularly known for one line which sums up a Spanish ideal of the time of Philip II:

> Un monarca, un imperio, y una espada.

Gutierre de Cetina, who lived in the first half of the sixteenth century, was by way of being an exquisite, and is especially noted for his love lyrics, as fluent and melodious as they are light and charming. He addressed them to ladies whom he called Doris and Amarillis, and it is suspected that one of them was the beauteous countess Laura Gonzaga. It is not known whether she was the recipient of the most famous madrigal in Spanish, *Ojos claros, serenos . . .,* of which this translation may give some idea:

> Clear eyes, sweet and serene,
> If for your gentle looks you are so praised,
> Why, seeing me, are you in anger raised?
> Since for their pitying glance
> They lovelier seem to him on whom they gaze,
> Dispel their angry haze
> Lest beauty's eyes thus look at you askance.
> Oh, rage and torture keen!
> Clear eyes, sweet and serene,
> E'en though your look be harsh, by you let me be seen.

Francisco de Figueroa, a modest and quiet gentleman of Alcalá de Henares, was born the year of Garcilaso's death (1536) and gained such fame for his poetry that he was given the surname of *El Divino*. At the end of a long life, he ordered that his poems be burned as useless trifles of youth, but some were saved to prove him a pleasant weaver of pastoral and amorous verse. He called himself *Tirsi* and the object of his adoration *Fili.* His sonnets and *canciones* are happy in imagery and expression.

In the later sixteenth century poets tended to center around different regions of Spain, notably Salamanca and Seville. Those of the so-called school of Salamanca were noted for classic sobriety, depth of thought, dignity of expression, greater attention to matter than to manner in contrast with the more exuberant manner of the School of Seville. The greatest of the northern school and in the opinion of most the greatest poet of Spain was Luis de León, who probably considered the writing of verse the least important of his several activities. Born in Belmonte (Cuenca) of partly Jewish descent, he studied first in Madrid and Valladolid, and at the age of sixteen went to the University of Salamanca. On January 29, 1544, he took vows in the Augustinian Order. He acquired several academic degrees and spent his life as a professor of theology or related subjects, at Salamanca. Because his orthodoxy was questioned by his academic rivals and enemies, he was haled before the Inquisition and spent from March 1572 to December 1576 in the Inquisitorial prison in Valladolid. He was declared innocent, and restored to his academic rights and privileges. After all these difficulties he returned to the University of Salamanca and began the first class after his return thus, "We were saying yesterday . . ." At least such is the legend, almost certainly apocryphal. The rest of his life was spent mainly at Salamanca. He died August 14, 1591, nine days after being elected Provincial of the Augustinian Order in Spain.

Among his colleagues and peers, Fray Luis de León was known mainly for his Latin compositions.

Of much greater general interest are the author's Spanish prose works, such as his translation of the *Song of Solomon,* and his *Exposición del libro de Job. The Perfect Wife* (*La Perfecta Casada,* published in 1583) is based on the last twenty-one verses of the last chapter of *Proverbs,* supported by the opinions of various church fathers and pagan worthies. The wife should be chaste, neat, charitable, industrious, generally virtuous and an early riser, well able to take care of the husband, household, and servants. The prose style is excellent, the ideas no doubt sound, but hardly original. Fray Luis knew very little indeed about women, and did not hold them in very high regard.

Of far greater beauty is *Los Nombres de Cristo,* published in the same year. It is a meditation, in dialogue form, upon the various names of Christ: Prince of Peace, The Shepherd, The Lamb, etc., in graceful and harmonious prose, breathing an inner peace.

Beautiful as his prose may be, his poetry is far lovelier. The comparatively small poetic production of Luis de León was not published until forty years after his death, when Quevedo made a very imperfect edition. León had intended to publish his poems, but never got around to it. He had divided them into three groups: I. Original Poems. II. Translations from Pagan Poets. III. Translations from Sacred Authors. The last came mainly from the *Psalms,* *Job,* and the *Song of Solomon,* and León says in his Introduction that he seeks to preserve the "sweetness and majesty that they possess." He succeeds admirably.

Among the Pagans, León translated mainly from Vergil (the ten Eclogues, the first two books of the Georgics) and from Horace. The translations are not literal, but they are smooth, graceful, in the spirit of the original.

It is, naturally, Luis de León's own poems which have lived on and given him his reputation as Spain's greatest poet. He has been called, with considerable justification, a Christian Horace. The great Latin poet was León's chief master, but the pupil was no slavish imitator. He possesses much of Horace's delicate charm, combined with greater seriousness, for León meditated more upon the things of heaven than upon the fleeting graces of a Chloe or a Lalage. That is, in León there is a fusion of two cultures, pagan and Christian. English readers will think of Milton, though the Spaniard, who was a devout Catholic, employed less mythological ornamentation, and achieved no long work comparable to *Paradise* *Lost.* He certainly achieved greater delicacy. About León's poems there is a deep seriousness and great beauty of expression, that gravity of matter combined with lightness of expression in which Coventry Patmore saw the crowning glory of Spanish literature.

One of León's most appealing poems is addressed to his friend Francisco Salinas, the blind professor of music at Salamanca. In it Fray Luis shows his love of the harmonies which calm the air and invest it with beauty and an unwonted light, but he desires too that music may ever awaken his senses to the perception of divine good, deadening them to all else. The calm night (*Noche serena*) and the heavens adorned with countless planets lead him to meditate on man's low estate and to seek to awaken to the immortal splendors for which they were destined. In his poem *To Felipe Ruiz,* Fray Luis longs to cast off the shackles of his fleshly prison and fly to Heaven, where he may not only see the mansions of joy and content, wrought of gold and light, but where he may also find all knowledge of the hidden causes of things. In this life (his *Vida Retirada*) he longs for plain and lofty living, freed from love, jealousy, hatred, hopes and fears. León's poetry is simple, free of artifice, tender, expressive, pure. His followers were not able to approach his excellence.

Quite different is the poetry of the south, of the so-called School of Seville, as best illustrated by Fernando de Herrera (1534-1597). This priest in minor orders is reported to have been rather unapproachable, forbidding, haughty, but for his verses he, like Figueroa, received the soubriquet of *El Divino*. He was a member of a group of poets and learned men who gathered in the palace of Don Álvaro Colón y Portugal, Count of Gelves and great grandson of the man we call Christopher Columbus. Herrera fell deeply in love with the countess, with a hopeless and apparently Platonic passion, and she inspired a large number of Petrarchian sonnets and elegies in which the subtleties of love are elaborated. It is not the amorous compositions of Herrera, however, that have given him his fame, but rather his heroic and patriotic poems. His most celebrated production is his poem "On the Victory of Lepanto," in which he thunders praises of Don Juan of Austria and Spanish arms, and hurls condemnatory epithets at the defeated Turks. Herrera clothes his lines with true pomp and majesty, and they roll on like surging seas. Their harmony is not delicate, but impressive; rhetoric, but excellent rhetoric. Herrera greatly admires Garcilaso, but Garcilaso's compositions are gentle and graceful, Herrera's strong and vigorous. The *Song on the Loss of King Sebastian* (*Canción a la pérdida del Rey Don Sebastián*), whose untimely death in Africa in 1578 constituted a tragic and unnecessary defeat for Portuguese arms, is a mighty lament, accompanied by sad resignation. Herrera displays a true Andalusian love of pomp and sonorousness, of exuberance and richness of language, of great attention to form. He is the proper ancestor of even purpler poets who are to follow him.

Among the most attractive of Herrera's acquaintances was that grand old Epicurean Baltasar del Alcázar (1530-1606). He was a soldier, and with soldierly fortitude he bore increasing poverty and the gout which plagued his old age. He regarded poetry as a pleasant avocation, but he wrote love poems of much charm, and religious poems of real sincerity. He is most noted, however, for his festive satirical pieces, which have caused him to be called the "Sevillian Martial." He possessed a true Andalusian verve and wit, which suffered from few restraints, notably in his delightful epigrams, such as the *Epitaph of a Very Thin Lady*, *To an Old Woman Who Found a Piece of Mirror on a Dunghill and Broke It*, *To a Man Hunchbacked in Front*. His *Cena Jocosa*, about a tale which he never succeeds in telling to his little Inés because the food and the wine are too good, is a model of its kind.

## THE RENAISSANCE EPIC

Homer and Vergil naturally suggested to cultured men of the Renaissance that modern epics might be produced, and Ariosto, Tasso, and Camoëns produced real works of art if not real Iliads and Aeneids. Spaniards, however, were less gifted in such matters. Attempts were made to sing in epic style of the deeds of Charles V, of Don Juan of Austria, and others, but the attempts were abortive. The Spanish narrative poem of the sixteenth century which has stood time's test is the *Araucana*, of Alonso de Ercilla (1533-1594). Ercilla was born and died in Madrid, but it was the years (1555-63) that he spent in South America that inspired his poem *La Araucana*. He wrote most of its thirty-six cantos on scraps of paper and leather at night, after spending the day campaigning in Chile. Although the poem is not entirely unified, and lacks grace and smoothness, it is vigorous, colorful, and presents real characters and bright descriptions of scenes and battles, notably in the part describing the defeat of the Araucan leader Caupolicán. The *Arau-*

*cana* is the epic of the Spanish conquest of America. It is a pity that Cortés had no such poet in his train.

There were several other epics during the same period, but they could not match the *Araucana* in merit.

## THE PASTORAL NOVEL

The production of verse in Spain at all times has been voluminous and important, but it is not to be thought that prose was neglected during the Renaissance and Golden Age. The novel throve and flowered in esthetic gardens both idealistic and realistic. The novel of chivalry was decidedly idealistic in tendency. Its materials were mediaeval, but it was after 1508, the date of Montalvo's *Amadís,* that its real popularity became evident, and Spain was filled with gaudily related imaginary deeds of high emprise. The feats of the Amadises and the Palmerins were in reality hardly more romantic or more startling than the actual achievements of Cortés or Pizarro or Cabeza de Vaca and many others, and these conquistadores were driven on not merely by greed for gold or craving for power, but by the same mystic spirit displayed by Amadis. The novel of chivalry was a literary form distinctly appropriate to its age.

The *Libros de caballerías* gave their readers vicarious adventures. Another sort of novel was on an even more ideal plane: the pastoral, Renaissance borrowing from antiquity. Pastoral poetry had been cultivated by the Sicilian Greek Theocritus and his Italian-Greek followers, Bion and Moschus. Indeed, there had been a charming bucolic novel attributed to the Sophist Longus (second century A.D.), *Daphnis and Chloe.* Unfortunately, this novel was not rediscovered until too late to influence the Renaissance. It was Boccaccio who originated the modern pastoral with his *Ameto* (1341). It was in prose and verse, like its successors. The most noteworthy pastoral was by an Italian of Spanish parentage, the short and lachrymose *Arcadia* of Jacopo Sannazaro (complete and authorized edition, 1504). His twelve tearful eclogues, connected with elegant prose, attracted hosts of readers and inspired many imitations. Most of the succeeding pastorals, such as Sir Philip Sidney's *Arcadia,* contained a smaller proportion of verse and were much longer. Honoré d'Urfée's *L'Astrée,* for example, was in course of publication from about 1608 to 1629, and ran to over five thousand average-sized pages.

The initial impulse, then, for the Spanish pastoral came from the classics through Italy, and the use of pastoral material by Encina and Garcilaso is to be remembered. The immediate production of the pastoral around the middle of the sixteenth century, however, was due to two Portuguese authors. The first was Bernardim Ribeiro, whose *Saudades* or *Menina e Moça* (1554) is partly autobiographical, and in Portuguese. The second was Jorge de Montemayor, who composed the best of the Peninsular pastorals, but in Spanish. Montemayor took his name from the village near Coimbra where he was born, Montemôr o Velho (in Spanish, Montemayor el Viejo). He was born about 1520, and, since his family was poor, was educated only in modern languages. He was a musician in the chapel of Philip II's sister, who had married a Portuguese prince. With her he came to Spain in 1554, and lived mainly in Valencia. He died in a duel over some love affair in 1561.

Montemayor's popular *Seven Books of the Diana* appeared probably first in 1559. Today most people find the pastoral novel depressingly soporific, but once it was not so. Montemayor's readers rejoiced in the verse part, and the author was really a polished and delicate poet, particularly in short lines, and the prose was considered the most elegant of its day. The main plot is simple, and contemporaries could take pleasure in identifying the false shepherds and shepherdesses who spread their amorous plaints over the Leonese countryside. The shepherd Sireno (Montemayor himself) loves the shepherdess Diana (some lady of Valencia de San Juan) and woos her assiduously and against all sorts of obstacles, but she goes and marries the shepherd Delio. Many enchantments, magic springs, spells, and other forms of the supernatural are included, and many episodes alien to the main plot are inserted throughout, as is the story of Felix and Felismena, which reappeared in Sir Philip Sidney's *Arcadia* and in Shakespeare's *Two Gentlemen of*

*Verona.* Although the *Diana* was left unfinished it was reprinted twenty-five times before 1800. Montemayor had intended to add a second part, but his untimely violent death prevented his doing so. There were others who were ready and willing, and the first continuation was made by Montemayor's friend and literary confidant, Dr. Alonso Pérez: the long, complicated and pedantic *Segunda Parte de la Diana* (Valencia, 1564). The best sequel was by Gaspar Gil Polo (died 1591): the *Diana Enamorada* (1564), in which Diana's husband, Delio, falls in love with Alcida, beloved of Marcelio and numerous other amorous complications ensue. They are all settled by the magic waters of the enchantress Felicia and the sudden death of Delio. So Sireno at last marries his beloved Diana, and the *Diana* series of pastorals comes to an end. But not the series of pastorals, for a score or so appear in Spain up to 1633.

Cervantes considered the genre highly enough to write his pastoral novel *La Galatea* (1585) for which he kept promising a second part up to the time of his death. Lope de Vega published his *Arcadia* in 1590.

Cervantes, in the *Coloquio de los perros,* described pastoral novels as "cosas soñadas y bien escritas, para entretenimiento de los ociosos y no verdad alguna." So imagination and good writing, or rather fine writing, are involved. No, the pastorals are not true: the adventures are concocted in silly fashion, the shepherd's dress has fine silk underneath, the sheep are about as significant as Mary's little lamb. The sentiment of the quasi-shepherds is sheer sentimentality, and nature looks like a stiff stage set. How could truly select Renaissance spirits take pleasure in such paste jewels of literature? For they undoubtedly did, and they were just as good men as we, with minds fully as good, too. The pastoral genre had its virtues. It represented an aspiration toward refinement, in sentiment as well as in literary style. After all, the pastoral disguise mattered very little. It was a convention like any other, and art has always been willing to accept certain conventions. No one regarded pastoral novels as manuals on sheep-raising. They were written on an idealistic, not a realistic, plane; their truth is poetic, not literal. They undoubtedly contributed to a growing refinement which the books of military

adventure, chivalresque novels, and pictures of reality, the picaresque, hardly emphasized. And perhaps most important of all,
they constituted a literature of escape. Those weary of life in the
armies of the Philips, tired of coping with crass realities, could take
up Montemayor and retire to Arcady and listen to shepherds' pipes
beside purling brooks in sylvan dells. They could savor poetry
and prose which, if it seems to us overdone, stilted, no doubt seemed
to them elegant, and was in any case polished, aristocratic, smooth.
So the pastoral enjoyed a century and more of very great popularity.

## THE *NOVELA MORISCA*

The novel of chivalry and the pastoral came from foreign sources.
Not so another kind of novel, the Moorish (*novela morisca*) which
is historical to a certain extent, but which stands between the idealistic and the realistic. It is a distinctly Spanish contribution to
world fiction.

The first example is called *El Abencerraje.* It appeared in 1565
in a miscellany called *El Inventario,* compiled by Antonio de Villegas. No one knows who wrote *El Abencerraje.* Surely not Villegas, who merely incorporated it in a longer work. It was similarly incorporated, in somewhat more elaborate literary style, in the
second and succeeding editions of the *Diana* and also appeared in
an undated Gothic-type book called *Part of the Chronicle of the
Famous Don Fernando Who Won Antequera. . . .* Since Villegas'
privilege to print was dated 1551, the story must have been in existence by that time.

At any rate, there exists the simple and moving story, telling how
the Abencerraje Abindarráez was in love from childhood with the
lovely Jarifa. They were parted when her father was promoted to
another place. While the Moor was on his way to be betrothed to
her secretly, he was overcome in single combat by the noble Rodrigo
de Narváez. The Spaniard was so affected by the Moor's story that
he gave Abindarráez three days' freedom. So Abindarráez was betrothed to his beautiful and spirited Jarifa, and they both returned
to be Narváez's prisoners. Rodrigo was so impressed by the gal-

lantry of the groom and the loveliness of the bride that he forgave them their ransom, interceded in their favor with the King of Granada, reconciled Jarifa's father, and they all lived in high-minded happiness thereafter.

The narrative is related in a straightforward style, and the characters are simply but firmly drawn. Abindarráez, for all his sturdy masculine virtues, has just a touch more sentimentality than Jarifa, though not nearly so much as the protagonists of the pastorals. The attitude of Christians and Moors as presented in the novel is of interest. There is no fanatical hatred despite the centuries-old struggle between them. They fight each other like gentlemen, and courage is admired when found. The generosity, the *caballerosidad* of Rodrigo de Narváez, is particularly emphasized, and he was presented as a model Spanish knight. The events were supposed to take place about a hundred and fifty years before the book was published in the reign of Philip II so it was easier to attribute virtues to past foes than to those of the moment, like the English, or even the surviving Moriscos in Spain.

## THE PICARESQUE NOVEL

The tone of the *Abencerraje* is aristocratic, like that of the pastorals and the novels of chivalry. There is another sort of novel which, like the *Abencerraje,* is a genuine Spanish development, but which is deeply, at times violently, realistic: the picaresque. It is influenced by the *Celestina,* but it also stems directly from the realities of Spanish life of the day.

One strange book which appeared in 1528 was based on reality and influenced by the *Celestina,* but it is not like the picaresque novels to follow. It was by a priest named Delicado, and was called *The Sprightly Andalusian Girl (La Lozana Andaluza)*. It has enjoyed a somewhat exaggerated reputation as the most obscene book in Spanish literature. For one thing, it is hardly literature, but rather a helter-skelter account of the adventures of Aldonza, a Spanish girl, one of the thousands of women who practised the world's oldest profession in Rome in the gay days of Pope Julius II. The book is a noteworthy social document, of great interest, too, to lexicographers, but obviously of no great interest or importance in its day. It had only one small edition and exerted no noticeable influence.

The real picaresque novel is of far greater interest. In 1554 there appeared three separate editions of *La Vida de Lazarillo de Tormes y de sus fortunas y adversidades*. It is the earliest and, to most tastes, the best example of the full-fledged picaresque novel. The plot could hardly be simpler: Lazarillo, a little ragamuffin, serves and goes through various adventures with a series of masters, a blind beggar, a priest, an hidalgo, a friar, a seller of indulgences, a chaplain, a constable, and finally marries and achieves a certain position of dignity as town-crier of Toledo. The form is autobiographical, the style colloquial and racy, and the satire keen. And such is the picaresque novel in general and at its best: the autobiography of a member of the lower orders (the *picaro*) who serves various masters and in passing satirizes the people and life he sees. Some have preferred to use the term picaresque much more loosely, applying it to any literary production that has to do with low life, with rogues and scamps. It does not greatly matter, as long as we realize that books like *Lazarillo* form a class apart. The autobiographical form is an important element in the esthetic formula, for the author takes that means of viewing and satirizing society from underneath, as it were, from the point of view of the humble. Only the naïve will be interested solely in the adventures of the *picaro* himself, amusing though they may be. In a way the picaresque novels constitute a parody on the books of chivalry. The *picaro* is a sort of Amadís de Gaula upside down, an anti-hero, as he has been called. His most lofty aspiration is to get enough to eat, the giants he fights are Dogberrys on his heels, and his highest achievements are apt to be acts of petty larceny. He serves not his king and his lady, but his stomach. There is one point in which conquistadors, knights-errant, and *picaros* resemble one another; they are all terribly restless and bat about the world, dashing from one thing to another not because anyone makes them, but because they want to, to satisfy some inner urge. The knight-errant, the Don Quixote, is superior to reality and moves in a different realm of spirit; the *pícaro* is very much of the earth, earthy, accepting the real just as it is, with no false ideals, no illusions. He is smart enough, like the Celestina, to observe the existence of ideal natures, and to use them for himself if he can. Witness the most beautiful chapter in the whole history of the picaresque novel: Chapter III of the *Lazarillo de Tormes*. The down-at-heels hidalgo of Castile whom the little scamp serves has very little nobility left except pride. Lazarillo looks up at him and sees his silly aristocratic mien, which accords so ill with a man who is starving: symbol of a Spain which kept up its front in spite of all economic realities, in spite of all defeats. And Lazarillo regards the attitude as silly, but he cannot help admiring it. So he shares his hard-gotten crumbs with his strange master. The satire of clerical greed and quackery is much more bitter and caused the book to be put on the first Spanish *Index Expurgatorius* in 1559. It was republished in expurgated form, but in the original was constantly bootlegged into Spain from abroad.

*Lazarillo de Tormes* is gay on the surface, bitter underneath. The *pícaro* himself is part stoic, part cynic, and part anarchist. He is no social revolutionary, because he accepts his hard lot with resignation and achieves a considerable insensibility toward pain and disaster. As a literary figure he comes straight from Spanish life and represents a large class of the downtrodden for whom society makes no provision. Literary precedents are many. Hints can be found in Petronius' *Satyricon*, in Apuleius' *Golden Ass*, in the *Book of Good Love* (autobiographical form, merry immoralities, satire), in the French *fabliaux*, the Italian realists of the Boccaccian type. It seems unlikely that authors like Pulci (*Morgante Maggiore*) could have had any real influence. Nor *Till Eulenspiegel* (1453), who was a mere prankster and wag. With Till, the jest was the thing, its own justification. The tradition of low class realism in the Middle Ages, existing in France, Italy, Germany, England, as elsewhere, is a part of the background of the Spanish picaresque, but the particular form, the most important step yet taken in the development of the modern realistic novel, was due to the anonymous author of *Lazarillo de Tormes.*

Ecclesiastical censorship may have accounted for the failure to develop the rich possibilities of the picaresque for half a century; at any rate, it was not until 1599 that a worthy second appeared. It is true that a short sequel or Second Part of the *Lazarillo* did appear in Antwerp in 1555. The anonymous author, much less skilled than Kingsley (*The Water Babies*), takes Lazarillo under the seas and puts him through a series of adventures among tunny fishes which make dreary reading. A more successful Second Part was composed much later (1620) by Juan de Luna, a teacher of French in Paris.

## DIDACTIC PROSE

The picaresque novels could be read by everyone, and everyone might catch their Erasmian critical spirit. More philosophically minded and sophisticated readers, who savored Lucianesque dialogues, could find pleasure in the works of the most fervent admirer of Erasmus in Spain, Alfonso de Valdés. His incisive *Dialogue of Mercury and Charon* was written specifically to show the injustice of the challenge to a duel sent in 1523 to the Emperor Charles V, whose secretary Valdés was, by the Kings of France and England. The technique is that of the *Dance of Death,* and the satire is keen, not failing to strike royal counsellors, dukes, bishops, and kings. Alfonso de Valdés' dialogue on the sack of Rome in 1527 struck hard at Pope Clement VII and the corruption of the Papal Court. The Papal Nuncio in Spain, no less a personage than Baldassare Castiglione, protested, but Valdés was exonerated by a board of judges.

Alfonso's brother Juan de Valdés was an excellent humanist and scholar, even though he was fond of reading books of chivalry. He was brought into contact with Erasmus by Alfonso, and was once tried by the Inquisition for ideas at least close to heterodoxy. He resided in Italy from 1531 to his death in 1545.

His theological works may not have passionate interest for moderns, but his *Diálogo de la lengua,* apparently written about 1535 in Naples, has a constant freshness, and is the pleasantest book ever written about the Spanish language. He champions naturalness, freedom from affectation: "Say what you want to say in the fewest words you can." In passing he makes acute comments on Juan de Mena, Jorge Manrique, the *Celestina* ("the Castilian book in which the language is most natural, appropriate, and elegant"), and many proverbs. Juan de Valdés is probably the master of the best prose before Cervantes.

Far more popular was the rhetorical prose of Fray Antonio de Guevara (c. 1481?-1545), of the Franciscan Order, preacher and chronicler of Charles V, bishop first of Guadix and later of Mondoñedo. Guevara's *Dial of Princes* (*Reloj de Príncipes*), also known as the *Golden Book of Marcus Aurelius* (Valladolid, 1529), is a pleasant mixture of history, legend, fable, and moral teaching, for the guidance of rulers, with dissertations upon peace, war, glory, justice, containing a series of invented letters of Marcus Aurelius on all sorts of subjects. The book is the most popular of its kind between the *Cyropaedia* of Xenophon and the *Télémaque* of Fénelon, and its public success was extraordinary. It was translated into French in 1531, and into English (by Lord Berners) in 1535. It then went into numerous other languages, including Armenian. Guevara's *Scorn of Court and Praise of Rustic Life* (*Menosprecio de Corte y alabanza de aldea,* 1539) also enjoyed considerable fortune. Guevara was obviously one of those authors thoroughly in accord with the spirit of his times.

Thus even before the Golden Age reached its apogee, the principal genres were well begun. The novel was established in various forms. The novel of chivalry was beginning to wane as the picaresque and the pastoral were established, and the Moorish had come to enrich what may be called the historical novel. Cervantes was to synthesize preceding currents in his immortal work. Lope de Vega was ready to mold the drama according to his own patterns.

Renaissance epic poetry, never strong in Spain, had almost disappeared, but the lyric had reached a high degree of perfection in Garcilaso, St. John of the Cross, Herrera, and Luis de León. Greater elaborateness was to be achieved by Quevedo and Góngora, poets of the end of an age.

El Greco: "Toledo in Storm."

*Culver Service*

El Greco: "The Burial of the Count of Orgaz." Only the lower part of the picture is shown.

El Greco: Detail from the picture above.

*Culver Service*

El Greco: "Crucifixion." Note the characteristic elongation of the figures.

El Greco: The Grand Inquisitor, Cardinal Niño de Guevara.

Velázquez: "The Surrender of Breda", (The Lances).

Velázquez: Equestrian Portrait of Philip IV.

Velázquez: "The Topers" (The Village Bacchus).

Velázquez: "The Count-Duke of Olivares."

Velázquez: "The Little Ladies-in-Waiting (Las Meniñas)." Velázquez himself is at the left.

Velázquez: "Philip IV."

# XVI

## Pícaros and Gallants

### PICARESQUE NOVELS AND TALES

THE picaresque novel which followed *Lazarillo de Tormes* was much later and much longer. Mateo Alemán (1547-1614?) was a contemporary though not a friend of Cervantes. He had more formal education but no happier life than that of the greater novelist, and both were in jail and both captured in Algiers. Both had spurious second parts to their works published by unscrupulous emulators. In 1608 Alemán went to Mexico, where he ended his days.

Although Alemán published a life of St. Anthony of Padua and one of Archbishop García Gera of Mexico, an *Ortografía Castellana,* and translated Horace, his fame rests on the two parts of the *Vida del pícaro Guzmán de Alfarache* (*First Part* 1599, *Second Part* 1604). A third part, thought to have been completed, was never published. The immediate popularity of the *Guzmán* was even greater than that of the *Quijote,* and it was translated into French, Italian, German, English (1630, by James Mabbe), Latin, and other languages.

One testimony to the attractiveness of the *Guzmán* was the spurious second part published in 1602 by a Valencian lawyer who signed himself Mateo Luján de Sayavedra, and whose real name was Juan Martí. This continuation was very inferior to the work of Alemán, and was soon forgotten. Alemán took vengeance in his own second part two years later.

To many it will seem that the *Guzmán* ought by all means to be shorter and funnier. Conciseness is not one of its virtues. It has the same structure as the picaresque novel in general, which is practically no structure at all. Guzmán, whose begetting was irregular,

157

loses his parents and has to start at fifteen to support himself. On his first night away he discovers some of the tricks of innkeepers and later discovers many more. Seventeenth century Spanish writers love to satirize innkeepers, as Molière loved to play with doctors. Guzmán serves all sorts of people, from cooks to cardinals and ambassadors, and engages in various professions, most of them involving thievery of one sort or another. So he lands in prison, is condemned to flogging and to six years in the galleys, and, for trying to escape, for life. Because he reveals an attempted mutiny, he is promised his liberty. The plan of the novel is purely episodical, like *Tom Jones,* like *Pickwick Papers.* The tone is one of disillusionment, of bitterness, and Guzmán has often been called a maturer and more experienced Lazarillo.

It was not only fear of Inquisitorial censorship that made Alemán insert a deal of moralizing in his work. He must have felt that there was something negative, something empty about the picaresque formula, and this he endeavoured to remedy by inserting some positive moral content. He did not wish his hero or, as Mr. Chandler (*Romances of Roguery,* New York, 1899) prefers to call him, his anti-hero, to be a mere manikin jerked against a dark social back-drop; he wished to give his show some real significance. Despite Alemán's best efforts his readers now, possibly like those in his own day, are likely to read the adventure, to look at the picture of society seen through Guzmán's beady eyes, and to run away from the moral edification. For most people it is enough to find in Guzmán what the author promises in his subtitle: "a watch-tower to view human life." The spectacles of the watchman are not rose-colored, but blue, and he reports in a style which fits the tone of his observations. It is rich in suggestions, leisurely in tempo (the style of Proust, even, has been suggested in connection with Alemán), and often of a popular savor.

If we feel that Alemán was unduly depressed by the behaviour of the human animal, we may reflect that he lived and wrote and his greatest book was licensed at the end of the reign of Philip II. A man had to be tougher or less sensitive or more philosophical than Alemán to be gay then.

Perhaps Don Francisco de Quevedo y Villegas (1580-1645) was all of these, for he certainly had his moments of boisterousness. Yet he too had a disillusioned and embittered spirit, sometimes concealed by his extraordinary cleverness.

His picaresque novel, the *Vida del Buscón,* called in English translations *Paul, the Spanish Sharper,* was not published until 1626, but it was written not long after the turn of the century, say about 1603. It is short, vivid, hard, no food for delicate and squeamish stomachs. The satire is ferocious, pitiless, and Quevedo does not snipe at his victims, he impales them and laughs at their writhings. He is a master of the grotesque, and his figures are composed half of gross reality and half of the exaggerated caricature of a gifted cartoonist. The style is full of merry conceits, thoroughly baroque in essence. Quevedo is a noteworthy practitioner of conceptism, the style delighting in play upon words and ideas. It is a far cry from the *Buscón* to the simple, apparently naïve manner of the *Lazarillo.*

It is quite possible that *La Pícara Justina,* ascribed to Francisco López de Ubeda, was written some years before its publication date, 1605, and touched up a bit at that time. Justina says at the end that she is married to Guzmán de Alfarache. The girl, of remarkable virtue, tricks various would-be lovers, as she wanders about like a true pícaro. The reader is likely to be more interested in her adventures, in her descriptions of *fiestas* in León, than in the society portrayed. The style of the novel, complicated, affected, difficult, did not keep it from finding readers at home and abroad. The full title is *The Book of Entertainment of the Rogue Justina,* and it is not very much more than that.

Vicente Espinel (1550-1624) had conversational, military, poetic, and musical talents, and not too much piety, though he was a priest. He was born in the lovely town of Ronda, and was a true Andalusian, even to being an excellent singer and guitarist. In poetry he is credited with the invention of the graceful stanza known as the *décima* or *espinela,* ten eight-syllable lines rhyming abbaaccddc. Espinel's best-known work, the *Vida del escudero Marcos de Obregón,* may loosely be called picaresque, but it is mainly a novel of adventure, with autobiographical elements and many digressions. Espinel's Andalusian temperament was gay enough to withstand misfortune, even the tragedy of his epoch, though he hated literal and spiritual cold and dampness. Hence the smoothly related adventures of his *Marcos de Obregón*. In fact, the author loves flowering orange trees and gardens and sweet smells, everything "that delights the five senses." The section describing Marcos' captivity in Algiers (where Espinel had been imprisoned, like Cervantes) contains a delicate love story, of a sort that would be quite out of tone in a true picaresque novel. Moreover, a majority of the people Marcos meets are likeable. The style of the novel is direct, unaffected, though pleasantly sophisticated, the style of a cultured man who is neither writing down to his readers nor seeking to be clever. Lesage drew heavily on Espinel for episode, as he did on many another seventeenth century Spanish novelist.

The Madrilene Alonso Jerónimo de Salas Barbadillo (1581-1635) was far more satirical than Espinel. He is facile, at times witty, and usually lively, though his work is uneven in value and has not much universality. *La hija de Celestina,* the very title of which suggests an influence often important to the author, is a deft picture of a conscienceless *pícara* whom no sense of delicacy or restraint keeps from gaining her ends. The novel in amplified form was called *La ingeniosa Elena.* This Elena bestowed her favors not for love but for profit. However, the novel is less concerned with its heroine as a prostitute of great charm than as a swindler, hypocrite, and generally gifted rogue. The style has the appearance of gaiety, but the implications are somber. After some dark red violence at the end of the book, Elena is apprehended, put into a sack, and thrown into the Manzanares. Scarron utilized the novel in his *Hypocrites,* which in turn contributed to Molière's *Tartuffe.* The other works of Salas, *El Sagaz Estacio, El Subtil Cordobés Pedro de Urdemalas, El necio bien afortunado* (*The Lucky Fool*), *Don Diego de Noche,* and more, all add to a somewhat depressing rogues' gallery. Salas did not belong to the "sweetness and light" school.

Cervantes' *Rinconete y Cortadillo* was first published at about the same time as *La hija de Celestina.* Are we to consider it as the great novelist's chief contribution to the picaresque? It is a question of definition. It is certainly one of the most artistic pictures of an organized gang of thieves ever painted in words, but one observes that the interest is in the members of the mob themselves, and not in their view of society; they themselves have rich artistic content. Such is not the case with *Lazarillo*.

Alonso de Castillo Solórzano (1584-1648?) is among the most urbane of authors who delved into the picaresque, and his style is unaffected. He has none of Quevedo's bitterness, either. His best-known work, *La niña de los embustes, Teresa del Manzanares (The Girl Who Tricked Them)*, 1632, is particularly concerned with thievery. The adventures of her husband, which should have come earlier, were published in 1637 as *Aventuras del bachiller Trapaza*. Their daughter Rufina plies the same trade, as reported in *La Garduña de Sevilla* (1642). *Garduña* means "weasel," though the English translation was called *The Pole-cat of Seville*. Rufina and her husband Jaime finally settle down as honest silk merchants in Murcia. Castillo also published several collections of short stories, such as *Jornadas alegres, Tardes entretenidas*.

Antonio Enríquez Gómez (1600-166?) was a converted Jew who went to France in 1636 to avoid difficulties, and was burned in effigy in Seville much later by the Inquisition. He wrote a number of poems and plays, but is much better known for his Lucianesque satire *El siglo pitagórico* (referring to Pythagoras' theory of trans-migration), in which a soul dwells successively in the bodies of a lady, a thief, a miser, a hypocrite, etc., and finally in an honest man. Loosely attached to this work is the *Vida de don Gregorio Guadaña*, a brief work of not too amusing picaresque adventure.

A picaresque novel which enjoyed great popularity was *The Limping Devil*. To many Europeans it was *Le diable boiteux*, but that was only Alain-René Lesage's adaptation of the original *Diablo cojuelo* of Luis Vélez de Guevara. Vélez was better known as a dramatist than as a novelist, but he had at least this happy idea of having a scapegrace release "the imp in the bottle." The little devil then took the student with him, lifting the roofs of houses and showing all that went on within.

Toward the middle of the seventeenth century the picaresque novel was declining, as Spain was. One of the later samples of the genre was *The Life and Deeds of Estebanillo González* (Antwerp, 1646). The unknown author claims he was a court jester. He was probably a servant of the Duke of Amalfi. He has his Stevie commit too many thefts and devote too much attention to wine, puts him through too many paces; but the work offers real information on historical personages and events in Italy, Flanders, Germany and Spain. The supposed hero even goes to Poland and England.

There were of course many more novels of a general picaresque character, though none as good as the *Lazarillo,* the *Guzmán,* and the *Buscón*. These Spanish novels offered inspiring suggestions not only in Spain but also abroad, and made a vital contribution to the development of modern realism.

## THE HISTORICAL NOVEL

Another form of novel which arose in the sixteenth century contributed more to romanticism than to realism: the historical novel, especially the *novela morisca*. *El Abencerraje* may stand as the first example, unless that honor be awarded to Pedro del Corral's fantastic history of Roderic, the last of the Goths, called *Crónica sarracina* (c. 1443). The most significant *novela morisca* was the *Civil Wars of Granada* (*Guerras Civiles de Granada*), properly called *Historia de los bandos de los Zegríes y Abencerrajes,* first part 1595, second part 1604. The author was a native of Murcia, Ginés Pérez de Hita (1544?-1619?), who fought against the Moriscos when they made an uprising in 1567. This campaign is described in the second part of the *Guerras Civiles*. The first part, however, is of far greater interest. In it Pérez de Hita gives a highly romanticized account of the last days of Granada: bloody feuds, treacheries, tournaments, gallant and dashing Abencerrajes and passionate sloe-eyed Moorish women and many a dark or brilliant deed. No wonder Chateaubriand and Washington Irving found ready-made material in the *Guerras Civiles*.

# XVII

## *Cervantes*

### BIOGRAPHY

HOLY oil was put on the head of an infant christened Miguel de Cervantes Saavedra in Alcalá de Henares on Sunday, October 9, 1547. There was probably not much excitement over the matter, because the parents already had three children, and the father, Rodrigo de Cervantes, was a doctor anyway.

Really nothing is known of Miguel's childhood, but he must have seen various Spanish cities as his father wandered around, presumably in search of better fortune. The boy studied in Madrid, in the *Estudio* of Juan López de Hoyos, but was he also educated in Seville and Salamanca? Some have thought so. A legal warrant has been found dated September 15, 1569, for the arrest of some Miguel de Cervantes "for having wounded a man," but was the man wanted by the police the future novelist? Did he flee the country on that account? There is no proof.

He was indeed in Rome in December 1569, and in 1570 he was a soldier in a Spanish regiment in Italy, which was mainly a Spanish possession at the time. On October 7, 1571, he fought gallantly in the great battle of Lepanto, and received gunshot wounds in the chest and the left hand. He spent the following winter recovering, but his left hand remained useless, and he gloried in the title "The Cripple of Lepanto."

He went back in the army, and remained there until 1575. He was returning to Spain in September of that year, to sue for promotion, when his galley, *El Sol,* was attacked and taken by Barbary pirates. Since he carried letters of recommendation from Don Juan of Austria, half-brother of Philip II and victor of Lepanto, and from the Duke of Sessa, viceroy of Sicily, his captors thought him a man of importance and set his ransom high. It had been an Albanian renegade who captured him, and a Greek renegade owned him as a slave. Cervantes' doings in captivity read like an adventure novel. He organized five attempts to escape, one of which (1578) brought him two thousand lashes. He survived, however, and next year almost succeeded in getting away, but a fellow conspirator betrayed him. By September, 1580, his family and friends had got together two hundred and eighty *escudos* for his ransom, but Hassan Pasha, King of Algiers, who now owned him, demanded five hundred. So Cervantes, in chains, was put on board a galley to be taken to Constantinople. At the last moment the Trinitarian Friars, who took charge of ransoming Christian prisoners, collected the remaining two hundred and twenty *escudos* and Cervantes was rescued, as his brother Rodrigo had been before him.

Having returned to Spain, Cervantes made unsuccessful efforts to secure lucrative employment. He engaged in an amorous intrigue with a certain Ana Franca de Rojas, and a daughter, Isabel de Saavedra, was born to them about 1584. In that same year, he wrote a pastoral novel, *La Galatea,* and sold the printing rights, and on December 12, 1584, he married Catalina de Salazar y Palacios, who was nineteen years younger than he, and had a fair dowry. He was also writing plays, most of which are lost, but apparently he found the pen even feebler than the sword as far as material support was concerned.

In 1585 Cervantes was in Seville, engaging in financial business. Finally he secured a government position as a commissary collecting supplies for the Spanish Armada. Even after the defeat of that expedition (1588) he continued in the government service, but he was paid slowly and irregularly. In 1590 he had to buy on credit enough cloth for a suit of clothes. His total experience as a government employee was quite unhappy. He must have been a very poor bookkeeper, and his luck was certainly bad, though there is no reason to consider him dishonest. A subordinate of his was untrustworthy, and a banker with whom he had deposited official funds went bankrupt, so Cervantes landed in jail (Seville, 1597). He came out after three months, on bond. The Treasury kept bedeviling him about his shortage and he was in jail again in 1602 for a short while.

During all this time, he may not have been enjoying life, but he was learning an extraordinary amount about it. He evidently was doing a bit of writing too, in spite of his difficulties. In 1603-4 he was in Valladolid, where the court was, negotiating for the publication of the *Quijote*. He secured the privilege to print September 26, 1604, and the book was published in Madrid in January 1605. It was popular and five more editions appeared the same year, but Cervantes was still a poor and struggling author.

On June 27, 1605, a nobleman was murdered outside the house in Valladolid in which Cervantes, his two sisters, his natural daughter Isabel, and a niece were living. They were haled into court, and though they readily proved that they had nothing to do with the murder, it turned out that Isabel's mode of life was at least open to suspicion. She later married twice, and brought her father much trouble, mainly over her dowry. The family was living in poor, even sordid surroundings, and Cervantes' advance royalties helped only temporarily.

Cervantes' later life was devoted more closely to literature. Just before his death he announced the names of four works upon which he was engaged. He died April 23, 1616, and was buried at the Convent of the Discalced Trinitarian nuns in Madrid. No stone marks his grave. Of the works that he had in hand, his widow published only one after his death.

## POEMS, PLAYS, AND PASTORALS

As in the case of many other masters of prose, Cervantes' first love was poetry and his first preserved works are poems. He contributed two to a necrological volume on the death of Philip II's queen, Isabel de Valois, when he was only twenty-two, and he wrote various poems from time to time to authors who were publishing works, even one to a man who wrote on kidney diseases (1588). There are poems within his short stories, notably his *La Gitanilla,* and in his longer works, including the *Galatea* and the *Quijote.* Many of his plays are, of course, in verse, and so is his essay in criticism, the *Viaje del Parnaso* (1614), in which he passes in review nearly a hundred and fifty poets in rather undiscriminating fashion. Cervantes was an indefatigable rhymster, but, despite the grace of some of his ballads and short-line poems, his true inspiration lay elsewhere. Lope de Vega, who did not like him, said there were many budding poets, "but none as bad as Cervantes," and the immortal novelist said of himself (*Don Quixote,* Part I, Chapter VI) that he was more versed in misfortunes than in verses. He did not have the happy combination of poetic ideas and grace of expression.

During his entire career Cervantes showed a great fondness for the pastoral novel, always a combination of prose and verse, and his first full-fledged work belonged to the literary Arcadian genre. Cervantes' *Primera Parte de la Galatea,* in six parts, was published in Alcalá de Henares in 1585. It was evidently suggested by Montemayor's *Diana* and does not differ markedly from other Renaissance pastorals. It does at least contain ideas on love (based on Leo Hebraeus' *Love Dialogues*), to which Cervantes remained faithful in his later works. The sweet pastoral names, such as Tirsi, Meliso, Astraliano, represent real persons among the author's contemporaries. Lauso is Cervantes himself, but the heroine Galatea was not the lady Cervantes married. We can admire the style of the better portions of this work, even if we find it difficult to develop an interest in the action or much admiration for the verse. It is a question of adapting ourselves to a mode of refined Renaissance expression which is outmoded. How many people now read Sir Philip Sidney's *Arcadia?* Cervantes was following a mode of his time. He admired the pastoral and kept promising a second part of his *Galatea,* up to the very last.

Cervantes began trying his hand at plays about 1585. In Seville in 1592 he signed a contract to write six. If they turned out to be the best yet shown in Spain, he was to receive fifty ducats apiece, and if not, nothing. Of the early plays only two survive, though the titles of eight more are known. *El trato de Argel* (*Life in Algiers*) is of interest chiefly for the light it throws on Cervantes' career as a captive slave in North Africa. *La Numancia,* on the famous siege of that city by Scipio, has a certain grandeur of conception, but it is poorly constructed and in itself would give its author little reputation.

In 1615 Cervantes published his *Eight Plays and Eight New Interludes, Never Shown* (*Ocho comedias y ocho entremeses nuevos, nunca representados*), even though he himself knew, as he said, that by this time Lope de Vega had "made off with the Kingship of the Spanish stage," and Cervantes, with more classic ideas on drama, did not approve of Lope's system. The public did not approve of Cervantes'. The interludes gave him better scope for his genius, and they are filled with bright pictures of contemporary types and scenes painted from life, with lively brush strokes and pleasant satire. All his dramatic works are important for the study of Cervantes' ideas.

## THE *EXEMPLARY TALES*

Prose was always Cervantes' happiest medium, and he virtually created the modern Spanish short story. No real progress had been made since the time of Don Juan Manuel, who had long since been forgotten. Cervantes was obviously inspired by the Italian short story, which he perfected with singular grace. In his preface to the twelve *Novelas Ejemplares* (1613) he tells us there is not one of his stories from which some valuable lesson may not be drawn, but suggests that they are fundamentally for entertainment, for the refreshment of the tired spirit. He tells us further that he is the "first to write short stories in Spain," a claim which is fundamentally true. The *Novelas Ejemplares* must have been written at various times in the twenty years preceding their publication.

The stories are twelve in number. They were written at different times and some are obviously better than others, though in every one at least an occasional flash of Cervantes' genius can be caught. *El amante liberal, La fuerza de la sangre, La española inglesa, La señora Cornelia* and *Las dos doncellas* are decidedly Italianate in manner. The interest is in the swiftly moving plot and the long arm of coincidence is badly stretched. Good stories, but by no means great. *El casamiento engañoso* (*Marriage through Deceit*) is the sad story of a man who tries to get a rich wife through trickery and finds himself badly out-tricked. This story serves as an introduction to *El Coloquio de los perros,* the conversation between two dogs endowed with the power of speech. One tells the other his experiences in serving various masters. This device, close to the picaresque novel, gives Cervantes an opportunity to use his own observation, to make fine thumb-nail sketches, to pen little paragraphs of satire.

*El celoso extremeño* (*The Jealous Estremadouran*) recounts the sad and oft-told tale of the jealous old husband and the young wife. The theme is not treated farcically as in the *fabliaux* or in Molière, but seriously, with emphasis on the tragedy of the old man who receives condign punishment because he has broken nature's law of fitness and harmony.

*El licenciado Vidriera* is more philosophical in tone than the other stories. The semi-mad *Licentiate* thinks he is made of glass, but apart from his mania he is wise and shrewd, and Cervantes obviously enjoys using him as a vehicle for witty statements.

The three gems of the collection are *The Little Gipsy Girl, The Illustrious Kitchen Wench* and *Rinconete and Cortadillo.* The first of the three, *La Gitanilla,* is a literary piece in which the story is the thing, and which overworks coincidence, but it is illumined by delicate characterization, sprightly narrative, bright observations of gipsy life, and charming idealism. Preciosa, the heroine, is portrayed with particular grace.

In *La ilustre fregona* there is an even more rollicking humor and realistic observation of life in Toledo, centering about an inn, the *Posada de la Sangre,* which still stood intact until 1936. The kitchen wench is really a girl of excellent family, and so is the student who becomes mule-driver in order to win her.

The very best of the twelve stories is one which has little plot but on the other hand contains most of Cervantes himself. Rinconete and Cortadillo are two tough and sturdy ragamuffins who roam about Spain in true picaresque fashion. They finally land in Seville, only to find that they cannot practise their chosen profession, thievery, without joining the union, so to speak. The mob of predatory ladies and gentlemen in Seville is presided over by Monipodio, whose firmness matches his dexterous capabilities. The reader through the author's guidance attends meetings of his mob, and becomes acquainted with a splendid assortment of male and female knaves. The effect is as if a composite group portrait by Rembrandt, Hals, and Velázquez were suddenly endowed with motion. Each denizen of Monipodio's patio is pictured with sympathy and understanding, and the whole is one of the most striking groups in all literature.

There is one more story which may or may not be by Cervantes. Authorities differ. It is called *The Pretended Aunt* (*La tía fingida*), and is decidedly Celestinesque in character, even scabrous. It was not published with the *Exemplary Novels,* and no wonder. It would be most difficult to find anything *ejemplar* about it.

A cultured person would hardly admit that he had not read Don Quixote, but he is likely to know *Los trabajos de Persiles y Sigismunda* only as a name. Yet Cervantes laid great store by it, and said that it dared to rival Heliodorus (*Theagenes and Chariclea,* or the *Aethiopica*). In fact, he even says it will be either the best or the worst book in the language. The *Persiles* is an idealistic and fantastic account of the wanderings and vicissitudes of a pair of lovers in some imagined northern region. After numerous shipwrecks and countless perils they travel by land, through Spain and France, to Rome, and are happily married.

This book, which narrates so many adventures and near tragedies of the chaste and idealistic lover Persiles comes to an end just as Cervantes' life ends. In a way it is a more youthful book than the *Quijote,* for it portrays the happy realization of a romantic dream. In its details it offers many happy descriptions, savory dialogues, delicate characterizations, well-rounded episodes, and the book contains some of the author's finest writing. It enjoyed ten editions in the seventeenth century, then suffered an eclipse. Only recently has it begun to be appreciated again, and that not universally. It would be unfortunate to overlook its importance for the study of Cervantes' ideas.

## THE *QUIJOTE*

If Cervantes had written nothing but his *Novelas ejemplares* and his *entremeses,* he would be an important author of the seventeenth century, but it happens that he wrote in addition to them the world's greatest novel. The first part of *Don Quixote* appeared in 1605, the second part in 1615. The oftener one reads it, the more one realizes its extraordinary depth and breadth, the author's penetration into human motives and actions, his profound sympathy, his gift of seeing life whole, his artistry in portraying it.

From an external point of view, one may consider *Don Quixote* as a sort of literary pot-pourri, like Alonso Quijano's own *olla,* containing all the ingredients of the preceding novel. Obviously the pattern of Cervantes' masterpiece is that of the Novel of Chivalry, with a knight and his squire running from one adventure to another. At the same time it is a parody. It contains pastoral elements, as in the episode of Cardenio. The picaresque is there too, as in the innkeepers, the galley slaves, Ginés de Pasamonte. The episode of Marcela and Grisóstomo is an Italianate short story, the *History of the Captive* an example of the Moorish. There are disquisitions on literary criticism, as in the famous examination of the books in Chapter VI of Part I, and in the discussion with the Canon in Part II. There are reminiscences of Ariosto's *Orlando Furioso* in the madness of the hero himself, though the author's technique is different. Many a conversation suggests a Lucianesque dialogue. Folk literature sprouts freely from Sancho's sly mouth, particularly in the form of proverbs. It is scarcely to be imagined that Cervantes put in all these elements unconsciously. He hardly needed so many ingredients if he intended to write merely an amusing satire of the exaggerations of the deluded followers of Amadís de Gaula.

How much planning Cervantes did before writing his great novel no one can know. There are suggestions, at least, that he changed the form of his hero's madness. At first Don Quixote thinks he is someone else, such as the Moor Abindarráez or the Marquis of Mantua. A commonplace sort of delusion. After his first sally, Don Quixote is himself, always, no matter how much he may try to emulate his favorite heroes. His actions therefore have more integrity and more significance for the reader. It seems more than likely that Cervantes added episode after episode, as they occurred to him, and not according to some prearranged schedule. Hence the novel seems loosely constructed. It is very different in form from *Madame Bovary,* for example—even though Flaubert claimed that his own origins were in *Don Quixote,* that he knew the book by heart even before he learned to read for himself. This relative formlessness has repelled a few readers, such as the pseudo-exquisite Barbey d'Aurevilly, but it does not seem to bother very many people. Next to the Bible, *Don Quixote* has been the world's most frequently published book.

How is that to be accounted for? There have been many books which won great popularity at the moment of publication but this one has been popular for more than three hundred years.

Cervantes did not have modern psychiatric training, but he managed to portray in his semi-mad literary creature an incarnation of many of humanity's dearest ideals, a synthesis of human traits. He is very foolish indeed, this anachronistic knight, tilting at windmills, mistaking women of the town for high born ladies, transforming a stable-smelly country wench into the Princess Dulcinea del Toboso, promising islands to his squire and pronouncing flowery discourses on the Golden Age to a hungry group of goatherds. Through it all he remains both dignified and noble, and we almost feel that reality itself is at fault rather than Don Quixote.

Those who are young actually or in mental age can enjoy *Don Quixote* merely for the adventure, the humor, the merry quips, the story. The middle-aged can find inspiration for constant endeavor, new light on their own problems, a penetrating commentary on life around them. The old may find consolation for dreams unrealized, communion with a spirit treated unkindly by life but never beaten.

It is trite enough to say that *Don Quixote* is an epic of humanity, not just of the realist and of the idealist separately, but of the two together, reacting upon each other. It is equally trite to say that Don Quixote and Sancho are one, for Cervantes said it before us. A consoling thought, that the earthy, over-practical and selfish Sancho within us is counterbalanced by a Don Quixote who will confront any danger, endure any hardship and suffer any pain in the steadfast pursuit of an unblemished ideal. Of course idealists fare badly in this world and are more than likely to be thought mad. And yet, do they fare badly within themselves? Don Quixote won his own victory. Perhaps the only salvation for humanity, at this moment in one of its least lovely moods, lies exclusively within the individual.

Sancho began by being about as free from idealism as anyone ever born, but association with his master changed him. He had no desire whatever to make the world over. His ideal was to get his stomach well filled with food and drink. He was crafty, shrewd in all matters covered by his limited experience, well supplied with popular wisdom, but faithful, devoted, capable of real affection, susceptible to influences which he had never even suspected. When his master lies dying, Sancho tells him movingly that it is very silly to die, that there are still many wrongs left for them to right, that they must go forth to new deeds of derring-do. Sancho had become infected with his master's idealism, as Don Quixote in Part II had under Sancho's influence made a closer approach to practical reality.

Although Cervantes was keenly aware of the cultural problems of the Renaissance, *Don Quixote* is by no means a manual of systematic philosophy. Yet every episode has a strangely stimulating quality, touching upon the deepest and most vital preoccupations of humanity. Every reader can make his own interpretation of the whole book and of its details, and each rereading suggests something new and fresh. It is quite possible to regard *Don Quixote* as a symbol of Spain: a country which in the time of Charles V and Philip II went forth to deeds of high emprise, trying to bring the world to what those sovereigns regarded as the true faith. Spain

Zurbarán: "Friar Jerónimo Pérez."

*Gramstorff Bros.*

Murillo: "Immaculate Conception."

Murillo: "The Melon Eaters."

Ribera (Spagnoletto): "The Martyrdom of St. Bartholemew."

*Cervantes.*

TERCERA PARTE
DE LAS COMEDIAS
DE LOPE DE VEGA, Y OTROS AV
ores, con sus loas, y entremeses, las quales Co
medias van en la segunda oja

Dedicadas a don Luys Ferrer y Cardona, del Abito de Santiago, Coad
jutor en el oficio de Portantvezes de General, Gouernador
desta ciudad y Reyno, y señor dela Baronia de Sot.

CON LICENCIA,

En Madrid, En casa de Miguel Serrano
de Vargas, Año, 1613.

A costa de Miguel Martinez,

Vendese en la calle mayor, en las gradas de
san Felipe,

Frontpage of the third part of the first edition
of Lope de Vega's Comedies, Madrid 1613.
(Facsimile in original size)

A typical seventeenth century title page. A *parte* consisted of twelve plays.

*Historical Pictures.*

Lope de Vega: "The Portent of Nature."

*Culver Service*

Gramstorff Bros.

Pedro Calderón de la Barca.

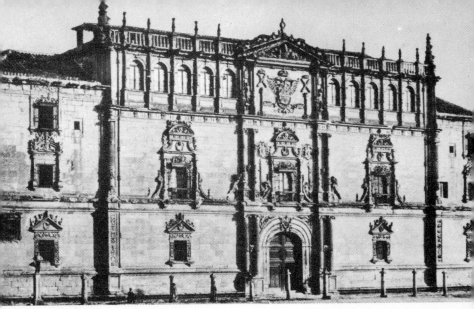

The University of Alcalá de Henares, founded by Cardinal Cisneros.

Francisco de Quevedo. He studied at Alcalá.

D. FRANCISCO GOMEZ DE QUEVEDO VILLEGAS.

failed, as Don Quixote failed, and the signs must have been evident to Cervantes. Nevertheless he thought the struggle for the ideal worth while. He himself never lost his sense of reality, but at the very end of his life he wrote one of his most idealistic works. He penned the touching dedication to *Los trabajos de Persiles y Sigismunda* just five days before he died.

*Don Quixote* received some unwelcome tributes in Cervantes' own lifetime. Two pirated editions of the First Part were swiftly published in Lisbon, and when in 1614 the author had reached Chapter 59 of his Second Part, a gentleman calling himself Alonso Fernández de Avellaneda published a spurious continuation in Tarragona. No one knows who this author was, though much learned ink has been spilled about the matter. Avellaneda possessed considerable skill in construction and narration, though his characters lack depth and subtlety. Cervantes told him off in his own Second Part, rather more mildly than we would expect. Perhaps Avellaneda made Cervantes hasten his work to completion. If so, posterity is deeply in his debt, for Cervantes might have died without finishing his great masterpiece.

# XVIII

## *The Theater of the Golden Age*

### LOPE DE VEGA. THE *COMEDIA*

DON QUIXOTE is the greatest masterpiece of Spain's Golden Age, but the Spanish *comedia* is its most typical product. The drama of the time is personified and summarized in the career of one of the most vital and fertile of all geniuses who ever made the welkin ring, the great Lope.

Lope Félix de Vega Carpio (1562-1635) was born, died and was buried in Madrid. At a tender age he started falling in love and writing verses and plays, and he continued the same pattern throughout his life. His two marriages and his multitudinous extra-conjugal amours brought him a flock of children, some happiness, some remorse and sorrow and constant excitement and inspiration. He also found time to run afoul of the police, to serve as secretary to various noble personages, to enlist in the Spanish Armada, to join various literary and religious associations. Also to compose some two dozen volumes of miscellaneous prose and poetic works and perhaps about eight hundred full-length verse plays and a very large number of *autos* in one act. Lope's disciple Pérez de Montalván credited him with eighteen hundred *comedias* and four hundred *autos*. He died in the odor of sanctity, possessed of the honorary titles of Familiar of the Inquisition and Doctor of Theology. His funeral was, naturally enough, a national event.

Since he displayed his principal merits as a poet and playwright, his pastoral novels, short stories, autobiographical "action in prose" (*La Dorotea*), his religious and ascetic works, his mythological narrative, epic, burlesque and didactic poems may be neglected. His lyrics and *comedias* cannot.

174

Lope's genius was essentially lyric. Some of his poems are among the most delicate in the language, for his taste was sure, his emotion omnipresent, his sense of melody pronounced, his technical ability extraordinary. Some of his poems were published separately, many are within his plays and other works. He uses with equal success the traditional metres and the Italian forms introduced by Boscán and Garcilaso. His ballads and sonnets are especially spirited and moving.

The lyric quality of Lope's dramas is also at once apparent, not merely because they are all written in verse and because they contain separate poems, but because of their general spirit. What sort of plays were these? Lope wrote, in verse, a *New Art of Composing Plays in These Times* in 1609. He says frankly that he does not follow the classic rules, because the audience pays for the drama and deserves to be pleased. Tragedy and comedy may be mingled. Of the three unities of time, place and action, only the last need be observed, though long periods should be supposed to elapse between acts, not within them. Speech should be appropriate to the character speaking; the clownish servant, the *gracioso,* should not talk like his master. Plays are to be composed in three acts, of about a thousand lines each, with metrical variety. Suspense must be maintained until the middle of the third act, to keep the audience interested. Lope makes various other recommendations in matters of detail.

The plays of this phenomenal improviser and of his contemporaries and successors can be characterized even more closely. In a typical *comedia,* the intrigue is complicated, and the development of character is less important than plot; hence no Hamlets, Othellos, Harpagons or Tartuffes, though certain particular characters of Lope and many another Spanish dramatist, possess life and validity, notably Tirso's Don Juan. The subjects might come from anywhere: Spanish or foreign history and legend, mythology, the Bible and lives of the Saints, pastoral material, the picaresque, or contemporary themes. Particularly noteworthy is the cloak-and-sword play (*comedia de capa y espada*), in which gallants of the upper middle class or the nobility pursue the maidens of their choice, and, after a complicated intrigue involving outraged or nearly outraged honor, duels, cases of mistaken identity, parental objections, love-making at the window, rivalries, misunderstandings and whatnot, the lovers win their beloveds, and joyous weddings are arranged. Such plays are clever rather than deep, but move along at a rapid pace and with a charming lyric spontaneity. The theme of honor is particularly prominent. The father or brother must wash out in blood any taint, perhaps only a suspicion of taint, upon the spotless mantle of the lady in his charge. Hence the development of real "honor tragedies," like the more sanguinary plays of Calderón. A striking feature of the drama of Spain's Golden Age is the absence of mothers on the stage.

The poetic gallantries and general high-jinks depicted in the *comedia* are, of course, romanticized. The plays reflect the spirit of the seventeenth century; they are not meant as literal portrayals of life. Naturally it is possible to learn many details of social classes, manners, customs and attitudes toward life from the *comedia,* but it can hardly be concluded that Spanish life consisted in the pursuit all over Spain of some reluctant gallant by a lady in disguise, or the summary private murder by irate husband or father of some lady on whom suspicion had unluckily fallen, and the slaying in fair duel of the man connected with the suspicion or even the reality.

The decidedly popular appeal of the Spanish theater in the seventeenth century is impressive. Lope saw to it that there should be something for everyone, and his successors followed in his tracks. The sophisticated could rejoice in his mythological references, his artistically turned sonnets, his occasional elaborate figures of speech, but the rapidly moving plots, the swift action, the gallant heroes and romantic though highly resourceful heroines, the physical and verbal antics of the *graciosos* could be appreciated by great and small. Even the treatment of the honor theme must have found some popular response.

Many of the themes used by seventeenth century dramatists were perfectly familiar to all, for they came from national history and legend or from contemporary life. Shakespeare, far greater than

Lope in psychological insight and grandeur of conception, nevertheless resembled his Spanish contemporary in offering something for every auditor. Not so the French, who have to this day found it difficult to understand the worth of the Spanish *comedia.* In France classicism prevailed, and a more refined, and more limited, type of drama was demanded, intended not for everyone, but for the elite, the highly cultured. The noble and beautiful dramas of a Corneille, a Racine, more carefully and artistically wrought than Spanish plays, show a profound knowledge of the human heart, but they have had less popular appeal. For all their virtues they have not attracted foreign audiences, and have furnished little inspiration to later dramatists outside France. The Spanish *Comedias,* on the other hand, furnished a rich mine of inspiration for future authors at home and abroad.

Since the cities were not large and the theater-going public was small, new plays were constantly needed: an invitation to rapid writing on the part of dramatists. Lope informs us that there were more than a hundred plays which he wrote within the space of twenty-four hours each. The first permanent theaters, rudimentary affairs called *corrales,* were established in Madrid in the 1560's and 1570's, and two, the *Príncipe* and the *Cruz,* continued as Madrid's only public theaters until the late eighteenth century. Spectators of high rank occupied boxes (*aposentos*) at the back of the courtyard, but elsewhere the sexes were separated. The "Stewpan" (*cazuela*) was a latticed gallery reserved for women, the groundlings stood in the pit (*patio*) and expressed rowdy disapproval of anything that did not suit them. Performances were held at two P.M. in winter and four in summer, but the theaters were closed by Lent, by a queen's pregnancy, by fits of austerity on the part of the sovereign or by other *contretemps.* Dramatic performances began with a *loa* or recited monologue to introduce the play. Between the acts *entremeses* (interludes) were put on, and after Act III some sort of *fin de fiesta,* with dialogue and dance. Dances were extremely popular, but alas! some, the *saraband,* for example, became such scandalous affairs that they were repeatedly forbidden. Spanish dances with which we are now familiar, such as *fandangos, boleros* and *jotas,* are more modern in origin, of the eighteenth and nineteenth centuries.

Lope de Vega had some dramatic tradition behind him, but he really created and sired the multifarious *comedia* himself. In view of Lope's incredible fertility, we are amazed at his variety, his invention, his scope. He did not concentrate his startling energies sufficiently to produce a masterpiece, and his dramatic production is better viewed as a whole than in its individual parts. Nevertheless many plays stand out as conspicuously excellent. *Fuente-Ovejuna* is a very dramatic portrayal of the rise of a whole town against an offensive overlord. *The Best Magistrate the King* (*El mejor alcalde el rey*) displays the king as taking the part of a peasant against a cruel nobleman. *The Peasant in His Own Corner* (*El villano en su rincón*) displays another admirable peasant type. Heroic women are portrayed in *Las famosas asturianas*. The theme of *El Abencerraje* is skillfully used in *Abindarráez y Narváez o el remedio en la desdicha* (*Remedy in Misfortune*). *Peribañez y el Comendador de Ocaña* is a noteworthy semi-historical drama. One scarcely knows which to pick among the very numerous *capa y espada* plays, with their rapid movement, romantic intrigue and charming heroines: *The Girl with the Water Jar, St. John's Night, Scorn Works Miracles, The Dog in the Manger, The Silly Girl, Toledan Night, Over the Bridge, Jane.* Yes, scores of others might be selected of practically equal sprightliness and grace. The "Portent of Nature" was remarkable for much more than mere quantitative production.

One of the best plays of Spain's Golden Age, formerly attributed to Lope de Vega without question, may not be his: *The Star of Seville* (*La Estrella de Sevilla*). Lope's or not, it is a powerful honor drama. The lovely Estrella is the fiancée of Sancho Ortiz. The King sees and loves her, and by suborning a slave girl, gets into her home. He is found by Estrella's brother Bustos Tavera, who reproaches him, but spares his life because he is King. To win vengeance, he gives Sancho Ortiz a sealed paper with the name of a man whom he must kill, for the man says the King is guilty of *lèse-majesté*. Sancho breaks the seal: his victim is Bustos Tavera.

After great hesitation he slays his fiancée's brother. She, dressing in her wedding finery to receive her bridegroom, receives instead her brother's corpse. Sancho Ortiz is jailed, and is ready to die rather than betray his sovereign. The King is too moved by such loyalty to remain silent. He confesses his instigation of the crime, and Sancho is set free. Estrella and Sancho part, for blood is between them; she goes to a convent, he to seek death in the wars.

Grant the validity of Sancho's sense of honor, and you cannot fail to be moved by the play's intense drama, its somber intensity.

## TIRSO DE MOLINA

One of Lope's most famous followers and defenders was the Mercenarian friar, Gabriel Téllez, better known as Tirso de Molina (1583?-1648). He was active in the business of his religious order and was its official historian but he found time to write some four hundred plays, all but eighty-six of which are lost. He also wrote two miscellaneous works—*Los Cigarrales* ("Country Places") *de Toledo* and *Profit and Pleasure* (*Deleitar Aprovechando*)—containing stories, dialogues, edifying instruction, plays and a defense of the Spanish *comedia* and of Lope's dramatic system. Needless to say, Tirso's plays, quite free in ideas and expression, brought sour looks to the faces of his pious and stricter confrères and censure, official censure, to the playwright. His were "profane plays, of evil incentive and example." Few would judge them quite so severely today.

Although Tirso frankly proclaims himself Lope's disciple, he is not a mere understudy. If his vitality is less titanic than his master's, his intrigues are not a bit less clever, his feminine characters no less alluring with perhaps a bit more of the devil in them, his clowns are funnier, and he created one of the memorable characters in literature, the figure of Don Juan.

Tirso could produce admirable historical plays, such as *La prudencia en la mujer,* on the Queen mother Doña María de Molina (early fourteenth century). He wrote many Biblical plays, such as the rather lurid *Tamar's Vengeance.* His *Doubter Damned* (*El con-*

*denado por desconfiado*) is a remarkable presentation of religious doctrine on the stage, involving unforgivable sin and the problem of God's grace. A holy hermit who doubts is damned, and a Neapolitan bad-man is saved because he repents at the last moment, like the Thief on the Cross. Tirso was particularly adept at the "palace play" (*comedia palaciega*), such as *The Bashful Man at Court* (*El Vergonzoso en palacio*). No one could devise more complicated plots for cloak-and-sword plays. *Don Gil of the Green Breeches, Madrid Balconies, Jealousy Cured by Jealousy, The Peasant Girl of Vallecas, Doctor Love* and many another attest his skill and charm. *Our Pious Martha* is a gracious hypocrite.

Tirso would have been famous if he had written no more than *The Deceiver of Seville* (*El burlador de Sevilla*), for it was in that play that Don Juan made his first seductive bow in literature. Certainly, the name of the world's first seducer and deceiver is lost in the mists of pre-history, but it was Tirso who gave literary and dramatic form and significance to the type. Tirso's Don Juan is a believer, an arrant individualist, a man of charm who makes his amorous conquests through trickery and promises of marriage. His servant, Catalinón, warns him that he must repent of his evil ways, that there is a Day of Judgment, and each time Don Juan says, "A long time before payment!" He has postponed over-long, for God's freely offered grace becomes inoperative if not accepted in time. Don Juan swaggeringly invites the statue of one of his victims, the *Comendador,* whom he had killed, to sup with him. The statue accepts, and Don Juan, not losing his swagger, accepts a return invitation. The dishes served are fire and brimstone, and finally the statue seizes Don Juan and drags him down to hell. Not, mark you, on account of his libertinism, which after all was nothing very extraordinary.

The figure of Don Juan was a real creation, fertile in suggestions and destined to inspire hundreds of authors up to our own day. Most of them were quite innocent of direct knowledge of Tirso's powerful drama, but something of the aura of Tirso has clung round Don Juan as his character has been transformed in different lands and different times. Molière (in *Don Juan ou le festin de pierre*) made him an atheist and something of a hypocrite, but he was still sent to hell. So is he in the familiar and perennially melodious *Don Giovanni* of Mozart. The nineteenth century Romantics could not bear to damn so vital an individualist, a figure who incarnated many of their dearest ideals, so they saved him. Zorrilla, for example, has him ransomed by love, and his sentimental soul flies up to heaven along with that of his beloved Doña Inés, accompanied by pink angels and sweet incense. Byron's *Don Juan* is unfinished, but his hero seems to be all dash, irresistible charm and insouciance. Some regard Pushkin's *Don Juan* as the most lyric of all. Many twentieth century authors have adopted Don Juan: Rostand, Bataille, the Machados and Hernandez Catá, Bernard Shaw, Ludwig Lewisohn and many more. He keeps changing, but he doesn't die. One of Spain's real contributions to world literature, more important than the plots from stories and plays which Spaniards so freely contributed to France and other nations.

## SECONDARY DRAMATISTS

Another dramatist who was influenced by Lope came from the east coast. Guillén de Castro (1569-1631), Valencian aristocrat who, according to legend, went from riches to rags, soldier, man about town, twice married, was also a poet and a dramatist with about fifty plays to his credit. He was a friend and admirer of Lope, whom he could match in vigor but not in delicacy and skill. His *Narcissus in His Own Opinion* caricatures a fop. Three of his plays take plots from Cervantes: *Don Quijote de la Mancha, El curioso impertinente* and *La fuerza de la sangre. Count Dirlos* and *Count Alarcos* are based on Spanish ballads, and so are Castro's two best-known plays on the Spanish national hero: *Las mocedades del Cid* and *Las hazañas del Cid*. They are very imperfect in structure, but are strong, fresh in spirit and action, reflecting and often quoting the ballads (not the *Poema del Cid*) which furnished their inspiration. To Guillén de Castro Corneille owed the suggestion for his most famous play, *Le Cid,* the keystone of French tragedy. Castro could inspire better than he could compose.

Luis Vélez de Guevara (1570-1644) is known to us as the author of a novel, *The Limping Devil,* but he was also a playwright of note. He is the author of one of the best plays on the tragic theme of Doña Inés de Castro. That drama is called *Reinar después de morir.* His dramatic version of the story of *Guzmán el Bueno,* who refused to surrender Tarifa to the Moors to save his own son, is *My King Rather Than My Own Flesh and Blood (Más pesa el rey que la sangre).*

One of the most popular plays of the entire Golden Age in Spain was *Del rey abajo, ninguno,* also called from the name of the protagonist *García del Castañar* and from his profession *El labrador más honrado.* The author was Francisco de Rojas Zorrilla (1607-1648), a man of excellent family who came from Toledo to Madrid and early won fame for plays and poems. He was once gravely wounded by another poet whom he had satirized, but apparently he suffered no harm from an actor also named Francisco de Rojas, by whose wife he had a daughter who became a well-known actress. Rojas later married a lady of the great Mendoza family, and in 1643 was given the habit of the noble Order of Santiago. Many of his plays were written in collaboration with others, such as Calderón and Vélez de Guevara.

The title of his most famous drama means *Below the King All Men Are Peers, García del Castañar, the Most Honest Peasant.* García, not really a peasant but a nobleman in retirement, mistakes Count Orgaz, who makes love to García's wife, for the King himself, and allows him to depart. Discovering his mistake, García kills the Count in a duel. He will bear anything from the King, but from no one else. The play is really better than one would think from the above, in plot, in the expression of emotion, in background. Rojas also wrote plays, such as the popular *Master Turned Servant (El amo criado),* in which the clown was the principal character (*comedia de gracioso*). He had somewhat feministic ideas. His *To Each His Due (Cada cual lo que le toca),* presenting a heroine who was quite capable of taking care of her own honor, did not please its public at all. The style of Rojas is by no means free from affectation. He furnished plots for Scarron, Thomas

Corneille, and perhaps Rotrou. Apparently he wrote only about six dozen plays, of which he published only twenty-four. *Merry Sport with Fools* (*Entre bobos anda el juego*) is a play called a *comedia de figurón,* in which the chief character is really a caricature. The genre was popular well into the eighteenth century, and such plays will be found in Antonio de Zamora (*El hechizado por fuerza*) and Cañizares (*El dómine Lucas*).

## JUAN RUIZ DE ALARCON

The poor Mexican hunchback, Juan Ruiz de Alarcón y Mendoza (1581-1639), was a solitary sort of figure and stood apart from his contemporaries. His disposition was not a happy one, and he inspired jealousy and dislike. Such men as Lope, Quevedo and Góngora lowered themselves to the point of poking fun at his physical deformity. He was born in Taxco, Mexico, though not in the present charming town of that name. He came to Spain and studied at Salamanca, lived in Seville, returned to Mexico, and in 1613 came back to Spain and remained there. His total production, twenty-four plays, is very small when judged by contemporary standards.

It was small for the simple reason that Alarcón was not an improviser, but an artist who polished and corrected his work. He was quite capable of writing a play in the Lopesque manner: witness his romantic and melodramatic *Weaver of Segovia,* second part. (The so-called first part was written by an anonymous author. They are both full-length plays.) It is, however, for his comedies on moral themes that Ruiz de Alarcón is justly famous, for they show the author as not only the skillful artist, but also as a true case of an upright and noble soul in a deformed body.

*Walls Have Ears* (*Las paredes oyen*) is directed against the vice of slander. *The Test of Promises* (*La prueba de las promesas*), based on a story by Don Juan Manuel, is a study of ingratitude. *Change and Thrive* (*Mudarse por mejorarse*), with a simple plot and finely drawn characters, portrays fickleness in love. The best-known of all Alarcón's plays is *Truth Suspect* (*La verdad sospechosa*), a glowing picture of a young nobleman who is a congenital and enthusiastic liar, and who finally comes to grief in the web of his own fabrications. The great Corneille said that he would have given any two of his plays to be able to write *La verdad sospechosa*. In fact Corneille adapted it as *Le Menteur,* so important in the history of French comedy, though the Frenchman did not improve the original when he changed the ending. Voltaire went so far as to say that Corneille's theater could not have existed without Alarcón. Even though that was an exaggerated statement, it remains true that the Mexican had qualities of universal appeal: earnestness, nobility of purpose, high ideals of craftsmanship.

## CALDERON

Calderón is the last great name in the history of seventeenth century drama, and some have thought him its greatest representative, superior even to Lope de Vega. Pedro Calderón de la Barca (1600-1681) belonged to the lower nobility. He was educated at the universities of Alcalá and Salamanca, and had a rather gay youth. He was in the army, in the service of the Duque del Infantado and the Duque de Alba, received the noble order of Santiago, and was ordained priest in 1651. He began to enjoy success as poet and playwright before he was twenty-one. After he entered the priesthood he wrote religious plays (*autos*) and *comedias* only for the court of the drama-loving King Philip IV.

Calderón wrote little beside drama. He has to his credit about one hundred and twenty-five full-length plays, including all the types popularized by Lope, plus about seventy *autos* and twenty miscellaneous short pieces.

In his historical plays, not the best in his repertory, Calderón shows little regard for fact. One, which merely refers to events in connection with Philip II's accession to the Portuguese throne, is admirable: *The Mayor of Zalamea* (*El alcalde de Zalamea*). It is a decided improvement over Lope's play by the same name on which it is based, and contains real characters: the silly broken-down nobleman Don Mendo, the gouty and fractious old soldier

Don Lope de Figueroa, the sweet heroine Isabel, and particularly the sturdy peasant mayor and hero Pedro Crespo.

In the cloak-and-sword play Calderón could concoct ever so ingenious an intrigue, worked out in detail, well-carpentered and trimmed, and possessed of grace and movement. Yet the characters are conventional, too much alike, quite lacking in depth. Examples would be: *It's Hard to Guard a House with Two Doors, You Don't Jest with Love, Still Waters Run Deep, April and May Mornings, The Quack Astrologer.*

The somber honor-tragedies of Calderón require for their understanding the acceptance of a code which is repellent to most. In *The Doctor Heals His Own Honor* (*El médico de su honra*), our hero, Don Gutierre, is forced to kill his innocent wife, poor fellow, because suspicion has fallen on her. The lady whom he next marries accepts his blood-stained hand with pleasure, presumably to the great satisfaction of the audience. *For Secret Wrong, Secret Vengeance* shows how honor is not tarnished provided dishonor be kept secret. It is to be doubted that such a code was perfectly in force in actual life. At any rate, Calderón did not invent it, for it was already to be seen in the plays of his predecessors. He used it in these and many other plays with great dramatic effect.

While the honor dramas are significant in the production of Calderón and form an interesting commentary on seventeenth century Spain, others of his plays have achieved greater celebrity. *The Constant Prince* is Ferdinand, son of King John I of Portugal (1385-1433), who suffers imprisonment and death in Fez rather than give up his faith. *La devoción de la cruz* has the theme that all crimes may win pardon through devotion to the Cross, as in Tirso's *Doubter Damned*. The drama possesses real pathos, if strange psychology, and is undoubtedly one of the world's great religious plays. *The Wonderful Magician* deals with the pact which St. Cyprian of Antioch made with the Devil: a suggestion of the Faust legend.

The most famous of Calderón's plays and probably the best known of Spain's Golden Age is *Life's a Dream* (*La vida es sueño*). Segismundo, Prince of Poland, is brought up in a cave, almost a wild beast. He is given a narcotic, and suddenly brought to court, where his violence, his untrammeled yielding to the impulses of the "natural man," causes the King, his father, to despair of him. He is taken back to his cave, and reflects that all must have been a dream. When a revolution takes him back to court, he has become the man of reason, convinced that all life is a dream, that we should so act on earth as to have a happy awakening in heaven. The play is undoubtedly poetic, moving, but that it presents a logically sound philosophy is very doubtful indeed.

Calderón was preeminent in a special form of religious drama, the *auto sacramental,* a one-act play devoted to the Holy Sacraments, to be performed on Corpus Christi Day. The theme was the mystery of transubstantiation, and many plots were used to present it symbolically. It is a typically Spanish production, a combination of naïveté, religion, and poetry, which has been practically unintelligible to many foreigners. *Autos* were splendidly put on in Spanish towns in the seventeenth century; by the late eighteenth they were forbidden. Calderón was merely continuing a tradition followed by Lope and others, and his *autos* contain some of his finest poetry.

Calderón was not an author who cultivated simplicity of style, but rather a baroque author who developed ornamentation to a high degree, whose rhetoric soars in complex spirals, whose thought is full of legal and theological subtleties learned in his university days.

## AGUSTIN MORETO

Agustín Moreto y Cabaña (1618-1669) had a relatively short period of dramatic productivity before he became a priest in 1657, but he wrote some fifty plays. His originality is slight, for most of his works are "honest thefts" from others, such as Lope, but he regularly improved upon his models. His plots tend more toward simplicity, his expression toward clarity, and he shows considerable gaiety and life. His *The Brave Justice-dealer (El valiente justiciero)* is a very successful and popular reworking of Tirso's *Rey don Pedro en Madrid*. On the Spanish stage, Peter I is presented not as "The Cruel," but as "The Justice-dealing," who champions the cause of his people against oppressive noblemen. Moreto's *El lindo don Diego* offers a neat portrait of a fop, based on Guillén de Castro's *Narcissus in His Own Opinion*. Certainly one of Moreto's best is *Scorn for Scorn* (*El desdén con el desdén*), a charming and witty development of the theme of the lovely lady who scorns all her admirers and falls into the arms of the wooer who had been shrewd enough to scorn her. Molière utilized it for his impromptu *Princesse d'Élide*.

The production of drama did not stop with the death of Calderón, Moreto, and their contemporaries, but by the end of the seventeenth century the flame of inspiration had burned very low.

# XIX

## Subtleties and Arabesques in Literature

### GONGORISM

AS artistic sophistication grows, a tendency often arises to depart from simplicity, to seek the complicated and difficult, the rare, the *recherché,* the highly ornamental. Compare Romanesque architecture with Gothic or Plateresque, plain-song with the music of Debussy or Hindemith, the Anglo-Saxon chronicle with *Euphues.* In the Middle Ages the Provençal poets and later the *Grands Rhétoriqueurs* set to subtilizing thought and complicating metrics. In Spain Juan de Mena sought to create a poetic language different from that of prose, enriched with borrowings from Latin and Italian, containing references known only to the initiated. And this tendency showed itself in Europe during or at the end of the Renaissance: *Euphuism* in England, *Schwulst* in Germany, *Préciosité* in France, *Marinismo* in Italy, all different, but with at least a common denominator. In Spain the tendency was two-headed, but the supporting body was the same. Some would prefer to put it in this way: that in the seventeenth century there were two horrendous literary vices, conceptism and *culteranismo,* or Gongorism.

*Culteranismo* followed the lead of Mena. Theoretically the terms should be applied to exaggerations in expression, in wording: "cultivated obscurity of style"; borrowing of foreign words, many of which, by the way, were accepted, naturalized, and are now regarded as simple enough. Distortions of syntax, Latin or Greek word order, even such delicacies as the use of the synecdochical accusative(!) (e.g., *azul los ojos* for *de los ojos azules*). Learned references to mythology (What about Milton?), history, geography,

188

anything. (Is it otiose to mention Ezra Pound, T. S. Eliot, and *dii menores* of our own day?) And elaborate figures of speech, especially metaphors. No one would quarrel with an effort, like that of the Pléiade, to enrich language and elevate poetry; the trouble was that enthusiasm might give rise to gross exaggerations, to taking that fatal step past the sublime. It did indeed.

Conceptism refers to intellectual subtlety, akin to that of the scholastic philosophers, the Provençal poets, even Petrarch. A *concepto* might be defined as a metaphorical quirk. The *conceptistas* labored manfully to produce striking conceits, to develop the ingenious turn, the startling metaphor: until the reader is almost ready to say, "Be good, sweet maid, and let who will be clever." Yet they, too, were seeking enrichment, some new way of emphasizing thought. And they developed enormous cleverness, for the best of them were heavily endowed with brains. Conceptism and Gongorism evidently meet in the metaphor. Supposedly "the silver serpent slithered over Libyan fire" (meaning the shining river flowed through hot Africa) would be *culterano,* whereas "su comida era eterna, sin principio ni fin" is conceptist (*principio* means beginning, first course; *fin* means end, dessert). In other words, they had nothing to eat. We learn further that their mouths were so unused that they had to be dusted off with feather dusters: another *concepto.*

The tendencies were not new, but they were more self-consciously pursued in the seventeenth century. A young courtier-soldier-poet named Luis Carrillo y Sotomayor (1583-1610) turned his aristocratic attention to poetic elegances in Spain and at the Court of Naples, and by 1607 circulated in manuscript his *Book of Poetic Erudition*. He and the Italian Marini (*Adone,* 1623) must have been subject to the same influences. Carrillo champions Latinization of Spanish vocabulary and syntax, wealth of obscure references, a poetry exclusively for the initiated. Unfortunately the poetry and prose of Carrillo, published the year after his death, are *curiosa* that interest mainly the literary historian.

## GONGORA AND THE *CONCEPTISTAS*

The truly great poet whose name has unfortunately been considered a synonym of poetic extravagance is Luis de Argote y Góngora (1561-1627). He was born in Cordova, the birthplace of the Senecas, Lucan, Mena. He was well educated, even though he spent some of his time at the University of Salamanca in writing poetry. He was made a prebendary of the Cathedral of Cordova, though he was only in minor orders, and his mode of life was not that of a model priest. He enjoyed the protection of royal favorites, and after being ordained priest he was appointed chaplain to His Majesty Philip III. He lived in prosperity in Madrid from 1617 to 1626, but his blood pressure was rising, and he suffered a stroke of apoplexy. He returned to Cordova to die at the age of sixty-six. He had many friends and some enemies who satirized him, notably Lope and Quevedo.

Throughout his whole poetic career Góngora wrote simple songs of lyric freshness and melody. He is unquestionably one of Spain's most gifted poets, and all anthologies would be poorer without some of his *romances, letrillas* (short satiric poems), and other popular forms, not to mention his sonnets and more ambitious pieces. He always possesses wit, grace, elegance, high polish.

It is therefore quite inaccurate to say that there was one Góngora, the "Angel of Light," who wrote simply until about 1609, and then another Góngora, the "Angel of Darkness," who wrote only unintelligible *"culto"* poems from that time onward. The works of Góngora which have so annoyed readers unwilling to make the effort necessary to understand them are mainly the *Panegyric to the Duke of Lerma* (1609), the *Ode on the Capture of Larache* (1610), the *Fable of Polyphemus and Galatea* (composed about 1613), the *Soledades* (unfinished, about two thousand lines in all, about the same time as the *Polifemo*), the *Fable of Pyramus and Thisbe* (1618). Yes, they are certainly difficult, but it takes very little good will to see their great beauty, their gorgeous imagery, their color, their poetic warmth; the poet's effort to grasp "the supernal loveliness."

Góngora could not found a successful poetic school, for his gifts were individual. Those who, not favoured by genius, sought to follow him, could imitate his technical devices, but they produced distorted syntax, high-flown metaphors, exaggerated bad taste. And so the Góngora of the *Soledades* was long condemned as the corrupter of poetry. In recent years, especially in the twenties of this century, he has been better understood, and his work has gone into the formation of contemporary poets in Spain and Latin America.

The chief *conceptistas* were Quevedo and Gracián, though the contagion spread far and wide in the seventeenth century. Francisco Gómez de Quevedo y Villegas (1580-1645), who wrote the picaresque novel, the *Vida del Buscón,* was a real artist. Quevedo hated fancy words, like those introduced by Góngora. Yet he loved to toy with ideas, and his prose and poetry, for he wrote a voluminous amount of both, are full of clever conceits, quips, puns (mainly good), startling comparisons, ingenious turns of phrase. He is therefore an author who is extremely hard to translate. His very great satirical and humorous gifts were also displayed in his visions (*Sueños*), his literary pamphlets, even in his works on specifically political, moral, and religious themes (*La política de Dios,* 1626, *La providencia de Dios,* 1641, and many others).

Quevedo's numerous poems were usually published in nine sections, one for each of the Muses. They are of great variety, from the most sprightly, jocose, slangy, festive or scabrous satire to tender love poems and religious verse of deep intensity, and he uses a large assortment of metres and stanza forms. His satiric and humorous pieces show his gifts to best advantage. Although he often displayed real earnestness, as in his *Epístola satírica y censoria al Conde-Duque de Olivares,* which showed him longing to have Spain's ills cured, he treated many lighter themes, as in his satire, based on Juvenal, against the perils of matrimony. Some of the satires can be digested only by a strong stomach, for Quevedo's wit was robust, not fit for tender virgins.

His love of the *"concepto,"* the cleverly turned phrase, is even more evident in his prose than in his poetry. In his *Sueños,* mainly published in 1627 though written about twenty years earlier, he pays a literary visit to hell and shoots satirical arrows at all sorts of types from contemporary society that he finds there: doctors, lawyers, tailors, innkeepers, barbers, bankers, ladies of various sorts, poets, lovers, and worse, in a style so scintillating that the eyes are dazzled, and at times perhaps a little wearied, and the reader longs for the plainness of the author of the *Lazarillo.*

Diego de Saavedra Fajado (1584-1648) modelled his style after that of Tacitus, but he could not entirely avoid the exaggeration of his contemporaries, and he is very erudite. His literary criticism is contained in his *República literaria,* written about 1612, though not published until 1655, and then as the work of another. It was far from complete since there is no consideration of the *Celestina,* Cervantes, or the theater. Artists as well as authors are included, despite the title. Better known is his work called *Empresas políticas, o idea de un príncipe político-cristiano* (1640), in which he used his long experience as a diplomat to proclaim his idea of what a Christian ruler should be and to combat the ideas of Machiavelli's *Prince.*

Baltasar Gracián (1601-1658) entered the Jesuit order at the age of eighteen. He was a learned theologian, a famous preacher, a gifted conversationalist, one of the solidest authors of his time. He was disciplined by his religious order at least twice, and requested permission to leave it, but was not allowed to. The Jesuits greatly honored him after his death.

His first published work was *El héroe* (1637), in which he sets forth the twenty qualities which should be possessed by the hero. The doctrine is anti-Machiavellian and the model prince one whom few would now select for admiration: Philip IV of Spain. Another model ruler, according to Gracián, was King Ferdinand, whom he praised in *El político Fernando* (1640). He also lavishes praise on the Count-Duke of Olivares. *El discreto* suggests twenty-five virtues, each with a historical example, desirable for the man of the world. *El oráculo manual,* which offers three hundred maxims for human conduct, influenced La Rochefoucauld and La Bruyère.

Gracián's masterpiece is *El criticón* (1651-53-57). There are two main characters, Critilo, the man of education, sophistication, and reason, and Andrenio, the natural man, who theoretically views society and the world without prejudice. The picture of society is pessimistic. No wonder Gracián so greatly appealed to Schopenhauer. The book is keen, witty, compact, the product of an enlightened, experienced, and highly cultivated man who had tried the world and found it wanting. The fundamental idea of the work is probably Oriental in origin, but various authors whom the talented Jesuit knew made their contribution.

Gracián's *Art of Wit* (*Arte de ingenio,* 1642), amplified in 1648 as *Cleverness and the Art of Wit* (*Agudeza y arte de ingenio*), is a sort of anthology and manual for writers who would be clever, who would practise conceptism with more than a dash of *culteranismo.*

There were those who followed Gracián's lead, only they did not have his wit and solid knowledge. Pulpit oratory was particularly affected, and the high-flown conceits of preachers furnished excellent material for satire in the next century (Padre Isla, also a Jesuit, in his *Fray Gerundio*).

Gracián, one of the most careful writers in the Spanish language, would probably be more read if he had cultivated subtlety less. His polished style is not easy, and one who would savor it cannot afford to let his attention wander. Every page is heavily packed, and the insignificant has been filed away.

The use of excessive cleverness or superfluous ornamentation could not be fruitful. There is something highly exaggerated about the productions of the last of the great authors of the Golden Age in Spain, and further development along the same lines was not possible. Those who tried to push Gongorism or Conceptism further were doomed to futility. Greater restraint and greater simplicity were needed. An effort was made to secure them in the eighteenth century.

## Spain's Golden Age in the Arts

### ARCHITECTURE, SCULPTURE AND HANDICRAFTS

THE splendid inspiration of the Renaissance could not fail to exert itself in Spain in realms other than literary. In architecture a new style developed which many would not think for the better, for the full splendor of the Middle Ages reached a glorious culmination in their cathedrals. The style characteristic of the fifteenth and early sixteenth centuries is called plateresque, and like the art of a *platero,* or silversmith, it emphasizes ornamentation rather than line and structure. The style was imported from Italy, and the basis was supposed to be the Roman column, but the distinction between the classic orders of architecture was not observed and various mixed styles can be noted. Moorish and Gothic influences were still in evidence. Within the sixteenth century there is a tendency toward a purer Roman style, a greater symmetry, a greater influence of the classic architectural ideals of Italy. A good example is the palace built (1526) for Charles V in the Alhambra. Its massive lines could hardly be less in keeping with the delicate lightness of the Moorish buildings adjacent to it. The severest example of classic architecture in Spain is the group of buildings begun by Philip II in 1559 at El Escorial: massive, stark, somber, impressive. The architects were Juan de Toledo and Juan de Herrera. The latter was also responsible for the Lonja (Stock Exchange) at Seville and the Cathedral of Valladolid, which was completed with numerous alterations after Herrera's death.

Spain has never been a land devoted to rigid classic ideals in anything and a greater exuberance began to reassert itself in the baroque in all forms of art. The emphasis is on the curved and broken, rather than the straight line, on crowded and swirling decoration, on ornamentation rather than on plane surfaces. At its worst such art is tortured, over-rich, excessively complicated, indigestible, but at its best it is vivid, splendid, gorgeous. It is mainly this style which was transplanted to Latin America, naturally, since it lasted until it was replaced by neo-classicism in the eighteenth century. The exaggerated baroque is also called *churrigueresco,* after the Spanish architect José de Churriguera (died 1725).

Some of the sculptors who flourished in Spain during the Renaissance were foreigners, like the Frenchmen Felipe Vigarni and Juan de Juni, and the Italians Francesco Pisani and Pietro Torrigiano. Many of Spanish origin, like Alonso Berruguete (c. 1480-1561), had studied in Italy. He and Gil and Diego de Siloé are among the best known, even if no one in Spain created statues to rival in fame those of a Donatello or a Michelangelo. Sculpture continued to flourish in the seventeenth century, as in the work of Martínez Montañés, Jerónimo Hernández, and Alonso Cano.

Some of the best work in Spanish sculpture was done in wood, not only in choir stalls, doors and altarpieces, but in statues. Many of the statues were painted and embossed with gold (*estofado*).

The sixteenth century was the great age of the Spanish goldsmiths, whose delicate crosses and monstrances can still be seen in cathedrals in many parts of Spain. Two families of goldsmiths were particularly distinguished, the Arfes and the Becerrils.

Spain had constantly been distinguished for fine ironwork, and the tradition continued through the Renaissance, producing admirable grilles for churches and convents as well as decorative stair-rails, balconies and gratings for private houses.

Furniture reflected Italian influences. Many examples of chairs, chests, wardrobes and desks survive from the sixteenth and seventeenth centuries, beautifully carved, often encrusted with gold, silver, ivory, or mother of pearl. Glazed tiles (*azulejos*), for which Spain has always been noted, now tended to show classic forms instead of the older *mudéjar* geometrical patterns. The best-known center for the production of pottery was Talavera, near Toledo, where some four hundred workmen were employed in the seventeenth century. The products were noted for their brilliant glaze and for their characteristic blue and white designs.

The raised embroidery on silk ecclesiastical vestments can still be admired, as in the Cathedral of Toledo, which has preserved many beautiful examples of the fifteenth and sixteenth centuries. One specimen is a mantle for the Virgin, embroidered in the early seventeenth century, which contains some eighty thousand pearls and other jewels. Tapestries and carpets were mainly imported from Italy and Flanders.

## PAINTING

The period of greatest splendor in Spanish painting came in the time of the first four Philips. The influences were mainly Italian, of the schools of Florence (Raphael), Venice (Titian), and to a lesser extent, of Bologna. Italian painters came to Spain, and Spanish artists studied and worked in Italy. Influence by no means implies Spanish imitation, and the greatest Spanish painters exhibit marked originality.

It is too bad to neglect the numerous Spanish painters who are only near-great, but even if the visitor to the Prado and other Spanish museums saw only El Greco and Velázquez he could store enough esthetic joy for a long time. Doménico Theotocópuli, better known as El Greco, was born in Crete slightly before mid-sixteenth century. Perhaps he was influenced by Byzantine art surviving there. He early went to Venice, and is mentioned as a pupil in Titian's studios. There is no record that he studied with Tintoretto, but he appears to have learned more from the latter than from the former. He did not imitate Michelangelo, whose canvases he must have known in Rome around 1570. He came to Toledo in 1577 and painted almost exclusively there until he died in 1614, two years before Cervantes and Shakespeare. Instead of aping the three great Italian masters, he was intensely Spanish, one of the world's most original and individualistic painters, worthy to stand with the best who ever put paint on canvas. A modern American critic (Sheldon Cheney, *A World History of Art,* New York, 1937, pp. 603, 612) has said of him, "No one else has so overlaid his subject matter and inner design with so rich a play of moving rhythmic forms, with so fiery an orchestration of visual elements. Yet underneath is the soundest plastic structure, the most nearly infallible handling of abstract elements known to Western painting. . . . Where painting touches upon the ecstatic and the supernal, he is master above all others." Externally he can be recognized not by his use of color, in which he was less lavish than the Venetians, but by his matchless use of light and shade, his contrasts of gleaming white darting and swirling into somber backgrounds, as one can see in his Crucifixions, his Resurrections, his Annunciations, even some of his portraits. The faces of contemporaries (self-portraits, the two Covarrubias, his son Jorge Manuel, Cardinal Tavera) are no doubt literal enough, but they look beyond the flesh into the spirit. The portrait of the Grand Inquisitor Don Fernando Niño de Guevara (Metropolitan Museum, New York) helps one to understand the Spanish Inquisition. The face is intelligent, intense, fanatical. Most of El Greco's work, however, was on religious subjects, and done for the Church in some way. The striking elongation of figure which upsets the literal-minded, responds to El Greco's inner vision, his longing to express something that transcends the merely terrestrial. That spiritual quality appears even in his landscapes, which he was one of the first Spanish painters to develop.

One of the most admired of all El Greco's numerous canvases and one of the world's great pictures is *The Burial of the Count of Orgaz,* painted for the Church of Santo Tomé in Toledo. An extraordinary group of spiritualized portraits appears in the lower half; an ecstatic vision of Christ, the Virgin and Heavenly hosts in the upper half. In it, perhaps better than in any of his other works, El Greco realized an aspiration of the Spain of his age, to spiritualize earth, and to lift it to heaven.

El Greco did not found a school. His technique could be imitated, but not his burning inner vision. His successors are realists, especially the Valencian José de Ribera (1588-1656), often called by his Italian nickname, Spagnoletto. He starved and studied in Italy until his canvases became fashionable at the Spanish court of Naples and in Madrid. Although he was a disciple of Michelangelo and Correggio, he seems to have learned most from the ardent realist Caravaggio, and he presented his figures, dwarfs, buffoons or saints with startling fidelity and with even a melodramatic note. His best-known canvas is the *Martyrdom of St. Bartholomew.* He painted many lean ascetic saints, and produced twenty-six fine etchings. His art was far better than his personal character.

Francisco de Zurbarán (1598-1663) was likewise a realist, possessed of a profound religious spirit. His *Monk in Meditation,* his various friars, painted with faithful detail and in deep reds and blacks, give a simultaneous impression of richness and somberness. He was a better man than Ribera, but not quite so good a painter.

Diego Velázquez de Silva (1599-1660) of Seville was one of the most prolific of painters. Some have thought him the world's greatest realist. He became rich, admired, successful, for kings and royal favorites smiled on him, and the Goddess of Fortune took him to her arms.

Francisco Pacheco of Seville, his teacher as well as his father-in-law, sent him to Madrid, where he won the favor of the Count-Duke of Olivares, and so of Philip IV, whose painter he was for nearly forty years. Forty of his canvases are portraits of that ugly long-jawed sovereign.

In his first period Velázquez painted religious pictures and crowded interiors (*bodegones*) with great fidelity of detail, but without realizing that the human eye cannot see very much at once. The most famous of his early pictures is *The Topers* (*Los Borrachos*), a fine group of attractive drunkards, with a half-nude village youth posing as Bacchus, cup in hand, vine leaves in his hair, receiving adoration. The portraits are individually splendid, the parts of the picture superior to the whole. The picture was painted in 1629, and in that same year Rubens, visiting the Spanish court, advised Velázquez to go to Italy.

The young artist spent two years there, and was influenced more by Titian and Tintoretto than by Michelangelo and Raphael. He learned greater concentration, greater balance in composition, greater depth. Back in Madrid after two years, he produced a long series of portraits of the King and court personages, even including court dwarfs. He did not then or ever completely forget the influence of El Greco. About 1647 he painted one of his great pictures, *The Surrender of Breda,* often called *The Lances,* a masterpiece of realistic and historic presentation.

In 1648 Velázquez paid his second visit to Italy. He was immediately commanded to paint Pope Innocent X, and the portrait, which Sir Joshua Reynolds considered the best picture in Rome, is an extraordinary canvas. It is reported that when His Holiness saw the artist's sketch, revealing the shrewd, hard face, he winced and said, "Too true."

It was after this second visit to Italy that Velázquez painted the only female nude known to have been put on canvas in Spain up to this time, the "Rokeby Venus." It is beautiful, but does not come up to the fleshly loveliness of the Venetian school. The Spanish Church forbade painting nudes.

It was in this last period that Velázquez painted some of his best pictures, when he had mastered the presentation of space and the effects of color, light, and shade. His radiant pearl-grey and rose are particularly remarkable in the picture of little Princess Margarita Teresa. *Las Hilanderas* (The Spinners) and *Las Meninas* (The Maids of Honor) show external naturalness, great selectivity, true harmony. His amazing craftsmanship makes up for a certain lack of imagination and fullness.

Bartolomé Esteban Murillo (1617-1682), also a Sevillian, was during the eighteenth and nineteenth centuries regarded as one of the world's great masters. Today his fame has suffered greatly. He painted popular types, which would make fine illustrations for picaresque novels, such as *The Melon Eaters, The Boy Drinking, The Flower Girl,* and many others. He also painted religious pictures, especially the twenty *Immaculate Conceptions,* with sweet blues predominating. To put it mildly, they are extremely sentimental. Murillo possessed zest and laughter and tenderness, plus craftsmanship, but he was never profound. After him Spanish painting showed little inspiration up to the time of the titanic Goya.

## MUSIC

Music, like the other arts, developed splendidly in Spain during the Renaissance and Golden Age, in both theory and practise. From the fifteenth to the seventeenth century, about a hundred books were written in Spain or by Spaniards on musical theory, and there were many world-famous performers.

Spanish folk music is generally considered the richest in the world (see, for example, Gilbert Chase, *The Music of Spain,* New York, Norton, 1941, Chap. XV) and we fortunately still possess many tunes used in Spain in the period mentioned for ballads and popular songs. Some are slow and solemn, evidently developed from church music, others sprightly and highly dramatic. The *Cancionero de Palacio* (*Palace Song Book*) contains some five hundred compositions of the fifteenth and sixteenth centuries, most of them for three and four voices. Juan del Encina, the dramatist, was a fertile composer and was represented in the collection by seventy-five songs.

One of the most famous musicians of the sixteenth century was the Valencian courtier, wit, poet and gallant, Luis Milán, born about 1500. In 1561 he published a book called *El Cortesano,* based, naturally, on Castiglione, in which he proclaims music to be one of the indispensable accomplishments of a gentleman. In his *El Maestro,* a theoretical and practical manual for the six-stringed *vihuela de mano* (guitar), Milán includes nearly seventy compositions, among them six lovely pavanes. There were other noted theorists who wrote for the *vihuela,* such as Luis de Narváez, *maestro de vihuela* to King Philip II, and Alonso de Mudarra, a canon of the Cathedral of Seville.

Everyone knows that the guitar, for which these gentlemen wrote, became the characteristic musical instrument of Spain. How did that come about? A primitive sort of guitar was known in Egypt nearly four thousand years B.C., and it was probably introduced into Spain by the Romans. At least the *guitarra latina,* of four-, five-, six- or seven-gut strings, was more like the modern instrument than the *guitarra morisca,* which bears closer resemblance to the lute. Luis Milán's tuning was g-c-f-a-d'-g', and the neck was always fretted for semitones. The composers were inspired by a combination of polyphonic music and dance and folk tunes. This style of playing, occasionally revived by contemporary guitarists like Andrés Segovia, remained in vogue until a Spaniard of Italian birth, Federico Moretti, published his *Principles for Playing the Six-stringed Guitar* in 1799 (see Gilbert Chase, op. cit., Chap. III).

The University of Salamanca had as professors of music several remarkable men. Ramos de Pareja, for example, who flourished in the later fifteenth century, wrote a noteworthy treatise on music, in Latin, and published it at Bologna in 1482. He abandoned the old theories, based on the Greek, of Boethius and Cassiodorus, and those of Guido d'Arezzo (eleventh century), and substituted a system based on the octave, as at present, divided into twelve semitones. He also used the consonant triad, the basis of the modern harmonic system.

A great organist and composer, called "The Spanish Bach," was the blind Antonio de Cabezón (died 1566). He was clavichordist and organist to Charles V and Philip II, and his fame spread over all Europe. His liturgical pieces, contrapuntal preludes and themes with variations were among the most remarkable composed in the sixteenth century.

Another blind musician, Professor of Music at Salamanca, was Francisco de Salinas (1513-1590), to whom the poet Luis de León dedicated one of the loveliest odes ever written to music (*El aire se serena* . . .). Salinas was performer, theorist and collector, and he preserved numerous folk tunes, to be found in his *Seven Books on Music* (1577, in Latin).

Salinas was for a while organist at the Spanish court of Naples, and many other Spaniards also contributed to European music in Italy, especially at Rome. One was Diego Ortiz, who published a treatise (Rome, 1553) on the improvisation of accompaniments over a given bass, which had great influence on the development of instrumental music.

The greatest of all Spanish religious composers was Tomás Luis de Victoria, of Avila (c. 1548-1611), usually mentioned with Palestrina, whose pupil he probably was. He wrote about 180 compositions, all connected with church worship, grave, grandiose, deeply spiritual. The greatest is probably the last he wrote, a Requiem Mass (*Officium Defunctorum*). Of the two great liturgists it has been said: "Palestrina is the Raphael of music, Victoria the El Greco. Each is great and unique in his own way" (Chase, op. cit., p. 85).

The full-fledged opera did not flourish in Spain in the seventeenth century, but a combination of spoken lines, dance, and music did, a sort of musical comedy or *opéra bouffe,* called a *zarzuela.* Philip IV enlarged a palace, originally a hunting lodge, which he had in the Pardo (a few miles from Madrid), and supplied it with gardens, fountains, and a theater. The place was called La Zarzuela. (The word means "bramble"; it must have been a bramble thicket once.) At this royal retreat the pleasure-loving king liked to hear short pieces, with music and singing, and they were called *fiestas de zarzuela.* The text of such a *divertissement* by Calderón survives: *El golfo de las sirenas,* performed January 17, 1657, in only one act. The zarzuela regularly has two acts, as did Calderón's *El jardín de Falerina,* performed earlier at the palace in Madrid. The sets for the *zarzuelas* were likely to be elaborate. In the eighteenth century *zarzuelas* came to be lighter in tone, for all the people and not just for court exquisites. They were extremely popular in the eighteenth and nineteenth centuries. The step to the full opera, entirely sung, was a short one. Calderón wrote two, *La púrpura de la rosa* and *Celos aun del aire matan,* the latter with music by Juan Hidalgo.

# XXI

## *The Bourbons Come to Spain. The Eighteenth Century*

### PHILIP V TO FERNANDO VII

AS the seventeenth century died, Spain was in desperate need of a housecleaning: all sections of Spain and all phases of Spanish life. There seemed to be no home talent available for the task, and it was time for someone else to try. After the sad days of Charles II the Bewitched, change in dynasty could not possibly be for the worse. It was just as well that Charles' will left the Spanish throne to a French prince, even though he was a man of mediocre quality.

Philip V, a Bourbon aged seventeen, grandson of Louis XIV of France, acceded to the throne of Spain in 1700. With a year's interlude (1724) he ruled until 1746. No small part of his reign was occupied with the Wars of the Spanish Succession, which brought Spain some military glory but little solid benefit. England gained an important section of Spanish soil, Gibraltar, the island of Minorca and numerous commercial advantages in the Spanish colonies, including the slave trade. Philip, brave enough in battle, was at home dominated by his first wife, María Luisa of Savoy, and her counselor, Madame des Ursins, and later by his second wife, Isabel Farnesio (Farnese) of Parma. Isabel, known as "The Spanish Termagant," was one of Spain's most energetic queens, but her energies were not exerted for the good of the country as were those of María de Molina four centuries before.

It was possible for more internal progress to be made in the time of Philip V's successor Fernando VI (1746-1749), because the latter's reign marked an era of peace. He died without issue, to be succeeded by his half-brother, son of Isabel Farnesio, Carlos III (1759-1788). This Charles III turned out to be one of the best sovereigns that Spain has had in modern times. His domestic policies were successful and the country made real progress. With regard to the Spanish colonies he was less fortunate, for his chief aim was to win revenues for the mother country. His difficulties were increased by the spirit of independence arising in the world as an accompaniment of the French and American revolutions, with attendant disorders in the Spanish possessions. On the whole, Charles III made Spain at home and abroad more powerful than she had been for a century.

During the reign of his weak heir, Charles IV, Spain received rough treatment from England and France and became less important in European affairs. Some of the internal reforms of Charles III were allowed to lapse. From 1792 onward the King was dominated by Manuel Godoy, a vigorous plebeian upstart who became the lover of Queen María Luisa, Prime Minister of the Kingdom, Duke and Prince.

Charles IV made the great mistake of trusting Napoleon Bonaparte. Napoleon had sworn he would never cede Louisiana to any power but Spain, but in 1803 it went to the United States. Nevertheless in the next year Napoleon persuaded Spain to chime in with French plans and to declare war on England. In 1805 the Spanish and French suffered the great defeat of Trafalgar. Then Napoleon and Godoy agreed upon the conquest of Portugal, which was to be divided between them. Portugal was won, but Godoy was left without his reward. French troops, coming from Portugal, made themselves at home in Spain. Godoy saw what Napoleon had in mind, that Spain was next on the list, but he could not prevent it for two reasons. King Charles favored Napoleon, and Godoy himself was very unpopular with Spaniards, who were sick of him, of the adulterous queen, and of Charles too. After a riot in which Godoy nearly lost his life, Charles abdicated on March 19, 1808, in favor of his young son Fernando VII.

Napoleon was glad enough to get rid of Charles and Godoy but not to have Ferdinand on the throne. He managed to lure him up to Bayonne, where Charles, María Luisa and Godoy arrived a few days later. Napoleon forced Charles to reaffirm his abdication, granted lands and privileges in France to all the royal group, including Godoy, and reserved to himself the right to name the king of Spain.

## THE WAR OF INDEPENDENCE

The French assumed the airs of conquerors below the Pyrenees, and feeling in Spain ran high against them. On May 2, 1808, French troops fired into a group of angry citizens in Madrid. The crowd scattered to spread the news, which reached the Spanish troops, strictly confined to barracks. Two captains, Daoiz and Velarde, rushed out to lead the enraged and scarcely armed populace against the well-drilled French soldiers. The result was inevitable and tragic. After a three-hour battle, Velarde and Daoiz were killed and the uprising quelled. The French were masters for the moment, but a national uprising had begun which was to drive Napoleon out of Spain and finally out of Europe. The Second of May has remained the great Spanish patriotic holiday.

Every region of Spain rose to fight the "War of Independence," now begun. Napoleon knew the French soldiers were greatly superior in training and equipment, but he reckoned without the furious Spanish patriotism, an indomitable spirit that refused to be defeated. In 1808 the French general, Dupont, with a sizable army, more than 20,000 men, began the conquest of Andalusia, only to find that the Spaniards rose in his rear as soon as his soldiers moved on. At Bailén, in the province of Jaén, Dupont put himself in a risky position, the Spaniards under Castaños won an impressive victory, and the French general was forced to surrender some 18,000 men. Napoleon finally had 300,000 soldiers in Spain, but they were not enough. The French usually won the pitched battles, but the Spaniards fought with terrifying bravery and stubbornness on defense, as in the sieges of Zaragoza and Gerona. The latter cost the French 20,000 men. Spanish resistance could hardly have been

finally successful, however, without the forces of Sir Arthur Welles-
ley, later Duke of Wellington, cooperating in Portugal and western
Spain, and without the support of the English fleet. Wellington's
Peninsular campaign would hardly have been successful, either,
without the intense bravery and constancy of the Spaniards.

Napoleon had put his brother Joseph on the Spanish throne, but
his authority was confined to occupied Spain. The Spaniards who
had not been conquered set up a temporary governing body which
they called the *Central Committee* (*Junta Central*). The *Junta* was
forced to flee from Aranjuez to Seville to Cadiz, but it performed
its function of appointing a regency council of five men to summon
a Cortes, and then resigned. The Cortes was indeed called, and met
in Cadiz in September 1810. It was not a very representative body
and its ideas were considerably ahead of those of the majority of
the population. Its achievement was the formulation of the Constitution of 1812, an advanced democratic document which provided
for a limited monarchy and popular representative government.

## INTERNAL CONDITIONS

The French were finally driven out, and Ferdinand "The
Longed-For" (*Fernando el Deseado*) returned to claim his throne
in 1814. He immediately began to show that he was a hard-headed
Bourbon who had learned nothing of the modern world, and he
proceeded to rule as absolutely as he could. He tore up the constitution of 1812 and declared all the acts of the Cortes of Cadiz
null and void. The liberals in his kingdom he sent to the gallows,
to prison or into banishment. He was not *Deseado* to many of his
people very long.

Six years later a liberal movement led by Colonel Rafael del Riego
forced Ferdinand to agree to reestablish the Constitution of Cadiz,
but Ferdinand appealed to France for aid against his own subjects.
Accordingly the Duke of Angoulême came to Spain with 100,000
troops, the uprising was crushed, and Riego himself hanged in
Madrid in 1823. Ferdinand ruled as a more savage reactionary than

ever. The ten years before he died were not a bright period in Spanish history.

While Spain was struggling for her own independence during the Napoleonic period, her colonies in America began to break away. The colonies held that their allegiance had been directly to the crown, and in 1809 they regarded that allegiance as ended. The separatist movement in America, furthered by such great leaders as Bolívar and San Martín, came to its climax in 1824, with the battle of Ayacucho. Of her once proud colonial empire Spain had left only a fragment: the Spanish Antilles, the Philippines and a section of North Africa.

Spain was in some ways better off in 1833, when Ferdinand VII died, than in 1700, but less well off than in the 1780's. From the time of the coming of the Bourbons through the reign of Charles III there had been a gradual improvement in Spanish national life. Charles III and his able ministers were ardent reformers, and wise and efficient provisions were made for improving agriculture, trade, industry, the army and navy, the Church and general education. Charles III was a pious Catholic, but he was jealous of the royal prerogatives in ecclesiastical matters, and the Spanish church became more subject to the king's authority. The power of the courts of the Inquisition, which had already grown much milder in the more liberal eighteenth century, was considerably limited. Charles III, like other European sovereigns, regarded the Jesuit Order as dangerous to his throne. Consequently the Jesuits were expelled from Spain and the Spanish colonies in 1767. They were expelled from France and the Kingdom of Naples at about the same time, as they had been from Portugal in 1759. Pope Clement XIV dissolved the whole Order in 1773.

Unfortunately the successors of Charles III, Charles IV, and Ferdinand VII, were by no means able men, and under them Spain lost the degree of internal prosperity and international power to which Charles III had brought her. The Napoleonic invasion of the Peninsula was a further disaster. Spain would have recovered faster in the nineteenth century if she had not been plagued by civil strife.

# XXII

## *Scholarship, Dullness and Brilliance. The Eighteenth Century*

THE eighteenth century marked a gradual rise in the general level of intellectual life in Spain. France was the dominating cultural force in Europe in the eighteenth century, and an effort was made in Spain to impose that culture from above, from the court and from aristocratic patrons of learning. In general there was much less intellectual ferment in Spain than in France, and the philosophic spirit, the Encyclopedists, even Rousseau, had a restricted influence.

The official encouragement to culture was shown by the foundation of the National Library of Madrid, 1712, the Royal Spanish Academy (of the Language) in 1714, and the Academy of History in 1735. In general, then, literature had an academic flavor in this age of strict regulation, of neo-classicism. Not that the people bothered about academies and rules. They stayed away in droves from neo-classic tragedies, for example, and went to see old plays of the seventeenth century, or new plays which had few literary virtues but which at least showed a little life and action.

### CRITICISM

The most influential literary critic of the eighteenth century was Ignacio de Luzán (1702-1754), a cosmopolitan diplomat and scholar. His *Poética* (1737), based not only on Boileau but also on Italian interpreters of Aristotle and Horace, holds up a neo-classic ideal of the various forms of poetry. Only poetry, for the novel was not regarded as artistic literature. Luzán and his supporters had a praiseworthy ideal: to raise the standards of Spanish literature, to correct what they regarded as excessive freedom, unbridled license on the part of the little gifted followers of Calderón, Góngora, and Gracián. Hence Luzán recommends following the doctrines of imitation, of verisimilitude, and urges that imagination should be curbed by reason. In drama, the unities of time, place, and action should be observed, and propriety maintained; the characters should be varied, but limited in number.

This implies a criticism of the master dramatists of Spain's Golden Age, and the condemnation in the second edition of the *Poética* (1789) was even stronger. Yet Luzán recognizes the genius of these earlier playwrights while deploring their extravagance. Toward Góngora and Gracián he is much more severe.

Unfortunately, while the recommendations of Luzán and his fellow critics were beneficial, they inspired no masterpieces. Nor did the criticisms of Lope, Calderón, and others pass unchallenged. The defense of the right of genius to work freely, to follow its own rules, a point of view maintained by minor critics throughout the century, was in accord with Romantic theory and practice after 1833.

The long-lived and learned Benedictine monk Benito Jerónimo Feijóo (1676-1764) had a keen mind and used it. He spent his years as professor of theology and philosophy at the University of Oviedo combating the false and superstitious notions of his countrymen. He approached most branches of learning in essays, which he published in eight volumes, 1726-1739, under the inclusive title of *Teatro Crítico Universal*. His five volumes of *Cartas eruditas y curiosas,* 1742-1760, form a supplement. His criticisms did not pass unnoticed, for they started an extensive controversy, one of a number of polemics in the eighteenth century. With regard to literature Feijóo believed in rules as a corrective to disorder, but he insisted that nothing could take the place of that something-or-other (*"no sé qué"*) called genius. He was a reformer and some of his ideas anticipate those of the later French Encyclopedists.

Feijóo was aware of the poor state of Spanish intellectual life because he could compare it with that of foreign nations. A man

who observed many phases of Spanish life much more directly was
that lively rascal Diego de Torres Villarroel (1693?-1770): runaway
boy, dancer, guitarist, bullfighter, street-singer, lock-picker, false
hermit, soldier, quack doctor, almanac writer, poet, university professor, churchman, philanthropist. He had other skills; despite the
irregularity of his life he was a reformer, anxious to contribute his
bit to social and cultural uplift. His autobiography (*Vida,* 1743) is
engagingly frank, slightly mendacious, constantly vivid. One of the
best commentaries on the times, it reads like a picaresque novel.

## THE NOVEL

The novel in eighteenth century Spain was mainly non-existent,
and the best to be published was not original but a translation: *Gil
Blas* (1787-88) by Alain-René Lesage. The Frenchman had based
his work on various Spanish models of the picaresque, so the excellent translation looked like a traveller returning home.

The translator was the Jesuit José Francisco de Isla (1703-81),
also known for his abilities as a preacher, letter writer, and satirist.
His most famous original work is a novel, the *Historia del famoso
predicador Fray Gerundio de Campazas, alias Zotes* (1758). Padre
Isla was quite familiar with the puffy bombast, the Gongoristic
oratory that issued from the Spanish pulpits of his day, and *Fray
Gerundio* helped to put an end to it. The book has relatively little
plot, and is definitely not characterized by terseness.

## COMPOSITIONS IN VERSE

At no time has poetry been lacking in Spain, even in the relatively prosaic eighteenth century, when erudition and criticism
tended to crowd out the creative spirit. Probably the poetic form
most in accord with the didactic tendency of the times was the fable,
best cultivated by Tomás de Iriarte (1750-91), inevitably called the
Spanish La Fontaine. Iriarte wrote a didactic poem on music, several literary pamphlets, and two good attempts at social comedy:
*The Spoiled Young Gentleman* and *The Ill Bred Young Lady,*

both finished in 1788. He also engaged in some of the many literary polemics which enlivened the age. He is best remembered, however, for his zestful *Fábulas literarias,* 1782. He employs with skill some forty different meters, invents interesting subjects, writes in good taste and with epigrammatic terseness, and satirizes with equal brilliance the general failings of mankind or the foibles of his contemporaries. Iriarte's fables were successful enough to arouse envy at the time of their publication. Since then they have been constantly read and quoted. Iriarte was a gifted man who died too young.

A fabulist of almost equal merit was Félix María Samaniego (1745-1801) who wrote his *Moral Fables* for pupils of a recently founded school at Vergara. Other authors who attempted the genre were less successful.

A large amount of didactic poetry was written in the eighteenth century. It is now dead. As a link with lyric poetry, it is pleasant to think of one of the most admirable figures that the age produced anywhere: Gaspar Melchor de Jovellanos (1744-1811), one of Spain's most enlightened patriots. His writing in prose and verse, though extensive, is incidental to his career as a statesman, his activities as a magistrate, educator, economist, and general reformer. His *Report on the Agrarian Law* (1795) suggested far-reaching reforms in Spain's fiscal system. The *Report on Spectacles and Public Amusements in Spain* has interesting things to say about the theater, and condemns bullfighting. Other reports on art and architecture contain new and stimulating ideas.

Jovellanos also wrote a tragedy of the neo-classic sort, on the hero *Pelayo* (1769), and a sentimental play (*comédie larmoyante*) called *The Honest Criminal* (*El delincuente honrado*) 1774.

The pastoral poems which this dignified gentleman wrote under the sweet Arcadian name of Jovino add little to his fame. His satires and epistles are better, making up in moral earnestness and sincerity what they lack in grace.

Jovellanos, strongly influenced by French culture, was patriotically and vigorously opposed to French domination. As a member

of the *Junta* he was pursued by Napoleon's minions and died flee-
ing from them, in Asturias, in 1811.

The chief lyric poets of the eighteenth century in Spain are
usually referred to as the "School of Salamanca" because they had
some sort of connection with that university city, and because they
admired if they could by no means equal the lofty songs of Luis
de León. One of the earliest was Fray Diego Tadeo González (1733-
94) who, despite his cloth, wrote various graceful though unimpressive lyrics to various lovely ladies. His best known is *The
Treacherous Bat,* a somewhat laboured trifle of nineteen eight-line
stanzas in which Delio (the author) curses the little animal for
frightening his timid and lovely Mirta.

A more virile gentleman was Colonel José Cadalso (1741-1782).
He traveled extensively in Europe and was a man of wide culture,
also of a passionate disposition. It is reported that he was so violently in love with the actress María Ignacia Ibáñez that on her
death he tried to steal her corpse and had to be banished from
Madrid. He went to Salamanca and exerted considerable influence
on younger poets there. He met his death fighting against the English at Gibraltar.

His prose works include a satire against affected scholars (*Los
eruditos a la violeta*), a satire à la Montesquieu called *Cartas mar-
ruecas,* criticizing political and social conditions in Spain, and a
sort of invocation to melancholy called *Noches lúgubres.* The title
was no doubt suggested by Young's *Night Thoughts,* but it is no
mere imitation. Cadalso's plays are decidedly neo-classic in construction and spirit, and his poems, admired in his day, are far less
passionate than might be expected. He is no full-fledged Romantic,
though he anticipates the men of 1830 in certain regards.

The sweetest singer of Salamanca was Juan Meléndez Valdés
(1754-1817), who assumed the poetic-pastoral pseudonym of Delio
and said pretty things in verse to several Phyllises and Rosannas:
twelve in all, he tells us. He possesses real grace and polish, and his
anacreontics, eclogues and ballads are still pleasant summer after-
noon reading. Later in life he became more philosophical, more
humanitarian, and his verse achieved a more serious tone. In his

sentimentality, he too anticipates Romanticism. He has even been called, with considerable exaggeration, Spain's first Romantic poet.

There was nothing sweetly effeminate about that sturdy patriot and poet named Manuel José Quintana (1772-1857), whose virile lyre reminds us of Herrera's. He remained of the eighteenth century, though he lived more than halfway through the nineteenth and saw Romanticism wax and wane. His vigorous efforts on behalf of the Spanish liberal cause, against Napoleon, even against the tyranny of Ferdinand VII, brought him imprisonment and banishment, but he lived long enough to be restored to favor on the accession of Isabel II. Crowned poet laureate, he died as Spain's grand old man, universally revered.

His prose *Lives of Famous Spaniards* was written to inspire the young by contemplation of past heroes. His plays are neo-classic in form. *El Duque de Viseo* (1801) is really a horror drama based on "Monk Lewis," of *Castle Spectre* fame, and his *Pelayo* breathes the patriotic fire which was part of Quintana's being.

Among the numerous poems of Quintana the best are the odes which show his love for Spain, such as the one *Al Combate de Trafalgar,* 1805, and the two in 1808, *To the Arming of the Spanish Provinces against the French* and *To Spain, after the March Revolution.* Although the poet is classic in form, it is emotion rather than reason that stirs him.

The same may be said of Juan Nicasio Gallego (1777-1853) who wrote the best poem on Spain's great popular uprising: *El dos de Mayo.* It is classic in style, furious in feeling, and is an excellent companion piece to Goya's painting, *The Shootings of the Second of May.*

A group of poets also existed in and around Seville in the late eighteenth and early nineteenth centuries. Poetically they went back to Herrera, Rioja, and Góngora, though they were neo-classic in theory. Some were actually professors, like the excellent critic Alberto Lista. The best known was probably José María Blanco y Crespo (1775-1841), an exiled Catholic priest who in England changed his name to Blanco White, turned first Anglican and then Unitarian. He wrote good poems in Spanish, but is particularly noted for his sonnet in English, *Mysterious Night,* a favorite with anthologists.

Just as in England Bishop Percy (*Reliques of Ancient English Poetry*) turned his attention to past poetic glories, a similar interest arose in Spain. Among Spanish scholars who displayed such interest, one might mention at least Tomás Antonio Sánchez, who published (1779-90) a highly valuable four-volume *Colección de poesías castellanas anteriores al siglo XV:* the first printing of the *Poema del Cid,* of Berceo, of the *Libro de Alixandre,* and of Juan Ruiz. López de Sedano also published inaccessible old poems in his nine-volume *Parnaso español.* Later anthologies were made by Quintana, by the German Böhl von Faber, and others. Spain's mediaeval literature was being opened up.

## THE DRAMA

The learned literary critics of the eighteenth century from Luzán onward glorified the classic tragedy as an admirable art form. At about the middle of the century attempts were made to compose tragedies "con todo el rigor del arte." They were written according to all the rules, but they turned out to be frigid and lifeless, and even official government encouragement could not keep them on the boards. One in 1778, *La Raquel,* had much more sparkle than the rest. It was based on a well-known Spanish story, the Jewess of Toledo loved by King Alfonso VIII, was in three acts, not five, and in assonating eleven-syllable lines. In other words, it was like a *comedia* of the preceding century. The author was García de la Huerta (1734-1787), translator of Sophocles and Voltaire, and declared enemy of the school of Lope. In fact, in a sixteen-volume selection of older Spanish plays he includes neither Lope nor Tirso nor Alarcón.

The people, however, as distinct from literary aristocrats, refused to be converted to what most critics considered good taste. They continued to go to see plays by Lope, Calderón, Rojas, Moreto and others, and plays by contemporaries who were not good dramatists but who managed to put a little vividness and movement into their productions. Such, for example, as Luciano Francisco Comella (1751-1812). His plays are exaggerated, but they do have movement and life. There were others like him.

A number of authors made recasts (*refundiciones*) of Golden Age plays, either to restore worthy authors and forgotten plays to favor, or to make others more suitable for modern presentation. Cándido María Trigueros (1736-1801?), for example, made *La Estrella de Sevilla* into a more regular five-act *Sancho Ortiz de las Roelas*, which was long played. He also adapted Lope de Vega's *La moza de cántaro, El anzuelo de Fenisa,* and *Los melindres de Belisa.* The later Dionisio Solís (1774-1834) prompter and adviser to the great actor Isidoro Máiquez, made quite a number of *refundiciones.* Others were made and played on through the Romantic period.

One gentleman of neo-classic taste made a real success in the drama. Not in tragedy, but in comedy. His name was Leandro Fernández de Moratín (1760-1828). His father Nicolás had written tragedies and one good poem with lots of color and picturesqueness, the *Fiesta de Toros en Madrid.* The son was apprenticed to a jeweler: a Rousseauesque idea on the part of the parent. Leandro early showed a literary bent, and began to win prizes for poetry. He traveled, held government positions, even under Joseph Napoleon, so when the French were driven out he was considered an *afrancesado* and fled to France, going from one place to another for fear of persecution.

Moratín's early satire, *The Overthrow of the Pedants,* showed scorn for the wrong kind of scholars. He gave proof of his own abilities as an investigator in *Los orígenes del teatro español,* which is still consulted with profit. His poems do not amount to much. He translated Molière (*L'Ecole des Maris,* and *Le Médecin malgré lui*) and *Hamlet,* by an author of whom he did not approve.

His fame rests on five comedies: *El viejo y la niña* (1790, in verse), *La comedia nueva, o el café* (1792, prose, an amusing satire of bad plays and bad dramatists like Comella), *El Barón* (verse, performed in 1803), *La Mojigata* (*The False Prude,* performed 1804), and *El sí de las niñas* (*When Girls Say Yes,* prose, 1806).

The last is his masterpiece, even though the lesson that girls should not be forced into marriage by oppressive parents is not very timely now that parents have lost their dictatorial complexes. The play is admirably constructed, moves rapidly, and possesses power and grace. The dialogue is excellent, the expression clear and direct. The best one can say of the characters, except perhaps of the comic mother Doña Irene, is that they serve their purpose. They are not great creations, and the lovers Charles and Fanny are more than a little wooden. Those who termed Moratín the Spanish Molière were exaggerating grossly.

Another dramatist of the time, Ramón de la Cruz (1731-1794), a native of Madrid, was less elegant than Moratín, but he gave more amusement to more people. He is quite Spanish in his realism and in his fecundity; sixty-nine tragedies, comedies and musical plays and four hundred and seventy-three *sainetes,* or other short compositions. His more ambitious full-length plays are almost forgotten; it was in the bright, highly colored popular short piece, regularly in one act, for about fifteen or twenty minutes' entertainment, that he excelled. Therein he was following the tradition of the *paso* of Lope de Rueda, the *entremés* of Cervantes or Quiñones de Benavente. The populace was delighted with the result. These *sainetes* usually deal with a slice of life in the humbler quarters of Madrid, with little plot and still less stuffy dignity, but they present a bright gallery of popular types, a set of deftly sketched portraits that immediately remind one of Goya, who did so much the same thing on canvas. Such satire as the *sainetes* contain is light and gay.

*El petimetre,* for example, is a fine picture of a fop. *La maja majada* describes a quarrel arising between two women because one tries to get a turkey and two jars of jelly which a gentleman had presented to the other. *La presumida burlada (She Puts on Airs and Gets Taken Down)* recounts tersely but vividly the career of María Estropajo, a servant girl who has the good fortune to marry her master, the widower Don Gil. She grows vain, temperamental and has a terrible temper. Her husband meets her mother, sister and uncle-in-law on the street in Madrid. They are as countrified, uncouth and rustic as can be. Instead of shaking them off, Don Gil takes them to his house at the very moment when his wife, entertaining some "top-drawer" friends, is putting on her most affected airs. At first María wishes to deny her family, but, urged on by Don Gil, she repents, falls on her mother's neck and becomes a different woman for life. At least so one is led to think. A great many *sainetes* have even less plot, merely giving brief scenes or episodes from Madrilene life, high or low, but all presented with verve and naturalness. About three dozen *sainetes* have something to do with the theater or with plays, such as *The Play Given at Home* (*La comedia casera*), *The Theatre from Inside* (*El teatro por dentro*), *The Interrupted Sainete* (*El sainete interrumpido*). Cruz also wrote many *sainetes,* parodies of the neo-classic tragedies which the élite favored and which he himself had composed or translated in his earlier period.

In the vivid local color and picturesqueness of his short pieces, Ramón de la Cruz anticipates the Romanticists, especially the writers on customs and manners. It has often been said that Cruz's *sainetes* and the etchings and cartoons of Goya tell more about eighteenth century Spain than many volumes of learned historians.

## EIGHTEENTH CENTURY ART

Spanish architecture, art in general, in the earlier eighteenth century continues the exaggerated Baroque. One has only to look at the Cathedral of Cádiz, for example. In Italy a neo-classic reaction set in, and progressing to France, came to Spain along with the French dynasty. Architects like Ventura Rodríguez and Juan Villanueva left, in Madrid and elsewhere, buildings whose straight lines and relative plainness contrast vigorously with the Baroque. A good example is the Prado Museum, in Madrid.

The Bourbon sovereigns of Spain in the eighteenth century brought to Spain many foreign artists, especially French and Italian. The most important, however, was the German eclectic painter Raphael Mengs, who was quite influential.

After the creative brilliance of the Golden Age, the eighteenth century in Spain seems painfully dull. It was enlivened, however, by one irrepressible genius of titanic artistic stature, Francisco Goya y Lucientes (1746-1828). He was born in a tiny village in Aragon and died in Bordeaux. No doubt his youthful excesses cut short his life.

Legend, which does not love nonentities, has lavishly enriched the biography of Goya, and even serious treatises contain fantastic statements about him. He was not born in abject poverty from the dregs of society, as has been more than once stated. His father was a gilder, came into contact with artists, and put young Francisco in school at Zaragoza. Did the young artist have to leave home hurriedly because he was involved in a murder? Did he really abduct a nun? Was he really stabbed and left for dead by a jealous rival on another occasion? Was he really a good bullfighter? Was the Duchess of Alba really his mistress (one of his mistresses) and did she really pose for his celebrated *Nude Maja?* Did he really have a couple of dozen legitimate children?

Goya certainly indulged in plenteous deviltries, and his talents for loving, roistering and brawling were extensive. Far more important than that, part of his exuberant vitality was devoted to the outpouring of his genius in pictorial expression. He makes his academic contemporaries seem anemic, lifeless, for everything that he did, good or less good, had conspicuous vitality, zest and vividness. He could be careless but never dull. He rose to be court painter through sheer force and ability.

Goya's range is enormous, from tenderness to savagery, from love to hatred, from sentimentality to harsh realism, from light gaiety to brooding despair, from sanity to madness. In subject matter from the gutter to the palace, from the church to the brothel, from innocent children to vicious degenerates, from over-dressed courtiers to undressed courtesans, from earthworms to horses, low and high, small and great. He paints children (e.g., *Manuel Osorio*) with loving tenderness, he brings out the stupid viciousness of silly courtiers, even of his King and Queen. It is hard to see why the sovereigns let him live after they saw themselves as he shows them, the King Charles IV, a nincompoop who deserved to be the cuckold that he was, the Queen María Luisa of

Parma, a nasty and vicious old harridan. Godoy, the Queen's paramour, was painted with the same brush. Realism and satire, psychological penetration and graceful technique have never been better fused. The distance from satire to fierce bitterness is traversed in the album of etchings called *The Disasters of War* and in Goya's various paintings of war such as *The Shootings of the Second of May*. War's brutality has never been more poignantly depicted. While French painters, including Goya's acquaintance David, are glorifying Napoleon, Goya shows Napoleon's soldiers massacring Spanish captives who wallow in their blood while their women are raped. Goya had no illusions about the cruelties and vices of humanity. His tortured spirit also produced a series of *Caprices* (*Caprichos*), possibly even more terrible.

Goya also painted numerous scenes from the life of his time, filled with picturesque vigor and brightness, scenes of types of people, popular fiestas, dances, bullfights. He was so fond of the national sport that he was nicknamed Don Francisco de los Toros.

His most-talked-about canvases are the beautiful *Maja Nude* and *Maja Dressed*. No more sensuously vivid portrayal of a loved body exists in all painting than the *Maja desnuda*. In the *Maja vestida,* painted in precisely the same pose, the clothes suggest rather than conceal.

Goya was more than a great realist and a talented technician. His realism served as a means, his skill in organization and execution as an aid, to conveying to posterity the inner fire of spirit that possessed him. By himself he makes up for the hundred years of dullness after Velázquez. A century that could produce him was more alive than its generally chilly academic tone would lead anyone to suspect.

## MUSIC

Sophisticated music in eighteenth century Spain was largely Italian in flavor. The most popular form was the Italian opera. The best-known singer was the male soprano who created a furore in Europe, Carlo Boschi, better known as Farinelli. Coming to Spain in 1737, this famous eunuch made such a hit with the melancholy Philip V that he was given a huge salary, renounced his public career, and sang the same four songs for his royal master every night for nine years. He was a friend of the important Spanish personages of his time and for a total of twenty-two years he exerted great political influence at court.

Domenico Scarlatti of Naples settled in Madrid in 1729 and spent the rest of his life in Spain. It was during those thirty-seven years that he composed his sonatas for the harpsichord, which are regarded as so important in the development of instrumental music. Spanish popular music exerted much influence on him and he in turn greatly influenced such modern composers as Falla, Turina, Granados, and Albéniz. Scarlatti's most important pupil was the Spaniard Antonio Soler.

Goya: "Majas on a Balcony."

Goya: "Carnival Scene." Fresco in the Academia de San Fernando.

Goya: "The Maja Dressed." A comparison is "The Maja Nude."

Goya: "The Bull-Fight." Goya was extremely fond of bullfighting.

Goya: Her Majesty Queen María Luisa of Parma, wife of Charles IV.

The romantic poet, José de
Espronceda.

The realistic novelist Benito Pérez Galdós.

Vicente Blasco Ibáñez.

Pío Baroja.

Juan Echevarría: Portrait of Ramón María del Valle-Inclán.

Zuloaga portrays "Miguel de Unamuno" author of *The Tragic Sense of Life, in Men and Nations.*

Zuloaga portrays individual dejection: "The Victim of the Fiesta."

# XXIII

## Romantic Color Returns. The Nineteenth Century

### POLITICAL BACKGROUND

DEATH released Spain from the noxious presence of Ferdinand VII in 1833, but national problems, political, economic, and cultural, were not solved merely by his departure, and have not reached even a reasonably satisfactory solution to this day. Ferdinand, without a son, had declared the Salic law abrogated, and left the throne to his infant daughter Isabel. The more conservative, some might say benighted, elements in Church and State declared in favor of Don Carlos, Ferdinand's brother, and thus the First Carlist War broke out. It plagued the country for seven years, and was brought to a close by General Espartero in 1840. There were further Carlist uprisings in 1848, 1855 and 1873.

The regent, Isabel's mother Cristina, and her ministers were forced to accept more liberalism than they liked so as to oppose the conservative Carlists. The political exiles were enabled to return upon the declaration of a general amnesty. Despite the unreliability of Cristina, the ideal of liberty was more widely accepted. Cristina was forced to resign in 1840, and Isabel II, though only thirteen, was declared legally of age. During the twenty-five years of her reign Spain was really ruled by a succession of generals, who under the form of a constitutional government managed to impose a control by the army. General Narváez was one of the most conservative and the most vigorous. This anecdote is related of him. When he was dying, his confessor said to him, "General Narváez, have you forgiven your enemies?" He answered in a still firm voice: "I

221

have no enemies. I have had them all shot." He was indeed severe, but he kept order. General O'Donnell, Spanish in spite of his Irish name and ancestry, was somewhat more liberal, but was a firm supporter of the Bourbons. He died in 1867 and Narváez in 1868. Isabel's reign had been disordered, and her personal character dissolute; in late 1868 she was dethroned by an army group under General Prim.

During Isabel's reign the Cortes had met more frequently than before. The question of the new form of government was left up to that body, which voted for a monarchy and not a republic. Considerable difficulty was encountered in finding a suitable person to occupy the throne. Amadeo of Savoy, Duke of Aosta, finally consented. The one man who might have given Amadeo the strong support he needed, General Prim, died by assassination December 30, 1870, just as the new king reached Spain. After an unhappy two years fraught with much political strife, Amadeo resigned the crown and left the country in February, 1873.

A Republic was proclaimed. No one of the four presidents was able to govern successfully, and the Republic quickly fell. The son of Isabel, Alfonso, was invited to come back.

Alfonso XII (1874-1885) issued a proclamation of amnesty in December, 1874, and promised constitutional government. His reign was comparatively peaceful. The constitution promulgated in 1876, under which Spain operated until 1931, provided for a Cortes of two houses, more like the British Parliament than the American Congress. The King was not responsible to the Cortes, but his decrees had to be signed by a responsible minister. Catholicism was the state religion, though other faiths were tolerated. In practice the toleration was not complete. The King's personal life was far from exemplary, but he came to be regarded as at least a symbol of political order.

Queen María Cristina (an Austrian) was pregnant when Alfonso XII died in 1885. Alfonso XIII was born in 1886 and died in 1941. His mother held the regency until 1901, when the boy was declared of age.

## ROMANTICISM

Spanish authors have constantly shown a tendency toward freedom and individualism, a dislike of formal rules. Spain's Golden Age was to that extent Romantic rather than classic. In a way the strict theorists of the eighteenth century were trying to interrupt a national tradition. The people, however, liked forms such as the drama of Ramón de la Cruz, which had more exuberance, less restraint. The native tradition, including the Siglo de Oro drama, had its defenders. After the middle of the eighteenth century there is found too an increasingly sentimental tone appearing here and there, as in the poetry of Meléndez.

To confirm and enlarge this native tendency there came in the late eighteenth and early nineteenth centuries influences from abroad: from Germany, Italy, England, especially from France. Young's *Night Thoughts,* Thompson's *The Seasons,* MacPherson's Ossianic prose poems, helped to create a sentimental mood and a new love of nature. Later Spaniards exiled for political reasons, notably the future Duke of Rivas, came to know English and French literature at first hand. Sir Walter Scott, for example, was furiously translated and read and later imitated. Chateaubriand contributed his share of influence, and so did a number of minor French novelists, such as Mme. Cottin. Goethe's *Werther,* first translated into Spanish in 1803, helped to produce sad young men. French melodramas were translated and played on the Spanish stage. At moments the influx of translations was so great that the Spanish theaters seemed almost more French than Spanish.

In all countries, including Spain, the Romanticists emphasized the emotions rather than the intellect, the heart rather than the mind. Their work constituted a protest against the Goddess of the eighteenth century, which was Reason. The Romanticists further claimed the right of each individual to proceed as he saw fit, to express not the universal but the specific, the particular. Their writings were not to be bound by rules and regulations, but each man was to compose as his own inidividual genius dictated. That genius might easily run afoul of the established practices of society, and many a Romantic felt that he was in conflict with a world that did not understand him, that repressed him and might bring him to a tragic end. The typical protagonists of Romantic dramas, for example, were doomed before they started their sad careers.

In matters of detail, the Romantics were likely to go to the Middle Ages for subjects, and they sought to supply their works with picturesqueness and local color. They made no distinction between dramatic genres, for comedy and tragedy were supposed to go hand in hand, as in life. They discarded the unities of time and place. They sought a grotesque contrast between humor and sadness.

Such characteristics are all to be found in the varied works of a gifted Andalusian nobleman who wrote one of the most violent Romantic dramas on record.

## POETRY

Angel de Saavedra, later to become Duke of Rivas after the death of his elder brother, was born in Cordova in 1791, and died in 1865. His education was neo-classic, and he early began to write poems and dramas in the eighteenth century manner. Although he came of a noble and rich family, he was a liberal as well as an ardent patriot. He fought against Napoleon. Banished by Ferdinand VII in 1823, he lived for five years on the island of Malta, where the Hispanophile John Hookham Frere introduced him to English literature, including Byron and Scott. Indeed, Frere suggested that Rivas write a modern Spanish epic after the manner of *The Lady of the Lake* or *Marmion,* and Rivas considered the subject of the Seven Princes of Lara, although the resulting poem was not published for several years. In 1828 Rivas published a poem *To the Lighthouse of Malta,* which is decidedly Romantic. The remaining five years of exile were spent in England and France. He became a full-fledged convert to Romanticism, and wrote a number of works not published until his return to Spain. He was fond of painting and for a time gave art lessons to support himself.

In 1834, when he returned to his country and succeeded to the title of Duke, he published in Paris the work he had planned in Malta: *The Bastard Moor* (*El Moro expósito o Córdoba y Burgos en el siglo x*). The poem carries a preface by Alcalá Galiano which is a sort of Romantic manifesto, and Rivas' treatment is definitely Romantic throughout. The theme, coming from Spanish ballads, is the vengeance taken by Mudarra for the murder of his half brothers, the Seven Princes of Lara, by their uncle. Rivas is not gifted in the creation of vivid narrative; it is the color of his description for which he is remarkable. The picture of Spanish and Moorish-Andalusian civilization in the tenth century is brilliant rather than historically accurate. The poem is composed in eleven-syllable verse, with assonance in the alternating lines.

Rivas further displayed his interest in Spanish history and legend in his *Romances históricos,* published together in 1841, though written earlier. They possess the same virtues as the long *Moro expósito,* with more vigor of narration, and really constitute Rivas' most valuable contribution to the poetry of his time. Conspicuous is the patriotic note, the interest in poetic material which belonged specifically to Spain's past.

It did not take Rivas long to grow more conservative. His later years were little devoted to literature, much more to politics and diplomacy. He was ambassador to Naples from 1844 to 1850, and to France from 1859 to 1860. He retired to his estates in Andalusia for the remaining five years of his life.

The glory of Rivas in presenting to his contemporaries the traditions of the Middle Ages is shared by the younger José Zorrilla (1817-1893), who is particularly noted for his *leyendas,* which gave definitive form to many a Spanish legend. Zorrilla was little concerned with history, nor did he quite possess Rivas' pictorial sense, but he could compose more vivid narrative in more varied and harmonious verse. He is much more given to the use of the fantastic and the supernatural. Some of his best-known *leyendas* are *Time Brings Truth, God Brings Justice* (*Para verdades, el tiempo, y para justicia, Dios*); *King Peter Judges* (*Justicias del rey don Pedro*); *el Capitán Montoya;* and *Margarita la Tornera.* The last is the well-known story of the nun who abandons her nunnery with a gallant; worn, broken and repentant she returns to the convent, to find that the Virgin Mary has all the time been taking her place.

The *leyendas* are relatively short. Zorrilla's attempt at a full-length epic was the unfinished *Granada* (1852). The nine books of the poem recount the life at the Court of Granada before its fall in 1492, but it is the gorgeousness of the descriptions and the lilt of the verse that count, not the historical narrative.

Rivas and Zorrilla were also of capital importance in the development of the Romantic Drama. In poetry, they represent the legendary and the descriptive. The poet who best rhymes his sufferings in moving lyrics is José de Espronceda (1808-1842). He was a wild and passionate youth, and the neo-classic teachings of the judicious critic Alberto Lista could not calm him. By the time he was sixteen he was in jail for conspiracy, and he spent exiles in Lisbon, London, and Paris. Since he was in Paris in 1830, it was natural that he should fight on the barricades.

It was in Lisbon that the poet met Teresa Mancha, and conceived for her a passion that might mildly be termed volcanic. He abducted her from her husband and children in London, and the two lived a stormy life together, with violent separations, until she died of tuberculosis. Apparently Espronceda was about to settle down, and was engaged to marry a sensible girl in 1843 when he died of a laryngeal infection.

The first poems of Espronceda, written under the encouragement of Lista, were neo-classic and not remarkable in merit. Such is the fragment of what was to be a long poem on Pelayo, the hero of Covadonga. The dramas, *Blanca de Borbón, Neither Uncle nor Nephew* (*Ni el tío ni el sobrino*), and *Love Avenges Its Own Insults* (*Amor venga sus agravios*) add nothing to the poet's fame, nor was he a good novelist (*Sancho Saldaña,* 1834).

It is in the lyric that Espronceda was preeminent. His poems, appearing separately at various times, were published in a collection in 1840. Although they display various influences, Ossian, Béranger, Lamartine, Victor Hugo, and, most of all, Byron, they show still more of Espronceda's passionate feeling and his poetic virtuosity.

He is one of the most skillful versifiers in Spanish, a language which seems particularly apt for lyric expression. *The Song of the Pirate* and the *Song of the Cossack,* Byronic in inspiration, are among his most rhythmical compositions. *To the Executioner, To the Beggar, The Condemned Criminal,* show the Romantic interest in anti-social types and a humanitarianism which stems from Rousseau. The sonorous *Hymn to the Sun* owes much to Ossian. The *Farewell of the Greek Patriot to the Apostate's Daughter* is deeply sentimental.

The theme of disillusionment, so characteristic of Espronceda's spirit, is evident in the extremely well-known *To Jarifa at an Orgy* (*A Jarifa en una orgía*). The poet's thought is something like this: the first principle is doubt, the chief reality of life is suffering, pleasure is the world's main illusion, the only solution for all problems is death. Is it surprising that Espronceda was an unhappy and tortured soul?

*El estudiante de Salamanca* is a much longer poem, a *leyenda,* on the subject of the young libertine who witnesses his own funeral, dancing off with his skeleton bride with the same swagger he had in life. The metrical variety of the poem is astonishing.

In the long (six cantos) but unfinished *El diablo mundo* (1840-41), Espronceda was going to attempt a sort of epic of humanity. Adam, rejuvenated like Faust, goes from one disillusionment to another as he encounters all classes of society. The elements that make up the poem are highly realistic, strikingly fantastic, thoroughly heterogeneous. The whole seems disordered, the separate parts impressively artistic. Canto II, *A Teresa,* is a poetic history of Espronceda's passion for his beloved, a masterpiece of self-revelation, one of the most deeply lyric poems in Spanish.

José Zorrilla (1817-1893), less pessimistic than Espronceda, was a poet quite in the tradition of Spanish fecundity. He said that he was born to write verses, and that was indeed his chief occupation throughout a long life. His *leyendas* were many, his dramas were rapidly written. These forms and his very numerous lyrics are all of a piece: the same brilliance of description, the same diffuseness of thought, for Zorrilla was no intellectual, the same harmonious flow of mellifluous cadences. Zorrilla was truly gifted. If his smooth lines do not captivate the brain, they always fascinate the ear. If they do not stir the deepest emotions of mankind, their imagery appeals to the imagination and stirs the senses. His several poems *To the Moon,* his *Orientals,* his addresses to various fair ones, his *Sunless Day* are all rich in sentimentality, with a faintly purple melancholy.

Zorrilla liked to call himself a wandering troubadour, the last of the minstrels. He retained a youthful, some would say an adolescent, zest in his poetry to the very end. On June 22, 1889, his country crowned him in Granada as national poet. The newspapers reported that he received five crowns of gold, eight hundred and forty-three of laurel, and many other tributes, in the presence of sixteen thousand people. Yet by that time the hoary bard had long outlived his poetic generation, for the times had changed and he had not. He had once been the best representative of a vague, sentimental, lyrically gushing Romantic moment.

Lyric poetry as represented by Espronceda and Zorrilla was the most characteristic manifestation of Romantic literature. The number of versifiers in the eighteen-thirties and -forties was very large indeed. Many are now remembered for a single poem, most are forgotten.

The Valencian Juan Arolas (1805-1849), a priest without vocation who died insane, published two admirable volumes of verse. His religious poems are ardent, sincere, filled with mystic longing. He was also much influenced by Hugo, Byron, and Zorrilla, and in his *Orientales* he evidently seeks to escape from the voluntarily incurred restraints of his religious life in sensuous imaginings, in thinking of a heaven of luscious houris rather than of ascetic saints. His love poems, no doubt expressing longing and not realization, were in harmony with his real spirit, but not with his profession. Hence the conflict that ended in madness.

Enrique Gil y Carrasco (1815-1846), who died of tuberculosis in Berlin, the author of a well-known historical novel, *El Señor de Bembibre,* is particularly remembered for a sweet little poem called *The Violet,* gentle and melancholy as the author.

A more vibrant note is struck by Gertrudis Gómez de Avellaneda (1814-1873), a Cuban who lived mostly in Spain. Her *Poesías líricas* (1841) are passionate in tone, vigorous in expression, sincere in feeling, whether they refer to her own sorrows or to religious or profane subjects. In Spain she has even been called, without sufficient justification, the greatest poetess of modern times. Foreigners have not been quite so lavish in praise. She was also the author of novels and dramas which show both spirit and skill. *Sab* (1839), an anti-slavery novel, came long before *Uncle Tom's Cabin. Baltasar* (1858) is one of Spain's best Biblical dramas.

Much more to the taste of many contemporaries is the heartfelt verse of the Galician Rosalía de Castro (1837-1885), post-Romantic in time, highly Romantic in sentiment. Her poems, both in Galician, *Cantares gallegos,* 1863, and in Castilian, *On the Banks of the Sar* (*En las orillas del Sar,* 1885), were a purely personal expression with her, and she left an injunction that all unpublished manuscripts should be destroyed at her death. Her simplicity and lack of pose make her quite different from many of her predecessors and contemporaries. She is unashamedly sentimental, as Galicians are supposed to be, but she avoids the mawkish, and her melancholy is by no means trumped up. No doubt she had many emotional conflicts, for she was illegitimate, a priest's daughter, and her marriage was unfortunate. Although she was little known in her lifetime, her reputation has grown while that of famous altisonant contemporaries like Núñez de Arce has dwindled.

Another belated Romantic was the Sevillian Gustavo Adolfo Bécquer (1836-1870), who lived, married, and died unhappily. He was apprenticed to his uncle, a painter, but at the age of eighteen he came to Madrid in search of a literary career. He found it, but he remained unhappy up to the time of his early death.

Bécquer's nature was dreamy and sentimental, and he had a penchant for the vague, mysterious, and fantastic. These qualities show in his prose legends, which are peopled with green-eyed pool nymphs, strange white does who are really women, supernatural organists, and mysterious statues. His settings, in gloom-haunted castles, breathe an atmosphere of eery melancholy. The style is polished but florid, and one senses strongly the influence of the German Hoffmann.

Bécquer's *Rimas,* not published in collection until the year after the author's death, are among the most popular poems ever composed in the Spanish language. They resemble the short *Lieder* of Heine when the German was not in a cynical mood, and the question of influence has been much debated. Bécquer also knew and admired the poetry of Byron. The *Rimas* form a poetic autobiography of Bécquer's sentimental life, and he comes close to achieving his ideal of "taming rebellious, wretched language with words which would be at once sighs and laughter, colors and musical sound." His sadness is not feigned, and his simple and polished lines are sincere. So is his artistry.

## THE DRAMA

Even at the height of Romanticism, many sorts of plays held the stage in Spain. In the eighteen-thirties and -forties *Siglo de Oro* plays, Moratinian comedies, operas, translations from the French, especially Scribe, out-and-out melodramas, "plays of magic" (the most popular play of the time was an absurd thing called *The Goat's Hoof*), even classic tragedies, were all to be seen in a disconcerting medley, and strictly "Romantic" plays, even in the banner year of 1837, never constituted more than a part of the repertory. Because of their sentimental and melodramatic exaggerations these Romantic dramas have stood time's test less successfully than the lyrics of Espronceda, Rosalía de Castro, Bécquer.

Francisco Martínez de la Rosa (1787-1862) was a Grenadine who received a neo-classic training and remained essentially a middle-of-the-roader throughout his life. He was a liberal and a patriot in politics, but when he became prime minister in 1834 he was too moderate for his more excited coreligionists. His abilities and his uprightness won him a distinguished career.

He spent years of exile after 1823 in France, where he saw the triumph of Romanticism, and even presented a mildly Romantic play, *La révolte des Maures sous Philippe II,* on the stage of the

*Porte Saint-Martin.* It was played in Spanish in Madrid in 1836 as *Aben-Humeya.* Previously he had written neo-classic comedies and tragedies, including an excellent *Edipo.* It was also in 1830, in Paris, that Martínez de la Rosa wrote *The Conspiracy in Venice* (*La conjuración de Venecia*), which was shown in Madrid on April 23, 1834, and is thought of as the first Spanish Romantic drama. It is in prose, breaks the unities, is well supplied with mediaeval conspirators (the time is 1310 A.D.), masks, carnival scenes, heartless judges, hopeless love amid the tombs; has a hero who finds out only too late that he is the son of the mighty Dux of Venice, and a heroine whose beauty is exceeded only by her love and her distress. She goes mad as he is executed for conspiracy.

The play was one of the most successful of the year, though hardly a mighty triumph. It was followed by French melodramas such as Ducange's *The Headsman of Amsterdam,* operas, such as *Norma, Don Giovanni, Siglo de Oro comedias* and other sorts of plays. The author's *Aben-Humeya* was much less successful two years later. Martínez de la Rosa was an innovator, but he is really significant in the history of Romanticism for only one play.

Certainly one of the most Romantic temperaments of the period belonged to Mariano José de Larra (1809-1837), who struggled with an insoluble conflict between head and heart. Intellectually keen and well-educated, he was, as we shall see, far and away the best critic and satirist of his time. He wrote or translated about a dozen plays, none of which won great success. The most significant is his *Macías* (September 24, 1834), which had a first run of only five nights. Larra himself says he does not know whether his "feeble composition" is Romantic, of the "colossal and naked" school of Victor Hugo and Dumas, or not; the Galician troubadour Macías is just "a man who loves." His beloved is married to a cruel tyrant, by whose hired assassins Macías is slain as Elvira commits suicide. The play comes closer to observing the unities and has much less local color than *La Conjuración de Venecia.*

The Duke of Rivas produced in March, 1835, his *Don Alvaro o la fuerza del sino.* Most people know it best in Verdi's operatic version, *La forza del destino.* It contains approximately the maximum number of Romantic exaggerations which can be packed into a single play. Local color by the stageful, dashing illustrious hero of at first unknown ancestry, lovely clinging aristocratic heroine, bitter quirks of fate (or blind chance), pitched battles, duels with avenging brothers of Leonor, accidental death, a whole gallery of popular characters such as gypsies, innkeepers, soldiers, choleric lay brothers, sly-tongued servants; palaces, military camps, convents, wild rugged nature. At the end Don Alvaro, though now a pious monk, is provoked to kill Leonor's second brother, who with his dying strength mortally stabs his sister, and our hero, cursing the human race, hurls himself to death in the abyss amid lightning, thunder, and the chants of the horrified religious community. The play is in five acts, shatters the unities, has comic elements to make the tragedy deeper by contrast, and is partly in verse and partly in prose. There is a famous monologue of Don Alvaro on the theme of the repeated line: "It is a dreadful thing to be born."

With this play, the Duke of Rivas practically tendered his resignation as a Romantic dramatist. Perhaps he even repented of *Don Alvaro* as he grew old and conservative.

March 1, 1836, saw the presentation of *El trovador* by Antonio García Gutiérrez (1813-1884), who produced in all about eighty plays, and two small volumes of verse.

*El trovador,* also in prose and verse, less wild and much more poetic than *Don Alvaro,* is certainly one of the better Romantic plays, and Leonor is one of the more appealing Romantic heroines. García Gutiérrez deserves more credit for the success of Verdi's *Il trovatore* than is sometimes accorded him. (Verdi's *Simone Boccanegra* is also based on a play by the author of *El trovador.*) García Gutiérrez wrote plays with better-drawn characters than *El trovador,* with fewer technical faults, but he never surpassed the youthful freshness and the delicate versification of his early triumph.

Juan Eugenio Hartzenbusch (1806-1880), son of a German cabinet maker in Madrid, was born to be a sober scholar, but he began his literary career with the production of plays, some even a bit lurid. His most celebrated drama was *Los amantes de Teruel* (prose and verse, 1837), on the well-known legend of the lovers, who, kept apart by adverse fate, by a torrid and wicked Sultana (of Hartzen-busch's invention), and by cruel parents, die of broken hearts before the theater-goers' astonished gaze. The verse is somewhat more than adequate, the action rapid and plentiful, and the sentiment ardent. Hartzenbusch wrote a number of Romantic and historical dramas, spectacle plays (*comedias de magia*), and social comedies. He found his true métier, however, in his position as Director of the National Library and editor of *Siglo de Oro* plays.

José Zorrilla (1817-1893) has been called the spoiled darling of Spanish Romanticism. He wrote a great deal, enjoyed great popu-larity as poet and playwright, and, as we have seen, was lavishly crowned laureate in his old age, but public esteem never expressed itself solidly enough to satisfy his champagne tastes. He came into public notice when he read a poem of his at the funeral of Larra, and verse dripped sweetly from his pen ever afterward.

Zorrilla's first real success on the stage came with *El Zapatero y el rey,* first part 1840. (The Second Part is really a separate play.) It concerns King Peter the Cruel, known to most Spanish dramatists rather as "the Justice-Dealer," the King who champions the people against oppressive nobles. The action, as in all Zorrilla's plays, is highly melodramatic. He never lacked for swiftly moving plots or for characters with real vitality, even if their reactions are simple, their psychology rather rudimentary. The Second Part of *The Shoe-maker and the King* ends with the murder of King Peter I at the hands of his bastard half-brother and successor, Henry of Trasta-mara.

The legend of Roderic, the last of the Goths, has been of peren-nial interest in Spain. Zorrilla dramatized it in a short play called *El puñal del godo* (1842).

The year 1844 marked the production of the most popular Span-ish play of modern times: Zorrilla's *Don Juan Tenorio,* which gradually became a sort of national institution. The character cre-ated by Tirso has undergone a gland operation and has had his face lifted. He is even more dashing, vital, invincible to men and irresistible to women, and he has acquired a deep Romantic senti-mentalism. And he is dragged down to hell by the statue of the

*Commendador* whom he has murdered? Oh, no, he repents after his death and, in company with the beauteous Inés, is wafted up to Paradise, accompanied by little angels and sweet incense. Romantic authors could not bear to damn such an ideal representative of vital force, of arrant individualism. The captious can find all sorts of faults, a host of improbabilities, in Zorrilla's play, but no one can deny the lyric gush of its verse. Thousands of Spaniards go "to hear the verses recited" year after year, as the play is put on throughout much of the Spanish-speaking world around All Souls' Day. Many of the sweetly flowing lines have no intellectual content whatever, but Zorrilla was writing poetry, not philosophy, and he has charmed generation after generation. Performances of this strange play are still attended by people of all conditions and ages, literally from babes in arms to tottering grey-bearded men.

Zorrilla's most perfectly constructed play was *Traitor, Unconfessing and Martyr* (*Traidor, inconfeso y mártir,* 1849), based on the story of the pastry-cook of Madrigal, who tried to palm himself off as King Sebastian of Portugal, slain in Africa in 1578. The drama is one of the best that nineteenth century Spain produced, though it never approached the celebrity of *Don Juan Tenorio.* After that Zorrilla wrote practically nothing for the stage.

All during the Romantic period other sorts of plays had been presented constantly. One of the chief purveyors of social comedies was the fertile Manuel Bretón de los Herreros (1796-1873), who has more than a hundred plays to his credit, plus an almost equal number of translations, and a large number of miscellaneous poems and newspaper articles. He is a typical bourgeois, and he satirizes, gaily, amusingly, but not too vigorously the foibles of his fellows. A good sound man, whose plays recommend a sound morality and good common sense.

## THE NOVEL

The novel in Spain for the first half of the nineteenth century was dominated by one man, not a Spaniard: Sir Walter Scott. The Scotch author was plentifully translated and read, and native novelists imitated him closely. The imitators were numerous, but hardly deserve mention for any permanent contribution to literary art. The first imitator was Ramón López Soler (1806-1836), whose *Los bandos de Castilla* (1830) owes much to *Ivanhoe*. It at least shows the tendency, which characterizes most of the products of Spanish Romanticism, to use native Spanish subjects and materials.

The year 1834, as has been seen, was noteworthy for the production of the first Romantic long poem, *El moro expósito,* and a play, *La conjuración de Venecia.* It also marked the publication of two historical novels by authors who shone much more brightly in other fields. Espronceda wrote *Sancho Saldaña* and Larra *El doncel de don Enrique el Doliente.* They both owe to Scott their general plan, method, and technique, but both show a decidedly personal note, a frank passion which would have made Sir Walter blush. To that extent they are different from *Ivanhoe,* for example, and more subjective, more Romantic. No little can be learned about their authors from reading them, and they do not quite deserve the condescendingly slighting remarks with which most critics mention them.

Enrique Gil's *El Señor de Bembibre* (1844) displays a greater sentimentality, more love of nature, and a more picturesquely presented scene. The events take place during the last days of the Knights Templar in Spain. Hence by many Gil's novel is rated as Romanticism's best, even as the best historical novel produced in Spain. It is only fair to note that the love of hero and heroine is lush and lachrymose, and that the novel drags most languidly.

There was nothing languid about the three hundred novels (five hundred volumes) of the "Spanish Dumas" Manuel Fernández y González (1821-1888), practically all on Spanish historical themes. Most of them were published in installments in newspapers. They have vigor and a crude sort of imagination, though no literary polish.

## *COSTUMBRISMO.* CRITICISM

The name *costumbristas* is applied to a number of writers who composed sketches on contemporary life and manners in the early nineteenth century. Something of the sort had been done in the seventeenth century, by Juan de Zabaleta, Francisco Santos, Liñán y Verdugo. Foreign ancestors were Addison and Steele in England and Jouy and L. S. Mercier in France. Sebastián Miñano, with his *Letters of a Poor Loafer* (*Cartas de un pobrecito holgazán,* 1820), was an immediate predecessor. The Spanish *costumbristas* were contemporary with Washington Irving.

Ramón de Mesonero Romanos (1803-1882) was a native of Madrid, vastly interested in his home town, a man of good digestion and a pleasant sense of humor, never given to exaggeration, always a *bon bourgeois.* He retired from a successful business to devote himself to writing, and he contributed sketches to important Madrid papers such as *Cartas Españolas, El Español* and the *Semanario Pintoresco Español.* These articles were later collected as *Panorama matritense, Escenas matritenses* and *Tipos y caracteres.* Mesonero also wrote a series of descriptions called *El antiguo Madrid,* still highly useful, and a book of memoirs called *Memorias de un setentón.* His works are invaluable to one who wishes to get a picture of social conditions of his time. He was highly patriotic, and did a great deal to renew interest in Spain's past literature, notably the drama of the Golden Age.

Serafín Estébanez Calderón (1799-1867), who used the pen-name *El Solitario,* did for Andalusia what Mesonero did for Madrid. Estébanez' *Escenas andaluzas* were published in various newspapers, and collected into a volume in 1847. They give a vivid picture of Andalusian popular life and customs, with considerable color and verve. The language is at times difficult, a bit stilted.

There were many others who wrote sketches from which we can learn a great deal about life in Spain in the first half of the nineteenth century. The fashion for such articles was shown by the publication in 1843 of a large collection of them, *Los Españoles pintados por sí mismos,* and later even *Las Españolas pintadas por sí mismas.*

It would be a grave error to class Mariano José de Larra, *Fígaro* (1809-1837), as merely a *costumbrista,* for he was much more than that: the greatest critic of his century.

Larra came of a good middle-class family, and was educated partly in France. He began publishing in his 'teens and crowded an extraordinary amount of writing into a life of less than twenty-eight years. At the time of his death he was the highest-salaried newspaperman in the country. He was married when only twenty to a woman older than himself, and his marriage was unsuccessful. He had the misfortune to fall deeply in love with a dark Andalusian beauty named Dolores Armijo, who was also married, and on her account he committed suicide on February 13, 1837.

Larra wrote a few poems of no great merit, made several translations of French plays, and wrote some comedies of his own. He made a bow to the Romantic drama with his *Macías* (1834) and produced a novel à la Walter Scott on the same subject in the same year (*El doncel de don Enrique el Doliente*).

His greatest work, however, appeared in the form of newspaper articles. He published one periodical all alone, *El Pobrecito Hablador* (fourteen numbers, 1832-1833), which made his reputation, and he contributed to various others under the pseudonym of "Fígaro."

As a dramatic critic he was far ahead of anyone in his country, as is easily seen by reading his reviews of such plays as *Hernani, Antony, El trovador, Los amantes de Teruel.* He was able to see the faults, the exaggerations in the works of his contemporaries, as well as the merits, and he was not bamboozled by Romantic hocus-pocus. Constantly evident in his numerous articles concerning the theater is a desire for reform, for improvement in the cultural level of Spanish dramatic production.

Larra's articles on various aspects of Spanish life are unmatched for incisiveness and penetration. He is not content, like Mesonero, to describe surface picturesqueness, but seeks the underlying causes of political or social behaviour. His *Marry in Haste and Make a Bad Job of It* (*El casarse pronto y mal*) is a vivid little preachment on a subject all too familiar to the author. *Come Back Tomorrow* (*Vuelva Usted Mañana*), *You Can't Come in without Speaking to the Porter* (*Nadie pase sin hablar con el portero*), and *Buenas Noches* are excellent political satires. *The Old Castilian* (*El castellano viejo*) is a fine satirical portrait. By 1836 an increasing bitterness in Larra's spirit is evident in his articles, culminating in the terrible *All Souls' Day, 1836* (*El Día de Difuntos de 1836*), in which

*Fígaro* describes all Madrid as a cemetery, with each building a grave of lost hopes. He ends, "The cemetery is in our own hearts."

Larra's style is one of the most natural, expressive, and brilliant since Cervantes. His death, when he was only twenty-eight, was a major tragedy for the thought and literature of Spain.

# XXIV

## *Realism in the Later Nineteenth Century*

L ARRA and the *costumbristas* had a far greater sense of reality
than was displayed in lyric poetry or drama during the brief
Romantic period. The work of the *costumbristas* prepared
the ground for the growth of the realistic novel. It was only natural
that the stage should become more realistic too, and should concern
itself less with unhappy troubadours of the Middle Ages and more
with everyday people and contemporary problems. Poetry showed
the same tendencies.

### VERSE

Ramón de Campoamor (1817-1901) was a prosaic gentleman who
fancied himself a philosopher and wrote verse. He lived a calm life,
though three times governor of a province, devoting himself mainly
to writing. He is an excellent representative of the positive, bourgeois spirit which was a natural reaction against excessive Romanticism, and his poems constitute a critique of the exaggerated
sentiment in vogue when he was young.

Campoamor in his early volumes of verse, now mainly forgotten,
yielded for the moment to the Romantic inspiration of the time.
Almost forgotten, too, are his polemics and his dissertations on
*El personalismo* (1855), on *Lo absoluto* (1865) and on *Poetics*
(*Poética,* 1883). His ambitious long poems such as *Colón* (1853),
*El drama universal* (1869), containing a little bit of everything in
twenty thousand lines, and the pseudo-historical *El Licenciado To-
rralba* (1888) are now read by few.

Great popularity came to Campoamor for three sorts of poems, which he claimed to have invented. It would be more accurate to say that he invented the names. In 1846 he first published his *Doloras*. He was enamored of "art for the sake of the idea," and a *dolora* was supposed to be a graceful, delicate, short poetic composition which would display truth through irony, which would briefly touch some universal problem. Campoamor does indeed achieve grace in these little poems, and since the thoughts were by no means above the heads of his contemporaries, he was bound to be a popular poet. The best known of the *Doloras* is *¡Quién supiera escribir!* An illiterate peasant girl tries to make a stern priest write a love letter to her absent swain, and each time he reproves her for exaggerated expressions of sentiment, she ends the stanza with the words, "If I could only write, myself!"

Campoamor's second form consisted of his thirty-one *Little Epics* (*Pequeños poemas*), usually anecdotes of a sentimental or philosophic nature. They were published at various times from 1872 to 1894, and are much longer than the *Doloras*. Their thought is always readily assimilable without effort on the part of the reader.

The *humorada* is very short, and Campoamor intended the form to combine all the best of the epigram, the ode, the madrigal and even other poetic forms. The *Humoradas* (1886-1888) are far more like epigrams pure and simple than like anything else, and some of them are extremely well-turned.

The tone of Gaspar Núñez de Arce (1832-1903) is far louder than that of Campoamor. He was engaged in politics as congressman, governor of Barcelona and Foreign Minister, and he constantly showed real solicitude for the best interests of his country and a deep preoccupation with the problems of his time.

It was Núñez de Arce's belief that poetry should be stirring, that it should plow furrows in the heart, that it should be intense. In practice he sought to achieve his ends by an extremely emphatic style, by shouting in verse. The title of his most important volume is significant: *Battle Cries* (*Gritos del Combate,* 1875). He cries out for a suppression of the evils of the past, though he believes in his nation and his religion. There is a noticeable tone of disillusionment, of pessimism in all his work, a presence of doubt that will not be banished. The same tone characterizes his other poems, such as *The Dark Forest* (*La selva oscura*), *Lord Byron's Last Lament, Brother Martin's* (*Luther's*) *Vision*.

Less resounding and more tender are *Un idilio y una elegía* (1878), a tale of love stilled by the chill hand of death, *Fishing* (*La pesca*, 1884), another love-tragedy, and *Maruja* (1886), the story of an old couple who achieve happiness by adopting a little beggar girl.

Núñez de Arce belonged to a rhetorical generation, like Echegaray and the great orator and statesman Emilio Castelar. The poet's cries seem less poignant with the passage of time and his fame has diminished. He was greatly esteemed in his day and there is no reason to question his sincerity.

## POST-ROMANTIC DRAMA

A nineteenth century dramatist who well represents the transition from the Romantic and historical play to the social and thesis drama was Manuel Tamayo y Baus (1829-1898). *The Snowball* (*La bola de nieve*, 1856) shows how jealousy increases like a rolling snowball. *Hard Cash* (*Lo positivo*, 1862) attacks excessive devotion to money. *Affairs of Honor* (*Lances de honor*, 1863) condemns the duel. Tamayo's best-known drama is *A New Play* (*Un drama nuevo*, 1867), a play within a play, involving Shakespeare and Yorick. It is highly declamatory and alas! poor Yorick tears his passion to tatters. The play was greatly admired for many years for an intensity which is close to the melodramatic. The construction is excellent. Tamayo also wrote sentimental and historical plays and a superior classic tragedy on the well-known theme of *Virginia*.

Adelardo López de Ayala (1828-1879) was a resounding orator, a pompous politician, and a fertile dramatist. He was familiar with the *Siglo de Oro* and might have aspired to be a Ruiz de Alarcón if he had had more intensity, more talent. He produced a number of well-planned realistic plays with pleasant intrigues, natural characters, and emphasis on some moral theme. *So Much Percent* (*El tanto por ciento*, 1861) shows love prevailing over base financial interest. *Consuelo* (1878) portrays a selfish minx who marries for money and is soundly punished. Some may prefer his first play, a historical drama called *High in Affairs of State* (*Un hombre de estado,* 1851). There were many minor dramatists who in general resembled Tamayo and López de Ayala.

Gaspar Núñez de Arce, best known for his lyric poetry, produced one of the best historical plays of the century in *The Fagot* (*El haz de leña,* 1872), on the death of Philip II's son Don Carlos. The theme had already been used many times in Spain and abroad, the best-known plays being Alfieri's *Filippo* and Schiller's *Don Carlos.* Núñez de Arce's play is noteworthy for its directness, its simple and moving plot, its preachment of religious tolerance.

The monarch of the Spanish stage in the last quarter of the nineteenth century was José Echegaray (1832-1916), the first Spaniard to receive the Nobel prize for literature, in 1904. Echegaray was a university professor of mathematics, engineer, statesman, and playwright who did not care how hard he pushed his plots and worked his characters. The result was a new sort of Romantic melodrama, emphasizing passion and leaving out minor considerations such as the Middle Ages, local color and other appurtenances of earlier Romanticism. Echegaray's scenes and characters are usually contemporary and apparently realistic. It is their volcanic passions and problems that now seem to us exaggerated, and give an impression of artificiality.

Echegaray's most famous drama was *El Gran Galeoto* (1881), showing how the world's base and unfounded suspicions can wreck true love and bring about gory tragedy. *Madman or Saint* (*O locura o santidad*) shows a meticulously honorable gentleman declared insane because he insists on making over his fortune to the real heir, amid much ranting. *The Son of Don Juan* (*El hijo de Don Juan*) shows the sins of the fathers visited upon the children, and is strongly reminiscent of Ibsen's *Ghosts.* Echegaray wrote some sixty more plays. Their glory has now vanished, lost in a welter of declamatory rhetoric.

The plays of Pérez Galdós, if less technically excellent, are more realistic, more an interpretation of actual Spanish problems which the author knew well. The title of Galdós' first play is significant: *Real Life (Realidad,* 1892). *Fancy (La loca de la casa,* 1893), *The Grandfather (El abuelo,* 1904), and others are based on the author's novels. *El abuelo* shows an old aristocrat converted by the fine qualities of an illegitimate granddaughter to the realization that ideas of inherited honor and pride of race are false. *The Duchess of San Quintín (La de San Quintín,* 1894) displays a decayed aristocratic family rejuvenated by work. *Electra,* 1901, won celebrity in excess of its merits as a drama. It portrays the conflict between blind traditionalism and progress, a theme dear to Galdós.

It has been said that Galdós' novels are highly dramatic, witness *Doña Perfecta,* and that his dramas are more like novels. He was not a master of stage-craft, but he is important in the history of nineteenth century drama because he brought plays back to earth, using themes of contemporary importance and developing characters taken from real life.

Of Joaquín Dicenta (1863-1917) it is usually said that he brought the proletariat to the stage, not for picturesqueness or for comic relief as in the *Siglo de Oro* drama, but as protagonist. Dicenta's *Juan José* (1895) is an honest workman who is turned into a criminal by the brutal treatment which his employer, of high social rank, accords him. The play enjoyed great popularity. *The Wolf (El lobo,* 1913) shows a convict regenerated by love, according to the Romantic formula, and stirs a vague memory of Victor Hugo's *Marion Delorme.* In fact, Dicenta has been called "a Romantic in a workman's blouse." His dialogue is the natural speech of the proletarians he presents, and he makes no attempt at prettiness or elegance. He certainly enlarged the scope of the Spanish stage.

## THE REGIONAL NOVEL

The Romanticists sought to re-create the local color of the past or the exotic, and the *costumbristas* presented the savor and peculiar atmosphere of their own country and time. Yet the latter produced only sketches, or later *cuadros de costumbres,* more extended pictures of local milieux and customs. Their contribution was great, but they did not evolve a novel of manners. It remained for authors of the second half of the century to produce the combination of plot plus background, to develop the regional novel which characterizes the period from 1850 onward.

This combination was first made by Cecilia Böhl de Faber (1796-1877), better known by her pseudonym Fernán Caballero. She was the daughter of the consul to Cadiz from Hamburg, the ardent Hispanophile Johan Nikolas Böhl von Faber. Though born in Switzerland and educated, mainly in the French language, in Germany, she spent most of her life, including three marriages, in southern Spain.

Her first and most important novel was *The Sea-Gull* (*La Gaviota,* 1849). The plot, concerning the sad life of a German doctor, Fritz Stein, and his marriage to Marisalada, the Sea-gull, is not remarkable. Marisalada wins fame and the love of a bullfighter because of her beautiful voice. Stein goes off to die of chagrin and yellow fever in Cuba, the bullfighter is gored to death, and La Gaviota loses her voice and marries the village barber. It is the background which is attractive, for Fernán Caballero lovingly describes the life of the simple peasants of Andalusia, their songs, stories, and superstitions, their sweet charity and simple faith. Unfortunately she loves to sentimentalize and to preach, and her style is no model of clarity or grace. She deserves credit for founding the realistic regional novel in nineteenth century Spain, for setting an example to be followed by authors of greater culture and penetration. Next in popularity among her numerous works was *La familia de Alvareda* (1856) and *Un servilón y un liberalito* (1857).

Antonio de Trueba (1819?-1889), an author of no great culture and with a careless style, began to write at about the same time as Fernán Caballero. He is remembered chiefly for stories which have his native Basque region as their background.

Far more important was the highly cultured arch-sophisticate Juan Valera y Alcalá Galiano (1827-1905). His profession as a diplomat took him to Naples, Vienna, Lisbon, Washington (he found the United States somewhat crude) and elsewhere. He wrote poetry, drama, much literary criticism, and made translations, for example, of *Daphnis and Chloe,* but his most famous work is his novel *Pepita Jiménez* (1874). It was inspired by his reading of the Spanish mystics, and is a simple and psychologically penetrating story of a young theological student who gives up the priesthood to marry a charming widow. The scene is a small town in Andalusia, the author's native and beloved region. His other novels are *El Comendador Mendoza, Doña Luz, Pasarse de listo, Las ilusiones del doctor Faustino, Morsamor,* and *Juanita la larga.* Valera's style is always elegant, polished, in excellent taste. His achievement as a regional novelist marks a great advance over his predecessor Fernán Caballero.

Pedro Antonio de Alarcón (1833-1891), a far more ebullient Andalusian than Valera, was a born storyteller. His *The Finale from Norma* (*El Final de Norma*), written at the age of eighteen, is a dime-novel string of puerilities, as the author later recognized. However, *The Three-Cornered Hat* (*El sombrero de tres picos,* 1874), based on Spanish ballads, is one of the best long short stories in Spanish, distinguished for rollicking humor, swift movement, well-sketched background, picturesque characters. *El escándalo* (1875) and *El niño de la Bola* (1880) are marred by excessive melodrama despite their virtues. *Captain Terrible* (*El Capitán Veneno*) suffers from over-simplification of characters, from exaggeration, but is a gaily told tale of scorn overcoming scorn: the infinitely sweet and virtuous Angustias wins complete surrender from the fire-eating woman-hating Captain Jorge. *The Prodigal Woman* (*La Pródiga,* 1881) was greeted with silence by critics, and Alarcón wrote no more novels.

Some have thought that Alarcón was really at his best in the short story, a form that necessarily restrained his native exuberance. The stories which he called *Historietas nacionales* are truly admirable, and some are contained in practically all collections of the best Spanish short stories. They have excellent background, swiftly flowing narrative, vigorously outlined characters. Good examples would be *El libro talonario, La buenaventura, El afrancesado.*

Alarcón also wrote good travel books (*De Madrid a Nápoles*) and war correspondence (*Diario de un testigo de la guerra de Africa*).

José María de Pereda (1833-1905) was born in the north and lived in Santander. He came of an aristocratic and conservative family, and intended to enter the army as an artillery officer, but he gave up a military career and devoted himself mainly to literature. At first he continued the tradition of Fernán Caballero and Trueba, publishing sketches in various Santander newspapers. They were later (1864) published in book form as *Escenas Montañesas*. He made unsuccessful attempts at drama and dabbled in politics. His first full-fledged novel was *The Hind Let Loose* (*El Buey Suelto*, 1877), filled with propaganda against selfish bachelorhood. *Don Gonzalo González de la Gonzalera* (1878) is better, and possesses real characters. *Pedro Sánchez* (1873) is a study of political corruption. *Home Flavor* (*El sabor de la tierruca*, 1884) is a sort of rustic idyl.

One of the best of Spanish regional novels is Pereda's *Fine-Spun* (*Sotileza*, 1884), a sort of prose epic of Santander. The chief characters, admirably drawn, are the orphan girl Silda (nicknamed "Sotileza," "fine-spun" for her extreme neatness) and her three suitors, who represent different classes of Santander society. The verbal sea-scapes, particularly the description of a storm, are admirable. *Climbing the Crags* (*Peñas arriba*, 1893) describes the patriarchal life in the northern mountains. These two novels are probably Pereda's best, despite the excellencies of many others.

Pereda is among the best artists of Spanish realism. He is noteworthy for vigor and sincerity, and possesses vital force and energy, a dignity, a sturdiness, which contrast strangely with the light Attic grace and somewhat weary cynicism of his contemporary Valera. His ideas we would consider old-fashioned, for he believed in the "good old ways," in a patriarchal system of government, docile peasants ruled by virtuous and unselfish overlords. He thought cities necessarily corrupt, and the country inevitably virtuous. He was an arch-conservative and no democrat, and he airs his views with frankness and with artistic and moral integrity. His style is massive and direct, his language rich and picturesque. He was one of Spain's best and most typical realists.

Countess Emilia Pardo Bazán (1852-1921) was the novelist of Galicia. Much more open-minded than Pereda, whom she matched in vigor, she was influenced by Zola, and sought to introduce naturalism into her country. However, it was her literary credo but not her philosophy which was naturalistic. She debated the matter in 1883 in a study which she called *La cuestión palpitante,* but the question of naturalism is far from *palpitante* today, and Pardo Bazán's literary methods seem as old-fashioned as Pereda's political ideas.

The countess' first novel, *Pascual López* (1879), had just as well be forgotten, but she is remembered for two works which give an excellent picture of life in her native and beloved Galicia: *The Manor of Ulloa (Los Pazos de Ulloa,* 1886) and its sequel *Mother Nature (La madre naturaleza,* 1887). The minor characters and the atmosphere are particularly well presented in a style which is picturesque if somewhat overloaded. Pardo Bazán wrote some excellent short stories and a number of novels much less good than her masterpieces.

Another proponent of the naturalistic method was the law professor, critic, and novelist, Leopoldo Alas (Clarín, 1852-1901). His chief work is a very long novel called *La Regenta* (1884-85), which dissects life in the city of Oviedo, sparing nothing and hesitating at no grim details. The characterization of the inhabitants, great and small, is vivid though bitter. The heroine, Ana Ozores, *The Wife of the Judge,* is a sort of Emma Bovary, who finally yields to a local Don Juan, bringing death to her husband, grief to a canon of the cathedral who loved her as much as his selfish nature would permit, and ruin to herself. The novel, despite its length, possesses real intensity. Alas wrote also a number of short stories. His critical articles show considerable acerbity, but also a desire to improve standards of writing. By the generation following, "Clarín" was esteemed while most of his contemporaries were scorned.

To Armando Palacio Valdés (1853-1939) one naturally applies the adjective pleasant. His numerous novels flow smoothly, idly, amusingly, with fairly interesting plots and natural and humorous dialogue. His analysis of character seems plausible without being profound.

*Marta y María* (1883), a study of the characters of two types of women, is one of Palacio Valdés' earliest and best novels, with the author's native Asturias as a background. *José* (1875) is a study of fishermen, less intense than Pereda's *Sotileza*. *La alegría del Capitán Ribot* (1899) presents Valencian customs. *Maximina* and *Riverita* are autobiographical, delicate, sensitive. The most popular of Palacio Valdés' works is *Sister San Sulpicio* (*La Hermana San Sulpicio*, 1899), a picturesque though rather tourist-like presentation of life and love in warm Seville. Our somewhat sickly Galician hero Ceferino, with appropriate wooings at barred windows, persuades his Gloria not to take final vows as a nun, and all is joy and happiness. Palacio Valdés' realism and sense of humor endeared him to hosts of readers at home and abroad.

The greatest novelist of the nineteenth century in Spain was unquestionably Benito Pérez Galdós (1843-1920). Born in the Canary Islands, he studied law in Madrid, though he never practised. He began publishing novels in 1870 (*La Fontana de Oro*) and continued to produce a constant stream of them up to the time of his death.

A very important sector of Galdós' work consists of his historical *Episodios nacionales* in five series, covering the history of Spain from the seventy years after 1808: forty-six volumes in all. Galdós was not seeking the picturesque, the glamorous à la Walter Scott in this remarkable presentation of his country's history. His main characters, his love intrigues, are imaginary and serve as pins on which to fix actual events, but he makes a strenuous effort, based on extensive documentation, to present not merely battles, uprisings, great events, but especially the true atmosphere of the Spain he is portraying. The statement is true that for the first time he enabled Spaniards to see themselves and their immediate past; their pusillanimity as well as their startling heroism, their failures and their successes. The first two series, beginning with *Trafalgar,* in 1873, are undoubtedly the best. The second ends with the defeat of absolutism in 1834, after the death of the tyrant Ferdinand VII. *Bailén* (1873), *Zaragoza* (1874) and *Gerona* (1874) are among the best volumes in the series. The *Episodios* are invaluable for the history of the Spanish people in the nineteenth century.

Yet this achievement by no means exhausted Galdós' energies, for all the while he was writing novels which bore on contemporary Spanish problems. *Doña Perfecta* (1876), one of Galdós' most compact works, is a somber study of fanaticism in an imaginary but plausibly presented Spanish provincial city. *Gloria* (1877) tells of the tragic love of a Spanish Catholic girl for an English Jew. *La familia de León Roch* (2 vols., 1879) shows how excessive religiosity can break up a family. *Fortunata y Jacinta* (4 vols., 1886-7) is a keen study of the middle classes of Madrid. *Ángel Guerra* (3 vols., 1891), with its scene laid in Toledo, presents contemporary mysticism. *Nazarín* (1895) suggests the mood of Tolstoi. *Misericordia* (1897) vividly studies the lower classes in Madrid. *Marianela* (1878) stands apart in Galdós' work, a sentimental idyl staged in the north, the life and death of a girl with a lovely soul in an ugly body. Her blind lover shrinks from her when he recovers his sight.

Galdós took no particular region but rather all Spain as the background for his novels, and he knew his country as no one else did. His *novelas contemporáneas* have been properly compared with Balzac's *Comédie Humaine*. No one has risen to take his place since he died.

Vicente Blasco Ibáñez (1867-1928), regional novelist par excellence of the Valencian district, belonged artistically to the nineteenth century. His first important novel, *Arroz y tartana*, appeared in 1894, and his fertile energy produced a plethora of volumes throughout his life. If one had to select two novels as his best, they would no doubt be *The Cabin* (*La Barraca*, 1898) and *Reeds and Mud* (*Cañas y barro*, 1902). The real protagonist of the former is the *huerta* or truck-garden district of Valencia, presented with singular vividness and life. The *Reeds and Mud* of the rice-growing lagoons or *Albufera* near Valencia form a fitting background for the somber tragedy filling the novel. As in the *Cabin,* the peasant characters are portrayed with deep intensity, and the reader gets a real feeling for the spirit and life of the region. Popular types are also portrayed in the short stories which compose the *Cuentos valencianos* (1896).

Blasco, ever vigorous and restless, was not content to stay actually or spiritually in his own corner. In *Sónnica la cortesana* (1901) he endeavors to re-create life in ancient Saguntum, after the manner of Flaubert's *Salammbô*. He puts forward his radical social and political ideas in a series of novels with scenes laid in various parts of Spain: *La catedral* (1903), anti-clerical, Toledo; *El intruso* (1904), Bilbao; *La bodega* (1905), stressing the evils of alcohol, Jerez; *Sangre y arena* (1908), so familiar to movie-goers as *Blood and Sand*, Seville; *Los muertos mandan* (1909), the Balearic island of Ibiza.

Blasco began to enjoy international fame, the greatest of any Spanish author since Cervantes, with *The Four Horsemen . . .* (*Los cuatro jinetes del Apocalipsis,* 1916), a stirring novel of World War I, with a moving description of the Battle of the Marne. As the author's fame and fortune grew his artistry declined. His later cosmopolitan novels such as *Mare nostrum, Los enemigos de la mujer, El Papa del mar, A los pies de Venus* (1926), are far below his earlier level. Blasco died in France, an exile from the Spanish dictatorship which he was fighting with all his force. He did not live to see the Republic, which would have delighted him, or the new dictatorship, which would have saddened him.

Literary exquisites have scorned Blasco for his turbulent naturalism, his lack of grace, delicacy, and restraint, even his lack of imagination. He was preeminently the gifted reporter, possessed of amazing vigor, master of picturesque detail, the simple and bold-lined sketch of uncomplicated characters, the skilled interpreter of his native region.

# XXV

## *The Road to Unhappiness*

IN 1898 Spain lost a war to a far more powerful nation, and Cuba and the Philippines were taken from her. In the ensuing years she was to suffer disasters in her remaining colonies, and to go through a devastating civil war, the result of which left Spain in the Fascist column. The democracies have reason to deplore that outcome, but at the moment France, England and the United States shilly-shallied and permitted the triumph of Franco, ally of Hitler and Mussolini. It was evident from the early years of Spain's last king to date that the country was restless and likely to be a prey to disorder.

### HISTORY—1898 TO THE PRESENT

Alfonso XIII was declared of age in 1902. He had considerable personal magnetism and force, and for some years at least was popular with large sections of the population, but the problems of his country were beyond his power to solve. Ever since the restoration of his father, Alfonso XII, the Conservative and the Liberal Parties had alternated in power, with no noticeable benefit to the country in either case. In the twentieth century smaller minority parties, such as the Catalan Party, the Labor Party and others won enough seats in the Cortes to make a majority vote on any question difficult to obtain. It was hard to settle any question by constitutional parliamentary means, and the result was a growing restlessness of the nation, a dissatisfaction with those who were supposed to govern it. Catalonia had long had aspirations toward autonomy,

251

and felt victimized by the central government. The Catalans were granted greater privileges (April, 1914) but were not satisfied.

The problems of the Spanish possessions in Morocco became even more acute after 1898. England and France made a secret treaty concerning North Africa in 1904, and William II of Germany broke into Moroccan affairs in 1905. The Conference of Algeciras in 1906 gave the "protection" of Morocco to France and Spain, defining their spheres. Spain had to cope with uprisings of the natives, and in the process suffered disasters at Melilla in 1909, and Annual in 1912. The Spanish public felt that affairs in Morocco were wretchedly managed, and confidence in the government was further undermined.

The agrarian problem, which had so concerned Jovellanos in the eighteenth century and various thoughtful patriots and Costa in the late nineteenth, was by no means settled, and the succeeding governments showed little interest. Practically nothing was done, either, about the great estates, the *latifundios,* owned by absentee landlords, which had existed and even grown since the Middle Ages.

There were some signs of progress, but not enough. Public works were being developed, spasmodic efforts were being made to reforest barren regions, and education was being better developed. The *Junta para ampliación de estudios* (*Committee for the Development of Study*), for example, founded for the furtherance of intellectual work on a level with the rest of Europe, marked real progress, and supplemented the decidedly old-fashioned universities.

It might be thought that the world war of 1914-18, in which Spain remained neutral, would have marked a parenthesis, at least, but it hardly did even that. Spain did prosper economically, but the other problems were only postponed. There was a near political crisis in 1917, glossed over for a time. The King, who had shown some democratic leanings, appeared to favor more and more the conservative elements in his nation. Popular discontent grew.

The season was just right for a dictator. September 13, 1923, Miguel Primo de Rivera initiated a military uprising in Barcelona, and triumphed without firing a shot. King Alfonso, who must have had previous knowledge of what was being prepared, accepted the establishment of a dictatorship involving suspension of the Constitution and of individual rights. The dictatorship was supposed to last three months. It lasted seven years. So the nineteenth century efforts toward constitutional and democratic government reached their end.

Primo de Rivera's government was first a Military Directory, then a so-called Civilian Government, because a few non-military men participated, but in reality there was but one authority: the dictator himself. His relations with the King were never well defined.

Primo de Rivera was a well-meaning and rather volatile Andalusian of no very great capability. He did manage to settle the war in Morocco with a Spanish victory over the Riffian tribes at Alhucemas in 1926. He established good roads. A new University City was begun on the outskirts of Madrid. Internal order was maintained for the moment, but Spain's problems remained the same. The country evidently wanted a functioning constitutional government, which Primo de Rivera showed no signs of approaching. He was forced to give up in January 1930, and went to Paris, to die there not long afterwards. The King called another general, Berenguer, who was supposed to observe the constitution, then an admiral, Aznar, but the system was doomed. Disorders of all sorts multiplied: strikes, five hundred and four of them in 1930 and even more the next year, student uprisings, military revolts. Anti-monarchical, anti-clerical pro-republican sentiment was growing rapidly. The military revolt at the airfield of Cuatro Vientos, near Madrid, and a civilian-military revolt at Jaca were suppressed, but two officers of the Jaca garrison who were shot became in the popular mind Republican martyrs. Many Republicans who signed a revolutionary manifesto were caught and jailed, but they continued their activities in prison. When they were tried, their leader, the former minister Alcalá-Zamora, and seventeen others were sentenced, but their sentences were remitted. This governmental leniency served only to increase Republican sentiment.

A coalition cabinet arranged to call municipal elections on April 12, 1931. All but four or five provincial capitals returned sizable Republican majorities. It was obvious that the parties of the left had triumphed and that the monarchy was doomed. Monarchists tried to temporize but Alcalá-Zamora would have none of it. Alfonso XIII, knowing that his rule was at an end, hurriedly left for the port of Cartagena April 14, leaving a manifesto declaring that he did so to avoid bloodshed.

The history of the second Spanish Republic (1931-1939), with most of whose ideals a large majority of Americans heartily sympathized, is a very tragic one. It would have had a chance of survival and success but for the doughty aid given to Franco by Mussolini and Hitler and the notorious lack of aid from France, England, and the United States.

Republican leaders in Madrid proclaimed Alcalá-Zamora as President. Catalonia had set up an autonomous republic, but was persuaded to remain within the Spanish Republic, which thus was instituted without bloodshed.

It was not to remain bloodless long. On May 10, a taxi-driver who shouted "Viva la República" was attacked by monarchists, whose club in turn was raided by Republicans, and the offices of a monarchist newspaper were torn up. A long-growing resentment against the clergy, who were supported in general by the Monarchists, showed itself, and several churches in Madrid and the rest of Spain were burned, and churchmen were attacked. Even if the extent of these excesses was exaggerated later by anti-Republican propagandists, they were bad enough and naturally induced some at home and abroad to think that the Republicans were the enemies of religion, unholy monsters who should not be trusted in a government. Further disorders were provoked by Anarchists and Syndicalists and other extreme leftists. Suppressing the disorders involved bloodshed. The provisional government proceeded with energy.

A constituent Cortes with leftist leanings was elected. The early Republic was indeed the product of intellectuals. The number of professors (sixty-five) and doctors (forty-one) in the assembly is astonishing. There were one hundred and twenty-three lawyers and twenty-four working men.

The constitution adopted by this group was liberal, socialistic in character. It began: "Spain is a republic of workers of all classes." It provided for an elected unicameral Cortes, a president, premier, and cabinet responsible to it, separation of Church and state with full freedom of worship, and secular education. A special law provided the dissolution and confiscation of the property of any religious order exacting more than the three canonical vows of its members. This was aimed straight at the Jesuits, whose influence in former governments was regarded as excessive.

With Alcalá-Zamora as president of the new Republic and Manuel Azaña as Premier, the Cortes passed a great many laws according to the leftist program. Civil marriage and divorce were provided for, agrarian reforms instituted, a new penal code adopted, various labor laws passed, the army reformed, and education greatly aided. The Republican support of popular education was especially admirable, and several thousand new schools were actually established. The Azaña government made a strenuous effort to renovate Spanish national life.

Many obviously regarded the reforms as too sweeping. The Government dealt vigorously with its opponents, and had opposition from both conservatives and extreme radicals. Hence when new elections were called for November 19, 1933, the Left won only ninety-nine seats in the Cortes. The Center held one hundred and sixty-seven, and the Right two hundred and seven. These conservatives and moderates accomplished very little, and incurred much enmity in settling a Catalonian outbreak and a general strike in Oviedo. The strike assumed the proportions of a rebellion (October 1934), and some thirteen hundred people were killed in fighting before government troops reestablished order. Political squabbles of various sorts marked the year 1935. New elections were called for in January 1936 and a leftist coalition, led by Azaña and called the Popular Front, was victorious. Unfortunately the victory was followed by violence: murders, strikes, burning of churches, attacks on priests and nuns. The conservatives were desperate, and it was no secret that Fascist groups were planning a rebellion. Their backing by Mussolini and Hitler was no secret, either. Political murders became more frequent, and the Government seemed unable to cope with the situation.

On July 17, 1936, the Spanish troops in Morocco under General Francisco Franco rebelled. The following day the commanders of various garrisons in Spain joined the "Glorious Movement," as its partisans called it. In Madrid and Barcelona it was quickly suppressed, with attendant disorders, but Franco began landing troops, including many Moors, in Southern Spain, and Andalusia was soon his. His support came mainly from (1) the rich, and the large landowners, including most of the nobility; (2) high officers of the army, most of whom had never liked the Republic; (3) many members of the clergy, who violently opposed and feared the radicals, and felt cruelly treated by them; (4) most of all by Mussolini and, to a lesser degree, by Hitler. Franco was far more to the liking of the dictators than any leftist government could possibly be. Moreover, Germans and Italians found Spain a splendid war laboratory, a fine ground for practical maneuvers. The Loyalists (Republicans) estimated the number of Italian troops fighting against them at a hundred thousand or so, plus an indeterminate and varying number of Germans, mainly in technical services. Supplies and troops could be landed for Franco in the South and through Portugal, whose dictator, Salazar, was favorable to the Fascists. It is perfectly evident now that Franco's rebellion in Spain was just one phase of the movement toward totalitarianism.

Spaniards have always been tough fighters when aroused and the Loyalists fought the combination against them with amazing tenacity. Madrid withstood a heroic siege, and was never stormed. Italian troops suffered a noteworthy defeat at Guadalajara. The Loyalists were at first aided by the Russians, and enjoyed air superiority. The Russians gradually withdrew their support and Franco's superiority in planes and *matériel* of all sorts became overwhelming. A farcical nonintervention commission, largely influenced by England, kept supplies from reaching the Loyalists, while they poured in to Franco's troops from Italy and Germany. Despite the preponderance of sympathy for the Loyalists in the United States (over seventy per cent, by Gallup poll), an embargo forbade supplies from there. There were Communists among the Loyalists, though never in a majority, and it seems that England during the Baldwin and Chamberlain governments, of unhappy memory, and the United States, if the Dies Committee meant anything, were mortally afraid of aiding world Communism. It was only later that the Democracies shook Stalin's hand and clasped him to their military bosoms.

Franco's progress was slow, but fairly steady. Loyalist resistance was crushed in the northwest by the end of 1937. In April, 1938, Catalonia was cut off from Madrid. Barcelona, since the Loyalists now had very few planes, was subjected to merciless bombings. In late 1938 the Loyalists could hold out no longer. The government and many troops fled north into France. Franco entered Barcelona in triumph on January 26, 1939. About a million Spaniards lay dead as war casualties, and there were some six hundred thousand prisoners. The latter number was reduced by Franco's firing squads. Special courts were quickly set up to judge Communists and Republicans.

Franco obviously had a most difficult task of rehabilitation on his hands. The war had done considerable damage, which he set about to repair, partly with the forced labor of prisoners. Probably half the country was still Republican in sympathy. Those who were not jailed or shot had to conform to Franco's dictatorial regime. In foreign policy there was no problem. Spain was necessarily allied with the Axis. But the chief problem was to get more food for Spaniards to eat. That problem has not yet been solved.

# XXVI

## An Introspective Generation: 1898

### 1898: REGENERATION

THE Spanish Republic of 1931 was the product of preceding intellectual ferment. In the last third of the nineteenth century there was developing in Spain a more critical attitude. Spaniards meditated more deeply on their own national problems. It was evident to any thinking person that things were not going too well with the country. Spanish colonies had been lost one by one. Internal strife, the Carlist wars, distressed the land, and the political system was obviously inefficient, even corrupt. The disasters of the Spanish-American War in 1898 were a sort of final blow and at the same time a symbol of national misfortune. Spain had assumed the forms of limited monarchy, even of democratic representative government, but the reality had changed very little indeed. For centuries Spain had exalted Church and King, and had put forth extraordinary efforts in furthering ideals which had not been achieved. It was only natural that a pessimistic soul-searching should be indulged in, and that many wished to make a complete break with the immediate past in pursuit of an obviously needed regeneration. Galdós and Leopoldo Alas had pointed out many of the evils of Spanish traditionalism, and their work, in a different mode, was continued by earnest successors.

### THINKERS AND ESSAYISTS

Joaquín Costa (1844-1911), for example, urged Spaniards to lock tightly the tomb of the Cid, that is, to break with the past and think of the present. He thought that the only cure for inefficient government was a dictatorship which would "Europeanize" Spain, impose upon her political and social procedures which had worked elsewhere. Costa's public speeches were even more influential than his books, which made challenging suggestions in various fields: law, education, politics, agrarian problems, and literature.

Pompeyo Gener (1848-1921) also called for a dictatorship, "a scientific dictatorship, exercised by a Darwinistic Cromwell grafted on to a Louis XIV, which would be at the same time implacable and splendid." No country has been blessed by anything of the sort thus far in the world's history. Gener expresses this ideal in a study of national decadence in his book *Heresies* (1887).

Angel Ganivet (1865-1898) is unquestionably one of the most important predecessors of the Generation of 1898. He was a sensitive Andalusian, a Grenadine who served as Consul in Antwerp, Helsinki, and Riga, and from the north he could meditate on his own country's ills. His attitude toward Spain must have paralleled a personal depression, for he drowned himself in the Dwina.

Ganivet wrote literary studies: *Men of the North* (*Hombres del norte*), a play, *The Sculptor of His Own Soul* (*El escultor de su alma*), an appreciation of his native city, *Fair Granada* (*Granada la bella*), letters from abroad, *Finnish Letters* (*Cartas finlandesas*), and two philosophical novels whose Spanish hero, Pío Cid, is an excellent conqueror and a poor administrator. His most significant work is his *Idearium español* (1897), a searching investigation of national diseases, with prescriptions for the future, brilliantly stated, though without logical order or system. Ganivet insists that Spain must make a strong effort of will to develop the best in her own tradition, modifying certain European contributions according to the peculiar individualistic genius of Spain.

One of the most vigorous spirits in modern Spain was the sturdy Basque Miguel de Unamuno (1864-1937): university professor of Greek, novelist, dramatist, poet, essayist, philosopher. He was driven from the rectorship of the University of Salamanca by the dictator Primo de Rivera, and exiled to the barren island of Fuerteventura. He returned and was in high favor during the early days of the Republic. He died in prison after Franco came to power.

Unamuno's dramas were not successful. His novels are hardly novels, and in fact he called them *nivolas* instead of *novelas*. External setting and action are mainly lacking, and the characters seem to be abstractions of intellect and sentiment, who go about discussing vital problems. Nevertheless the novels possess considerable intensity, much wit and real originality, as shown in *Peace During War* (*Paz en la guerra*), *Aunt Tula* (*La tía Tula*), *Mist* (*Niebla*), *Abel Sánchez, Love and Pedagogy* (*Amor y Pedagogía*). Some of Unamuno's short stories, as in the collections *The Mirror of Death* (*El espejo de la muerte*) and *Three Exemplary Novels and a Prologue* (*Tres novelas ejemplares y un prólogo*), show him at his best—intense, challenging, sparkling.

As a poet Unamuno is rugged in form, vigorous and sincere in expression, deeply personal. There is no grace and lightness in his poems, but the adjective spiritual properly applies. Unamuno uses particularly the sonnet and the *romance*. Unrhymed octosyllables are used in the remarkably intense poem, *El Cristo de Velázquez*.

The novels, plays and poems of Unamuno are not really very different from his essays, the genre in which he is happiest, in which his unsystematic but penetrating mind, his vast culture, can best display themselves. There is hardly any human problem or contemporary theme which he does not touch upon, and his obvious sincerity makes one overlook his inconsistencies, his excessive use of paradoxes. He has faith in the individual and belief in the possible progress of his beloved Spain.

Probably the best single book of Unamuno is his *The Tragic Sense of Life* (*El sentimiento trágico de la vida*). The tragedy comes from the conflict between reason and the longing for immortality. Unamuno writes with great earnestness, not only with his reason but with his feelings: "with his whole soul and body" he says. He believes in immortality because he needs to in order to live, even against logic.

Unamuno's *Life of Don Quixote and Sancho* (*Vida de Don Quijote y Sancho,* 1905) contains much more of Unamuno than of Cervantes. In fact the commentator says he wishes to free the living Quixote from the dead Cervantes. So the work is no literary commentary but rather a sort of tract in which Unamuno can develop ideas suggested by Don Quixote.

Unamuno was deeply admired by most literate Spaniards and greatly influenced them.

José Martínez Ruiz, better known by his pen name of "Azorín" (1874- ), is an essayist of a different sort, quiet instead of turbulent, delicate rather than rugged. Azorín is the observer and the critic, standing at one side and watching the performance of life. His observations are always keen, exact, reported in a style that seems gentle yet penetrating.

Azorín is thoroughly typical of the Generation of 1898 in his likes and dislikes, his vital attitude. He began, in his twenties, by lambasting older contemporaries then highly esteemed. The last third of the nineteenth century was an age of rhetoric in Spain, and Azorín was always the sworn enemy of rhetoric, which constituted a part of "lo viejo," and the young men of '98 disliked that which was old. Not necessarily "los viejos," because old men like Pompeyo Gener might be young in spirit.

The Generation of 1898, including Azorín, was characterized by a critical rather than a positive attitude, by *abulia* or lack of will. The title of one of Azorín's early works is *The Will* (*La voluntad,* 1902), which, along with *Antonio Azorín* (1903), constitutes a series of essays on Spanish life. The nostalgic *Confessions of a Little Philosopher* (*Confesiones de un pequeño filósofo,* 1904) describes the author's school days in a boarding school run by the Piarist Fathers, and presents a real and detailed picture of an important aspect of Spanish life in the 1880's.

Some of Azorín's most valuable contributions to the literature of his time will be found in his volumes containing articles of a critical nature on many aspects of Spanish life and literature. His attitude is decidedly unacademic, and he always seeks to give the particular and peculiar color and flavor of any man, place, or epoch he chooses to discuss, with delicate and sensitive appreciation. If in his earlier years he was severe toward the dramatists of the Golden Age, he later made amends. Noteworthy among his literary essays are the volumes *Al margen de los clásicos, Clásicos y modernos,* *Los valores literarios.*

Some of Azorín's works are entitled *"novelas,"* but they are at best novels without plots, descriptive and interpretive pieces which are no less valuable because they follow no set pattern. *Don Juan* and *Doña Inés* are admirable character sketches, conveying a delicate perfume of person and place. In his later years Azorín became at least a semi-convert to surrealism: *Féliz Vargas* and *White on Blue (Blanco en azul).* They are far from being his best. Nor do his poems add much to his fame.

Azorín possesses a style very much his own. It is quiet, in a minor key, apparently simple, direct, singularly expressive. The author has a passion for the exact word, the precise shade, and his writing is quite the opposite of the rhetorical burbling of an orator like Emilio Castelar (president of the first Spanish Republic) or of Azorín's contemporary Ricardo León. The lack of vigor in Azorín's writing may be more apparent than real. He is one of the best interpreters that Spain, and especially Castile, has ever had.

## POETS

Romanticism emphasized subjectivity. Realism and Naturalism sought objectivity in attitude, without too much care for form. "Modernism," a term applied particularly to a Hispanic poetic movement toward the end of the century, was in a way a protest against both. It parallels and often imitates the Parnassian and Symbolist efflorescence in France (notably Leconte de Lisle and Verlaine) and was a reaction in Spain against the verbose intensity of Núñez de Arce and the essentially prosaic verse of Campoamor.

The chief figure of the Modernistic movement was not a Spaniard but a Nicaraguan, Rubén Darío (1867-1916). His life was disordered, his art of singular perfection. His first poetic god was Victor Hugo, but he boasted of being widely read in Spanish literature also.

Darío's first significant book, *Blue (Azul)*, published in 1888, consisted of both prose and verse. It was praisefully reviewed in

Spain by Juan Valera. The other two most important volumes of Darío are *Profane Poems* (*Prosas profanas,* 1896) and *Songs of Life and Hope* (*Cantos de vida y esperanza,* 1905). In addition he wrote a considerable amount of prose.

Darío was always an exquisite, whose lines are pearls and silver, delicately chiseled, artistically polished. His was a highly aristocratic art, and he hated like the plague the commonplace and the crude. He was never trying to teach any noble lesson, to be a preacher to humanity, only to write verse of suggestive imagery, of marmoreal perfection, of deep musicality.

Darío's influence upon Spanish poets was decisive and can still be seen today, for he was one of the best versifiers who ever tuned lines in the Spanish language. Experiments in verse were being made in Spain, as, for example, by Salvador Rueda (1857-1933). He was a Malagan, with true Andalusian brilliance and melody. His experiments in verse were not always successful, for he was gifted with excessive fluency. If his poems are uneven in merit, at their best they are beautifully harmonious and colorful.

Eduardo Marquina (1879-   ), though a Catalan, wrote his poems and dramas in Castilian. He is distinctly a modernist in his verse, which often combines vigor and gravity with harmony. His *Odas* were published in 1900, and many consider *Vendimión* (1909) his best work. His *Canciones del momento* (1910) show him applying his serious muse to contemporary problems. His plays have won greater renown than his poems.

Francisco Villaespesa (1877-1935) was one of the closer imitators of Darío. He combines Oriental color with a perhaps affected melancholy. Some of his poems are sincere and moving, but the bright jewels of his verse are sometimes paste.

Emilio Carrere (1880-   ), inspired by Darío and even more by Verlaine, is the poet of Bohemia. Some of his poems of popular scenes are excellent, and his facile sentimentality won him many readers.

One of the best followers of Darío was the Sevillian Manuel Machado (1874-   ). That is to say, Machado follows Darío in his Parnassianism, but there are other strings on his lyre. With the refinements of Paris he combines the fire and delicate sensuousness of Seville. His technical mastery of modern verse forms is displayed in the early volume *Alma* (1902), containing some of his best poems, which possess a wealth of color and impressive descriptive ability. He is a painter with words and sounds, able to achieve vivid effects with economy of means. His volume *Caprichos* (1905) is more Andalusian; the poems are of unequal merit. *Cante hondo* (1912) and *Sevilla y otros poemas* (1918) are devoted to his native region, whose spirit he fully incarnates, with an artistic stylization of popular motifs and a warm suggestiveness. He is never profound, but few poets have hymned sensuous beauty more melodiously.

Manuel's brother Antonio Machado was also born in Seville, in 1875, but he spent his youth and most of his life in Castile, and he is the modern poet who best portrays the grave and even somber spirit of that region. His output is small, for he speaks only when deep feeling compels him and shuns the easy emotion, the facile phrase. His poems are concentrated, never diffuse, intense, serious, classic in line and sober in expression. His most characteristic poems may be found in *Campos de Castilla* (1912), in which he presents the windswept high plains, the almost barren landscape, the stern and even dark character of the peasants of Castile. The longish narrative poem in the volume, called *La tierra de Alvar-González,* is a poetic treatment in ballad meter of a sanguinary family feud, which harmonizes perfectly with its background. Many consider Antonio Machado the best Spanish poet of his generation (d. 1939).

Others might prefer the far more fluent Juan Ramón Jiménez (1881-  ). He has poured forth his verse in volume after volume, for he has the creative exuberance of the true Andalusian, and he is a poet who is best read in selections. Yet he is a poet of enormous talent. He began with *Violet Souls* (*Almas de Violeta*) and *Water Lilies* (*Ninfeas,* 1900) as a clear follower of Darío, but soon developed a far more personal and original style. His chief quality is refinement, his dominant tone one of gentle melancholy; one of his volumes, in fact, is called *Melancolía.* As in the case of other modernists, his subjects do not much matter. It is the emotion which he can draw from them and his delicate and melodious expression which are important. He evolved more and more away from ornateness, often an Andalusian curse, toward extreme simplicity. Yet he preserves the Andalusian's sensuousness and keenness of perception.

It would be hard to put José María Gabriel y Galán (1870-1905) in any literary school. Born in Salamanca, he became a country schoolmaster and retired to become a farmer. His poetry is simple and sincere, poetry of the soil, connected with ancient Spanish tradition rather than with any modern group. He sings of flocks, herds, nature, and country life with real emotion and sincerity. *Castellanas* and *Extremeñas* (about 1902) are noteworthy early collections, interpretations of rustic life in Castile and Estremadoura. *Nuevas Castellanas* appeared in 1905, *Religiosas* in 1906. He is not a profound or a highly cultured poet, but in his verse one will find much of the true Spanish spirit.

## DRAMATISTS

The second Spaniard to receive the Nobel prize for literature was, like Echegaray, a dramatist. His name is Jacinto Benavente (1866- ), but his plays are very different indeed from his predecessors'. Benavente is a Madrilene, an urban type, who carefully avoids Echegaray's screaming histrionics. Indeed, most of Benavente's plays are so quiet that they seem almost undramatic. They are mainly dramas of social satire, and the chief victims are the members of the upper bourgeoisie of Madrid. This is particularly true of the plays written between 1894 and 1903. The satire is keen, ingenious, pleasantly ironical, and the observation of life exact, artistically portrayed. The tone is one of mildly cynical tolerance and detachment. *Feeding the Animals* (*La comida de las fieras,* 1898) is typical of this earlier period. The theme is the eagerness with which supposed friends of a now ruined aristocrat pounce like Harpies on his remains at an auction of his goods. The play is based on an actual occurrence. *The Governor's Wife* (*La gobernadora,* 1901) satirized provincial social and political corruption.

With *Saturday Night* (*La noche del sábado,* 1903) Benavente seeks a more cosmopolitan milieu, though he continues to satirize his fellow Madrilenes in *The Evil Doers of Good* (*Los malhechores del bien*). The latter play raps supposedly beneficent reformers who insist on controlling the lives and actions of the objects of their charity.

Somewhat apart among Benavente's scores of plays is *Bonds of Interest* (*Los intereses creados,* 1909), often thought of as his masterpiece. It is in the form of the semi-improvised Italian *commedia dell' arte,* with characters named Polichinela, Silvia, Colombina, Leandro, Crispín, Pantalón, etc. Crispín brings his intrigues to a successful conclusion only because of the pure love of Leandro for Silvia. So, as the author practically says, Crispín and Leandro are two sides of humanity, the base and the ideal, inevitably bound to one another, earth and sky, impossible each without the other.

Another play which stands apart among Benavente's works is *La malquerida,* translated into English under the peculiar title *The Passion Flower.* The setting is rural, the theme the tragic passion of step-father for step-daughter. The play has real intensity, and is Benavente's favorite.

If this Nobel prize winner's attitude is cynical with regard to his fellow man, he at least has great sympathy for children, and has included among his scores of plays various charming plays written especially for the young.

Gregorio Martínez Sierra (1881-   ) wrote lyric poetry and novels, but he is best known as a playwright. Less talented than Benavente, he none the less possesses real dramatic ability and a feminine delicacy which may be the contribution of his wife and collaborator, María de la O Lejárraga—for example, in *Cradle Song* (*Canción de cuna,* 1911), which, with little plot, is the portrayal of the feelings of a group of nuns toward a foundling baby girl who grows up among them. The play possesses excellent characterization and a wistful atmosphere. Some of his other plays are *The Mistress of the House* (*El ama de la casa*), *Spring in Autumn* (*Primavera en otoño*), *An August Night's Dream* (*Sueño de una noche de agosto*), *Mother* (*Mamá*), *The Kingdom of God* (*El reino de Dios*). The grace and comic verve of Martínez Sierra's plays were well brought out by the chief actress in his dramatic troop, Catalina Bárcena.

Manuel Linares Rivas (1867- ) was particularly fond of the thesis play, with deft satirical touches. *An Old Family* (*El abolengo,* 1904) attacks pride of lineage. *The Claw* (*La garra,* 1914) shows the cruelty of law that does not allow divorce. Linares' characters are natural, his dialogue witty, his action rapid. Even though his plays have a certain sameness, they are good theater, and were quite successful on the stage.

The verse drama was best represented by Eduardo Marquina. He regularly selects themes from national history or legend and treats them with dramatic effectiveness, in ringing lines. *The Cid's Daughters* (*Las hijas del Cid,* 1908) comes from the *Poema del Cid. In Flanders the Sun Has Set* (*En Flandes se ha puesto el sol,* 1910), generally rated Marquina's best, has its scenes laid in the Low Countries in the time of Philip II, and the conflict between Dutchmen and Spaniards is vividly and dramatically shown. *The Flowers of Aragon* (*Las flores de Aragón*) is a good dramatization of the circumstances surrounding the marriage of Ferdinand and Isabella. Marquina's plays combine vigor of action with poetic charm and movement of verse.

The brothers Serafín (1871-1938) and Joaquín (1873- ) Alvarez Quintero were born in Utrera, south of Seville, and their very numerous plays show all the warmth, color, grace, and wit commonly attributed to Andalusians. Their works were written in collaboration and at their best have delicate characterization and real humor. No wonder audiences for a generation laughed until the tears came.

The Quinteros are, however, more than professional funny men. In short plays such as *El patio* (1900), *Las flores* (1901), they catch the poetry and not just the fun of Andalusia. *Los Galeotes* (1900) is a serious dramatic treatment of ingratitude, named after the galley-slave episode in *Don Quijote. Doña Clarines* (1909) is a good character study. *Don Juan, buena persona* is not much of a drama, but it is a most amusing study of a Don Juan whose ex-flames stick to him and keep depending on him for spiritual and material aid. He has a kind heart and they cause him a deal of worry.

The Quinteros are admirable in the *sainetes,* short bits taken from life, quite in the tradition of the *pasos* of Lope de Rueda, the *entremeses* of Cervantes, and the *sainetes* of Ramón de la Cruz. In modern times such little one-act plays have been termed the *género chico,* "little plays," and have had great vitality. Carlos Arniches (1866-  ) wrote similar skits, with scenes from the life of the popular classes in Madrid. Pedro Muñoz Seca (1881-  ), with longer pieces of foolishness on the stage, enjoyed a great if ephemeral success.

## THE NOVEL

The generation of 1898 tended to protest against what had immediately preceded, for example, to make the drama undramatic. So the novel, as in the case of Azorín, paid less attention, or practically none at all, to plot, to the development of intrigue.

This is true in the numerous novels of Pío Baroja (1872-  ), who was born in the Basque country which is the scene of some of his novels. He was trained in medicine, but practised only a brief while. For a time he ran a bakery in Madrid, but the itch for writing was too strong for him, and he became a novelist. That is, he wrote prose with a certain continuity, but without definite plan, and those who demand structure in a novel will not like Baroja. People's lives, he contends, do not fall into neat patterns, and so when he has written about three hundred pages about his characters, he just stops. He has grouped his novels in series, but the classifications ("The Race," "The Sea," "The Cities," "The Struggle for Life," etc.) are not very significant, except perhaps the number of novels making up the "Memoirs of a Man of Action." Baroja is a sedentary man himself, even if he has been about Europe a bit, and he takes his action in writing about it. He sees no solution of life's problems; the only thing to do is to act. Hence he writes about the man of action that he is not. Baroja has denied that there is any such thing as a Generation of 1898, but he surely belonged to a group whose gifts were for criticism, for reflection, rather than for action.

Baroja began by writing stories which were really impressionistic sketches of the Basque country, gathered into volumes called *Dark Lives* (*Vidas sombrías*) and *Basque Idyls* (*Idilios vascos*). His first full-length novel was *La casa de Aizgorri* (1900), the story of a distillery in the North. Much better is *The Lord of Labraz* (*El Mayorazgo de Labraz,* 1903) which presents vividly the atmosphere of a small moribund Spanish city. The blind hero finally burns his estate and, having "recovered his will," starts out with a girl to tramp the roads of Spain.

One of Baroja's best stories of pure action, strictly episodical in plan, is *Zalacaín el aventurero* (1909). Zalacaín, a fine Basque type, lives fully and dangerously until he is finally shot smuggling arms across the French border.

The trilogy of low life in Madrid (*Weeds, The Quest, Red Dawn,* all in 1904) is indeed drawn from life, and contains more vivid portrayals of characters and scenes, as far removed as possible from "castles in Spain."

All Baroja's novels contain his opinions about everything on God's green earth, which looks brown and sere to this hard-bitten Basque, but one might single out *The Way of Perfection* (*Camino de perfección,* 1902) and *The Tree of Knowledge* (*El árbol de la ciencia,* 1911) as particularly significant. *Silvestre Paradox* (1901) and *Paradox, Rey* (1906) are fantastic but sprightly.

Baroja has spoken freely about himself, as in *Youth and Self-worship* (*Juventud, Egolatría,* 1917). He admits the influence of Nietzsche, Dickens, Balzac, and Dostoievski, but no one formed his style, which is rugged, direct, but capable of descriptive power and at times even of lyric grace. His ideal, he says, would be to produce "rhetoric in a minor key." There is no reason to question the sincerity of the pessimistic views he holds, even if one feels he takes a certain perverse pleasure in being opposed to so much: an anti-miltarist, anti-clerical, an enemy of sham, of obscurantism, of politicians, and of professors. He has a great sympathy for the under-dog, the oppressed, the maladjusted, and he utters his opinions rapidly and directly. Force and sincerity are his obvious virtues.

Ramón María del Valle-Inclán (1869-1936) was the opposite of

Baroja in many ways. Baroja had an apparent scorn for art, Valle-Inclán was artistic to the end of his aristocratic finger tips. Baroja wrote along carelessly, turbulently. Valle-Inclán polished every melodious sentence. He was an exquisite with a limited range, but he achieved singular perfection within it.

Valle-Inclán wrote poetry and plays in addition to his novels. As a poet he followed Rubén Darío, producing poetry of form rather than of ideas, harmonious, rhythmic, suggestive. His dramas are also poetic in their suggestiveness, vague in construction, lacking in dramatic intensity. They read much better than they act. *Romance de lobos* (1908), filled with strange superstitions and somber characters, is usually considered the best of them.

Valle-Inclán began by imitating the decadent *Diaboliques* of Barbey d'Aurevilly in the six *Femeninas* (1894). They are by no means up to the author's best work, probably to be found in his four *Sonatas,* one for each season of the year. These harmonious literary sonatas constitute the sentimental history of a neo-Casanova, the Marquis of Bradomín, who was "ugly, a sentimentalist, and a Catholic."

Three of Valle-Inclán's novels are concerned with the last Carlist war: *Crusaders in the Cause* (*Los Cruzados de la causa,* 1908), *The Gleam of the Bonfire* (*El resplandor de la hoguera*), and *Gerfalcons of Yesteryear* (*Gerifaltes de antaño:* both 1909). In them the author endeavors to give the atmosphere of a period, not its history, which is merely incidental to his purpose.

*Tirano Banderas* (1926) is the story of a Latin-American, presumably a Mexican, tyrant who rules with blood and iron, and shoots himself and his daughter when he sees that his race is run. The series of novels under the title *El ruedo ibérico,* which treat Spain of the late nineteenth century, are of less value.

In his later years Valle-Inclán wrote a number of dramatized novels which he called *Esperpentos,* works filled with popular characters and a sort of stylized popular speech, fantastic and realistic at the same time, always satirical.

Valle-Inclán always insisted that in literature the essential thing is style. His own is a remarkable instrument in his hands, musical, bejewelled, smooth, sensitive, expressive. Like Darío or Juan Ramón Jiménez, he scorns the commonplace, the cliché, always seeking to "put words together for the first time." He is at the opposite pole from the tumultuous and helter-skelter Blasco Ibáñez, of whom he vigorously disapproved. In his earlier period he was affected by Gabriele d'Annunzio and the Portuguese Eça de Queiroz, but his later style, with his vocabulary enriched by popular terms from the whole Spanish-speaking world and his ironic spirit intensified, is more original and forceful. He achieves a fusion of the infinitely exquisite with the extremely popular. His characters are not cut by any pattern of Puritan morality, but they love and sin according to high esthetic standards, elegantly, amid the faded brocades of a palace in the picturesque countryside of Valle-Inclán's native Galicia or the torrid heat of tropical Mexico. His characters, high or low, always have an aura, an atmosphere. Valle-Inclán was throughout his career the conscientious artist who tried never to let his reader down.

Gabriel Miró (1879- ), a native of Alicante, also possesses a rich and polished style, embellishing the commonplace like Azorín, suggesting the rare and precious like Valle-Inclán. Many of his works he called *estampas,* literary prints of literal and symbolic beauty. One of his best works is his *Figures of the Passion of Our Lord.*

The Asturian Ramón Pérez de Ayala, born in Oviedo in 1880, is the most cerebral of contemporary poets and novelists. His subtle and restless mind was trained by the Jesuits, whom he violently attacked in his first full-fledged novel, *A.M.D.G.* (1910). He has published numerous articles of criticism on various subjects, for he is an excellent critic as well as a creator.

As a poet Ayala is quite apart from Darío and his followers, for with him thought is always of prime importance, and he seeks poetic expression of the idea, not merely beautiful form and emotional suggestiveness. Noteworthy volumes of his verse are *La Paz del sendero, El sendero innumerable* and *El sendero andante.*

By most readers Ayala is no doubt considered principally as a novelist. His *Shadows on the Heights* (*Tinieblas en las cumbres,* 1907) has episodes and characters of sub-marginal morality and is artistically not quite mature, but it provides rollicking fun and ironies both delicate and broad. *A.M.D.G.* (1910) is a furious attack on the Jesuits, which suffers from its very violence, but it contains impressive character sketches and vivid writing. *The Fox's Paw* (*La pata de la raposa,* 1912) shows greater artistic power, and *Go-betweens and Dance Girls* (*Troteras y danzaderas,* 1913) even more. They both deal with the literary and artistic *demi-monde* of Madrid, and they are helter-skelter in arrangement, but rich in characterization, highly stimulating in thought. Ayala constantly passes from bawdy episode to deep philosophical discussion. His attitude is always vital, not conventional. He is suggestive of Aldous Huxley, though he remains Spanish and broadly human.

Ayala's short stories, as grouped in *Under the Sign of Artemis* (*Bajo el signo de Artemisa*) and *The World's Umbilicus* (*El ombligo del mundo*), are remarkable for humor, irony, human sympathy, tragic intensity. The three stories which he calls "poematic novels" appeared in *Prometeo* (1916). The two stories included with *Prometeo* in this volume, *Sunday Sunlight* (*Luz de domingo*) and *The Fall of the House of Limón* (*La caída de los Limones*), are among the best in contemporary Spanish literature. They are all tragedies, painted in the tones of a Ribera, deeply felt, poignantly presented, with characters of full humanity who come to grief because of unfortunate surroundings, dragged down by fate, not by moral delinquencies.

*Belarmino y Apolonio* (1921) tells in somewhat rambling and rather intricate fashion of two cobblers of Ayala's favorite city "Pilares" which has strong resemblances to Oviedo, capital of Ayala's native Asturias. The story itself does not much matter, but the attitude of the characters and their philosophical implications do. Belarmino is the introvert, the dreamer; Apolonio the extravert, the man of dramatic action. Their rivalry continues even when they are both inmates of an asylum for the aged. The conflict gives rise to deep thought and real humor.

Most would agree that Ayala reached the summit of his powers in *Tiger John* (*Tigre Juan*) and its sequel *The Herb-Doctor Treats His Honor* (*El curandero de su honra,* 1926). Here Ayala's philosophical bent, his startlingly vital creative power, his humor, his deftness in description and characterization and his varied and vigorous though subtle style show at their best. "Tigre Juan" is rather more than a life-size figure, with faint touches of caricature, but he is also an intensely alive sample of humanity in its Spanish branch.

Ayala has one of the largest vocabularies in Spanish literature, but he uses his rich stock to fit an exact word to his meaning, to gain preciseness as well as picturesqueness. Political and other duties (he was ambassador to England during the Republic) have kept him from enriching his literary generation with further works to match or surpass *Prometeo, Belarmino y Apolonio* and *Tigre Juan*.

Ricardo León (1877- ) enjoyed considerable popularity for his novels, which may be said to mark a reaction against the spirit of 1898. León is a traditionalist, who loves to glorify Spain's past splendors in a fine old-fashioned rhetorical style which made a chair in the Spanish Academy his natural seat. His prose flows on in rotund periods, as do the "hours which fall isochronously, like beads from the rosary of eternity," to quote one of his own phrases. In *Casta de hidalgos* (1909) he shows the sad end of a young man who leaves his home and his secure fireside to expose himself to all the modern winds that blow. He returns ruined, broken. The novel contains, in the form of a dream, an evocation of the fifteenth century Santillana del Mar. Further novels of Ricardo León are *Comedia sentimental, El amor de los amores, Alcalá de los Zegríes, Amor de caridad*. In all of these we find a mystic note, poetic suggestiveness, a decidedly overblown style.

Other novelists of the first part of this century pleased a certain public. Concha Espina (1877- ) has numerous novels and short stories to her credit. She gives a wealth of realistic detail, most successfully in *The Sphinx of Maragatería* (*La esfinge maragata*), a portrayal of the picturesque customs of a remote region of León, near Astorga. Concha Espina is never profound, but her sincere sentimental note is pleasing to many.

Alejandro Pérez Lugín wrote a highly popular novel of student life at Santiago in *La casa de la Troya* (1915). Eduardo Zamacois,

Felipe Trigo, Rafael López de Haro and Alberto Insúa were among numerous cultivators of the erotic novel. They possessed considerable psychological insight and a certain grace of style.

## SCHOLARSHIP

Spain in the past has produced noteworthy scholars. The greatest of the nineteenth century was Marcelino Menéndez y Pelayo (1856-1912). Possessed of a phenomenal memory and extraordinary industry, he illumined almost every phase of Spanish literature in his numerous studies, which are obligatory reading for students of literature. Some of his important studies are *La ciencia española* (1876), *Horacio en España* (1877), *Historia de los heterodoxos españoles* (1880-82), *Calderón y su teatro* (1881), *Historia de las ideas estéticas en España* (9 volumes, 1883-89), an edition of the *Obras dramáticas de Lope de Vega,* with highly valuable prefaces in the thirteen folio volumes, *Antología de poetas líricos castellanos* (13 volumes, 1890-1908, up to the sixteenth century), *Los orígenes de la novela* (1905-1910, up to the sixteenth century). These are only the major works. The achievement is amazing. Even if Menéndez Pelayo's style is a bit florid and his prejudices all in favor of Spain and Catholicism, his critical judgment is keen and his information sound as well as extensive.

Among other scholars who follow him, the greatest is Ramón Menéndez Pidal (1869-    ), one of the best Romance philologists of the present day. His scholarly discipline is stricter than that of Menéndez Pelayo, and his texts of the *Cantar de mío Cid* (3 vols., Madrid, 1906-11, with a study) and the *Primera crónica general* (Madrid, 1906) have won unusual admiration. He has extensively studied the Spanish epic, the ballads, the Spanish *juglares* (minstrels), the origins of lyric poetry, and many another phase of Spanish literature. His *Manuel de gramática histórica* remains the standard work on the subject. His *La España del Cid* shows his keenness as a historical investigator.

The most noted historian in Spain is Rafael Altamira (1866-    ), who has written a great many volumes bearing on Spanish history.

His outlook is broad, his attitude liberal, and he has always sought to recount the whole history of Spanish culture and institutions, not merely dynastic changes, wars, and political vicissitudes. His fundamental publication is his *Historia de España y de la civilización española* (4 vols., 1900-1911).

The Spanish philosopher who is best known in the present epoch is José Ortega Gasset (1883- ), for many years professor of metaphysics in the University of Madrid, founder and director of the most important literary magazine in twentieth century Spain, the *Revista de Occidente*. If Ortega's views are often pessimistic and his statements arbitrary, they are at least challenging and always gracefully expressed. The seven volumes of *El espectador* (1916-29) contain essays on all sorts of subjects. *España invertebrada* (1922) is by way of being an attack on Spanish tradition, and was vigorously attacked in turn. The *Meditaciones del Quijote, La deshumanización del arte, La rebelión de las masas, Goethe desde dentro,* all show the subtle mind of the author and are filled with provocative ideas.

# XXVII

## *Recent Art and Music*

---

### MODERN PAINTING

THE first two-thirds of the nineteenth century in Spain did not produce any masterpieces of architecture, painting, sculpture, or music. There were some good painters, who were more influenced by French academic models than by Goya, such as Fortuny, Rosales, the Madrazos, and Pradilla, but they were far from great. The sculptors likewise left little impression. Toward the end of the century the artistic skies grew more luminous. There were several painters and sculptors who were excellent, and three painters who won great fame both at home and abroad. The three were very different.

Joaquín Sorolla (1863-1923) was a native of Valencia, and he never got away from the dazzling light of Spain's eastern coast. His pictures are all sunlight, of an overwhelming brilliance. He fuses his figures into this background, which is more likely than not to be the white sands and azure sea around Valencia, as in *After the Swim* (*Después del baño*). Some of his best canvases can be seen in America, in the museum of the Hispanic Society, New York. He exhibited several times in America.

Ignacio Zuloaga (1870- ), a hard-headed Basque, studied in Madrid, Rome, and Paris, but he was too independent to be subservient to any school or master. He copied pictures in the Prado Museum in Madrid, where El Greco, Velázquez and Goya impressed him most; merely another way of saying that he admired the three greatest Spanish painters. Perhaps the chief lesson he learned was that he should be himself.

Zuloaga eschewed academic polish, and many of his canvases

seem stark, bare. He has particularly interpreted the sober and brooding spirit of Castile, to such an extent that Spaniards accused him of spreading the legend of "somber and fanatic Spain," of exaggerating one side of Spanish character which foreigners for centuries have been all too ready to over-emphasize. His pictures contrast vigorously with those of the sun-loving Sorolla. Zuloaga uses background to emphasize his figures, and he employs black far more than gleaming white, as in his *Victim of the Fiesta* or *The Brotherhood of Christ Crucified*. In some of his portraits he has put more life and joy, for example, *My Cousins* and *Lucrecia Bori*. He has painted with true Spanish zeal, since more than four hundred canvases have come from his swiftly moving brushes.

Pablo Picasso (1881- ) is commonly thought of as the leader of the modern school of Paris. He was not born in the French capital, but in Málaga. His father moved to Barcelona to become professor of fine arts, and Pablo studied at the Academy there, giving his first exhibit in 1900. He paid a visit to Paris in the next year, and in 1903 moved to France for good. In the early years of the century he produced some of his soundest work. He has been an untiring experimenter, an ardent seeker after form, and in his quest he has had many incarnations: "blue periods," "pink periods"; cubism, realism, abstractions, surrealism. Cézanne and Toulouse-Lautrec influenced him, but he has been blown by many winds. For all that, he has always maintained great originality, vigorous imagination and sureness of touch. His life was spent in France after he was twenty-two, but his fervor and independence are Spanish characteristics.

Salvador Dalí (b. 1904), who has established his residence in the United States, is an artistic resident of the realm of the subconscious, but a painter of undoubted talent and imagination. He has been known to write poems, and he was a friend of García Lorca, but it has been his Surrealistic canvases which have won him notoriety if not fame. The titles of articles concerning him in art magazines are significant: *Is Dalí Crazy?* (The man in the street would certainly answer yes); *Glubbel, glubbel, who's a mental cripple?*; *Freud + Minsky = Dalí; Dalí, Waster of a Great Painting Talent*, and the like. He has considerable gifts, which he has chosen to use in a region more familiar to the psychiatrist than to the average man. It is difficult to say what contribution he has made to the painter's art. His work is at least rich in suggestion.

## MUSIC

The opera, mainly Italian, continued to be very popular in Spain in the first half of the nineteenth century. The *zarzuela,* after a period of eclipse, came back into great vogue slightly before the mid-century. One of the best composers of *zarzuelas* was Francisco Asenjo Barbieri (1823-1894), who showed a real love for the Spanish popular spirit. Quite literally hundreds of *zarzuelas* were composed. One man alone, Joaquín Valverde, is credited with two hundred and fifty.

The popularization of Spanish music in Europe was mainly due to two composers, Albéniz and Granados.

Isaac Albéniz (1860-1909) gave his first public concert when he was four, and had lived a very full life before he was twenty. He was a noted concert pianist, but a still more remarkable composer. His masterpieces are in four books comprising his *Iberia:* "twelve new impressions" he called them. They are based on Spanish, mainly Andalusian rhythms and tunes, and are an impressive musical interpretation of the Peninsula. *Triana* and *El Albaicín* are particularly moving, certainly among the most original piano compositions of the century.

Enrique Granados (1867-1916) more sentimental and less violent than Albéniz, interprets Madrid and the age of Goya rather than Andalusia. In fact, the scenes of Goya's day served as inspiration for Granados' most celebrated compositions, the suite called *Goyescas:* six pieces for piano, 1912-1914, not independent, but thematically bound together. The best known is *Love and Death,* which is melodious and tragic.

Granados later made *Goyescas* into an opera, performed five times at the Metropolitan in New York in 1916. The music is much more interesting than the uninspired plot.

An engineer turned composer is Oscar Esplá (1886-    ). He invented a scale of his own and uses folk themes, but tries to make his music universal rather than merely regional. His most frequently played composition has been his *Don Quijote velando las armas,* in three connected movements.

Andalusia is again represented in the music of Joaquín Turina (1882-    ). He studied in Paris and his Andalusian pieces have at least a slight French accent. He is much less profound than Albéniz or Granados.

The best Andalusian music has been written by Manuel de Falla, born 1862 in Cadiz. He studied in his native city and in Madrid, where he was inspired by the important musician Felipe Pedrell. In 1904 he won a prize for his opera *La vida breve,* purely Andalusian in background, and the next year he won another prize as a pianist. Then he went to Paris, supposedly for a week, and stayed seven years. He was befriended by Debussy, Dukas, and Ravel, and by his fellow-countryman Albéniz. In Paris his most important composition was *Nights in the Gardens of Spain.*

Falla returned to Spain in 1914 and in 1915 wrote for the famous singer and dancer, Pastora Imperio, the lyric drama called *El amor brujo.* The *Fire Dance* from the play is now familiar to all concert-goers.

Falla's ballet *The Three-Cornered Hat* was produced in London in 1919 by Diaghilieff's *Ballet Russe,* with choreography by Leonide Massine and costumes designed by Picasso. It was then and has been since extremely successful.

*The Three-Cornered Hat* was based on Alarcón's story of the same name, in turn based on Spanish ballad material. Falla's *El retablo de Maese Pedro* is based on an episode in *Don Quijote.* Anyone who wants to know the fire, passion, vigor, and variety of Spanish music should listen to Falla.

# XXVIII

## Literature of the Present. Conclusion

### SCHOLARS AND TEACHERS

EVEN though the results of the Spanish Civil War produced a dislocation in the lives of many of Spain's scholars, artists, and authors, the continuity of Spanish culture has not been broken. A large majority of the Spanish intellectuals sympathized with the now deceased Republic, and can no longer live in Spain. A few have found it possible to remain. The venerable dean of Spanish scholars, Ramón Menéndez Pidal, has kept his residence in Madrid. Ángel Valbuena Prat, professor at the University of Barcelona, also remains in Spain. He has been a specialist in Calderonian studies, but has also written a survey of Spanish drama and a *Historia de la literatura española* (2 vols., Barcelona, 1937), which is uneven but particularly distinguished for perceptive esthetic judgments of Spanish authors.

The pupils of Menéndez Pidal are in many places. Federico de Onís has long taught at Columbia University, New York. Américo Castro, philologist, literary historian and critic, whose *El Pensamiento de Cervantes* (Madrid, 1925) marked an epoch in Cervantine studies, is now at Princeton. Also in the United States are the most notable Spanish phonetician, Navarro Tomás, and the collaborator in the work of the *Centro de Estudios Históricos,* Homero Serís. The career of Antonio G. Solalinde, who for many years led studies on Alfonso el Sabio at the University of Wisconsin, was cut short by untimely death. Dámaso Alonso, scholar and critic, who devoted special zeal to the study of Góngora, is in Argentina. Other scholars are in various parts of North and South America.

## PROSE WRITERS

For some years before the Civil War in Spain there had been signs of a change in artistic taste. The authors who dominated the literary scene continued to be those who had established themselves just after 1898: Baroja, Valle-Inclán, Ayala, Benavente, the Quinteros, Juan Ramón Jiménez, the Machados; but the so-called "Generation of 1898," which had protested so violently against that which it considered old, "lo viejo," was itself growing old. Younger authors sought something different. Typical of the tendency was the ebullient Ramón Gómez de la Serna (b. 1891), "RAMÓN," as he likes to style himself. He has shown a Lopesque fertility in the production of volume after volume of prose, rich with startling and suggestive metaphors, in which he artistically stylizes prosaic reality. At his worst he is grotesque, unbearably exaggerated and manneristic; at his best, richly imaginative and stimulating, as in *The Bullfighter Caracho* or *Six False Novels*. His multitudinous novels display the same exuberance as his personal whims, such as keeping a gorgeous nude wax statue in his apartment to embarrass his friends, or making a lecture in black face or from a circus trapeze, or writing a whole volume on *Breasts*. For all that he is a gifted artist, "ultraist" or "vanguardist" or not.

Akin to "RAMÓN" are other writers of undeniable gifts, who in the twenties and thirties sought to express a new attitude toward reality, a new use of artistic motifs. They are advanced writers, likely to be unintelligible to the average man. Their efforts may be laudable, but it is very doubtful if the future will regard their achievements as solid. Among these would be José Bergamín, E. Gímenez Caballero, Benjamín Jarnés and Antonio Espina. Their imagination exceeds their power of communication, though an occasional description, a rare metaphor, may reward the bemused reader.

One novelist, though sensitive to modern currents in thought and art, has spoken more plainly and has a more penetrating vision of human character: Ramón J. Sender (b. 1901). He was educated at a monastery school, at Zaragoza and in Madrid, but in the capital he gave up his law course to engage in revolutionary activities which caused him to run afoul of the authorities. His parents, small Aragonese farmers, claimed him as a minor, and for three years he busied himself editing a country newspaper. He spent his compulsory military service in Morocco, and his experiences there are described in *Imán* (translated as *Earmarked for Hell* by James Cleugh, London, 1934, and as *Pro Patria,* Boston, 1935). In 1924 he joined the staff of the liberal newspaper *El Sol.* He was imprisoned by Primo de Rivera, but naturally came into favor with the establishment of the Republic. In 1933-4 he went to Russia as a most sympathetic observer. In 1935 he received the National Prize for literature. Since the fall of the Republic he has been living and writing in Mexico. His works are numerous; they include books of travel, a life of St. Teresa, short stories, an account of his imprisonment, a work on Hernán Cortés, novels of Spain and Mexico. *Seven Red Sundays* (*Siete Domingos rojos,* Barcelona, 1927, tr. by Sir Peter Chalmers Mitchell, London and New York, 1936) is a stirring account of radical activities in Madrid, with vivid characterizations of the participants. *Contraataque* (Madrid, 1937, tr. as *Counter-attack in Spain* by Sir Peter Chalmers Mitchell, London and Boston, 1937) was partly written while Sender was fighting for the Republic. It is decidedly one of the best books on the Civil War from the Loyalist side. The last pages, which relate the shooting by Franco's men of the author's brothers and his wife, have a true poignancy.

*El lugar del hombre* (Mexico, 1939, tr. as *A Man's Place* by Oliver La Farge, New York, 1940) is more perfectly constructed than Sender's other works, and gives an admirable picture of a whole village which is terribly upset when a man supposedly murdered is suddenly found; an excellent study in human relationships.

Sender has a poetic vision combined with a keen sense of reality and a knowledge of people not gained from books. His style is straightforward and lively.

## CONTEMPORARY POETS

The greater achievements of Spanish literary art in recent years have been not in any form of prose, including drama, but in verse. Poets of the past generation still happily alive have continued their production, and younger poets have arisen to prove that no age in Spain can be without impressively intense poetic inspiration. The Spanish Civil War has brought banishment to some and death to one of the greatest of them.

The *Ultraists,* beginning in 1919, sought to create a new poetry on the basis of the poetic image, reflecting contemporary preoccupations, free from sentimentality and free from rhetoric. Their attempts were not fruitful. One poet who shared some of their aspirations but who was willing to add more of his own personality is Gerardo Diego (b. Santander, 1896). Diego is really eclectic: classic or cubistic, primitive or extremely modern, but always refined and elegant. In addition to his own verses (e.g., *Imagen,* 1922, *Soria,* 1923, *Versos humanos,* 1925, *Via Crucis,* 1931) Diego published a valuable anthology of contemporary verse called in its second edition *Poesía española. Antología,* Madrid, 1934.

Diego comes from the North. From the opposite end of Spain, Cadiz, comes Rafael Alberti (b. 1903), who seeks the intellectualization of the popular elements of art. He always retains the true Andalusian's sensitive grace, and he can be as complicated, as difficult, as Góngora, whom at times he specifically imitates, as in a *Soledad* of his own. He has even made his bow to Surrealism in compositions for which some of Salvador Dalí's paintings might serve as illustrations. For all their difficulty, Alberti's poems possess vital structure and give an impression of creative energy and strength. Three of his best volumes of verse are *Sailor on Land* (*Marinero en tierra,* 1925), the Gongoristic *Mortar and Stone* (*Cal y canto,* 1929) and *On the Angels* (*Sobre los ángeles,* 1929).

From the center of Spain, Castile, come two poets now resident in the United States, Pedro Salinas and Jorge Guillén, both men of wide and rich culture, and both at present professors.

To Salinas (b. 1892), poetry is not a form of literature meant for amusement, for distraction from care, even for inspiration; it is something from the spiritual life of the poet which will stir the reader, turn him in on himself. His is not a poetry of purple passages, of elaborate imagery, of complicated rhythms; it is simple in expression, suggestive, provocative, rich in poetic ideas, often subtle, always possessed of great refinement. His first works were in prose, and critics suggested a relationship with Marcel Proust, but they were a poetic interpretation of reality, not a realistic analysis. Salinas began his poetic production with *Presages* (*Presagios,* 1923) and has continued his mature work in a number of volumes: *Sure Hazard* (*Seguro Azar,* 1929), *Fable and Sign* (*Fábulo y Signo,* 1931), *The Voice Owed to Thee* (*La voz a ti debida,* 1934) and *Account of Love* (*Razón de Amor,* 1936). Two volumes of tasteful translations by Eleanor L. Turnbull, *Lost Angel* (1938) and *Truth of Two* (1940), have been published by the Johns Hopkins Press. Salinas admirably combines the intellectual with the emotional.

The poetry of Jorge Guillén (b. 1893) is definitely cerebral. He was born in Valladolid, the birthplace of Zorrilla and Núñez de Arce, and the classic perfection and intellectual design of his verse contrasts strangely with the poetry of his diffuse fellow townsmen. Guillén is far closer to the Frenchman Paul Valéry, whom he has translated. His is a stern sort of poetry, meant for reading and meditation rather than for reading aloud. The conventional harmonies in Guillén's carefully wrought poems may be deceptive; they may hide a lyric suggestion not immediately apparent. He avoids the merely picturesque "local color," and presents the essence with carefully chosen figures, as in his poetic interpretations of Castilian cities. Guillén's poetry, first published in periodicals such as *La Pluma* and the influential *Revista de Occidente,* and gathered into a volume, *Cántico* (Madrid, 1928), is small in bulk, as such highly polished poetry must be. Guillén is the classisict of the present, simple in form, infinitely rich in suggestions, in poetic concepts.

Luis Cernuda (b. 1904), an Andalusian resident in Mexico, has gained considerable celebrity in the Hispanic world for his mastery of poetic form, especially the quatrain, and for his vivid poetic imagination, which includes the Surrealistic, the inspiration of the subconscious. His first volume, *Profile of the Air* (*Perfil del aire,* 1927), suggests Guillén. He shows greater originality in the collection called *Invitation to Poetry* (*La invitación a la poesía,* 1933).

Poetry in the Spanish language has many more votaries but there was one fervent spirit who alone would have been able to fill the Hispanic sky with melody and thrill it with poetic imaginings: Federico García Lorca.

Lorca was born in a little town, Fuendevaqueros, near Granada, in 1899, and the heady aroma of Moorish Andalusia always clung to him throughout his far too short life. He studied in Almería and in Granada. In 1919 he went to Madrid, to the *Residencia de Estudiantes,* where he was a companion of the poet Moreno Villa, the critic Guillermo de Torre, who was later to edit his works, and the artist Salvador Dalí. He took his degree in law at the University of Granada in 1923. He was always interested in painting, and even gave an exhibition of colored drawings in Barcelona in 1927. His intense passion for music was increased by his visits to Falla's house in Granada. He loved to sing the folk songs of his native Andalusia, accompanying them on the guitar. He would do the same with poems of his own, and some have called him the last of the minstrels.

Lorca's first publication was a prose account of a trip through Castile, *Impresiones y paisajes,* 1918, a bit of juvenilia never reprinted. In 1920 he put on the stage his first play, *The Curse of the Butterfly* (*El maleficio de la mariposa*) which was a complete failure. His *Libro de poemas* appeared in 1921; his *Canciones* in 1927, his *Gypsy Ballad Book* (*Romancero gitano*) in 1927. The last was a resounding success, and has gone through edition after edition.

In 1929 Lorca went to New York, returning to Spain by way of Cuba. The effect of the clanging of the New World on his spirit is reflected in some of his later poems (*Poeta en Nueva York,* published after his death).

In 1931, on his return to Spain, Lorca published his *Deep Song* (*Poema del Cante Hondo*) and organized a theatrical troupe called *La Barraca,* with student actors, which toured Spain in classic plays, mainly Cervantes' *Entremeses,* Lope's *Fuenteovejuna,* Calderón's *auto, La vida es sueño,* and Tirso's *Burlador de Sevilla.* Several of his own plays were shown before he died, interpreted by the great Spanish actress Margarita Xirgu.

In 1933 and 1934 Lorca was in Argentina. On his return he busied himself with the production of plays and poems, and seemed at the height of his vitality when Franco's rebellion broke out in 1936. He had never paid any attention to politics. He was spending a summer holiday in his native Granada. One night he was seized by Franco sympathizers at a friend's home, taken to a cemetery in the outskirts of the city, and shot five times.

The *Obras Completas* of García Lorca, including much material unprinted during his lifetime or gathered from magazines, have been edited in six volumes by his friend Guillermo de Torre (Buenos Aires, 1938). Many of the plays and poems have been rendered into English.

Lorca's dramas, in verse, prose, or half and half, are essentially poetic, for they all transmute reality into art; their action happens in a realm a little apart from earth, occasionally even in the realm of the subconscious. The very successful *Blood Wedding* (*Bodas de Sangre,* 1933), for example, is realistic enough in essence: a bride flees with her former lover Leonardo instead of marrying her fiancé. Yet the whole atmosphere is impregnated with boding mystery. The moon stops in its rising when Leonardo is killed by the irate groom, the woodcutters are figures from a fairy tale, the beggar woman is a symbol out of nowhere. Poetry, for all its dark beauty, runs away with the drama. Much of the same may be said of the intense *Mariano Pineda,* and even of light comedies such as *Perlimpín* (*Amor de don Perlimpín con Belisa en su jardín,* 1931), called an "Erotic Hallelujah in Four Scenes."

García Lorca will be remembered less for his plays than for his verse, in which he has achieved a fusion of popular inspiration with the most delicate and sophisticated poetic procedures. In this Lorca is a true heir of Lope de Vega. His Andalusianism is no mere reflection of the externally picturesque region of castanets, guitars, tropical heat, bright shawls and bullfights, but comes from a penetration into the popular soul, with its lightness or its brooding, its gay effervescence or its sanguinary tragedy, its brilliant songs or its gloomy laments, its passionate sensuality or its refined stoicism.

Lorca's *Libro de poemas* (1921) contains works of his youth. The poems are technically excellent, delicate, imaginative, suggesting the style of Juan Ramón Jiménez, but they have not quite reached maturity. His *Songs* (*Canciones,* 1927) show considerable development, subtler interpretations of popular themes, deeper musicality. The *Songs for Children* contained in this volume are infantile in inspiration and appearance, highly sophisticated in execution.

It is in the *Romancero gitano* (1928) that Lorca shows the plenitude of his powers. The form, that of the centuries-old ballad meter, is traditional, but the poet tunes it with new harmonies and enriches it with new images, gives it a new depth. Lorca knew the Gypsies of the Albaicín of Granada from his infancy. Instead of using them for decoration, as objects for bright description, he makes an esthetic interpretation of their spirit. The expression can be direct, literal, as in the *Ballad of the Unfaithful Wife,* now so frequently recited throughout the Hispanic world, with its crude expression and deep though poetized sensuality; or it can be close to pure poetry, lulling, alluring, vague, impressionistic, as in the *Romance sonámbulo,* a song which ends:

> Verde que te quiero verde.
> Verde viento. Verdes ramas.
> El barco sobre la mar.
> Y el caballo en la montaña.

> *Green I want you naught but green.*
> *Wind that's green and deep green branches.*
> *Boat that rides upon the sea.*
> *Horse high up upon the mountain.*

The three ballads to three Andalusian cities, Granada, Cordova and Seville, are infinitely suggestive. One of the simplest and most polished ballads in the collection is that on the death of the Gypsy

Antoñito el Camborio. *The Ballad of the Guardia Civil* finely depicts the hostility of the Gypsies against their born enemies, the police. All the ballads contain daring poetic images, vigorous metaphors, beautiful harmonies of verse. The *Romancero gitano* is the most intense interpretation of the Spanish Gypsy spirit that has been offered to the world.

*Deep Song* (*Cante hondo,* 1931) shows Lorca still interpreting the life of his region, with no diminution of power or suggestiveness. Some of the poems gathered and published since the poet's death add bright facets to his production. Lorca is likely to live as one of the few true poets that the first part of the twentieth century has produced.

Lorca's death was one of the tragedies of the Spanish civil war, but the Spanish spirit cannot be killed. If Spain survived nearly eight centuries of fighting against the Moors and then rose to be the most powerful nation on the globe, at the same time pouring out her genius in splendid manifestations of art in all its forms, she can survive a Fascist régime or worse. She has always shown great toughness, great resistance to any spirit or influence not congenial to her special qualities. In a world which is tending toward uniformity, toward a fusing of the person in the organization, in the large group, Spain has a contribution to make to humanity. In her art and literature and attitudes she has enriched the world hitherto. There is no reason to think that she cannot do so in the future.

On all subjects connected with Spain, for information and bibliography, the great *Enciclopedia Universal Ilustrada,* often called *Espasa,* may be profitably consulted. Madrid and Barcelona, 70 volumes plus 10 of Supplements. Vol. 70 is dated 1930, vol. 10 of the Supplement 1933.

*History:* Working bibliographies will be found in Rafael Altamira, *Historia de España,* vol. IV; in Antonio Ballesteros, *Historia de España,* and Charles E. Chapman, *A History of Spain.* The *Hispanic American Historical Review* mentions current items on Spain.

*Literature:* Working bibliographies may be found in Hurtado and Palencia, *Historia de la literatura española,* Mérimée-Morley, *History of Spanish Literature,* Fitzmaurice-Kelly, *New History of Spanish Literature.* There are many older and partial or special bibliographies. An extensive bibliography is now in course of publication: Raymond L. Grismer, *New Bibliography of the Literatures of Spain and Spanish America,* Perine Book Co., Minneapolis, Minn. Four volumes (A-B) published to date. Current bibliography will be found in *Revista de Filología Española,* Madrid, 1914-1936, and *Revista de Filología Hispánica,* New York and Buenos Aires, 1939- .

Flores, Angel. *Spanish Literature in English Translation.* New York, 1926.

*Music:* Working bibliography will be found in Gilbert Chase, *The Music of Spain,* and in J. B. Trend, *A Picture of Modern Spain, Men and Music.*

*Art and Architecture:* See special bibliography.

## GENERAL BOOKS ON SPAIN

*The number of periodical publications which deal with Spanish history, geography, culture, science, literature and language, art and music is very large. The more significant of them are referred to in the various works mentioned in the following bibliographical notes.*

Ellis, Havelock, *The Soul of Spain*. London, 1908. New ed. with an introductory essay on the Spanish Civil War, Boston, 1937.

Krause, Anna, *España y la cultura española*. Chicago, 1929.

Madariaga, S. de, *Spain*. London, 1930.

—— *Englishmen, Frenchmen, Spaniards*. London, 1928.

Martín Echeverría, L., *España. El país y sus habitantes*. Mexico, 1940.

Peers, E. Allison, *Spain: A Companion to Spanish Studies*. London and New York, 1929. 3d ed., London, 1938. A survey by various contributors under Professor Peers' editorship of geography, race, history, literature, art, architecture and music.


## HISTORY

Altamira y Crevea, Rafael. *Historia de España y de la civilización española*. 5 vols. in 6. Barcelona, 1900-1930. Vol. 5, in two parts, on the contemporary period, is by Pío Zabala y Lera.

Altamira has written a great many other works connected with Spanish history. The one-volume *Manual de historia de España,* Madrid, 1934, is an excellent survey.

Ballesteros, Antonio, *Historia de España y su influencia en la historia universal*. Barcelona, 1918- .

Burke, U. R., *A History of Spain from the Earliest Times to the Death of Ferdinand the Catholic*. 2 vols. 2d ed., London, 1900.

Chapman, Charles E., *A History of Spain*. New York, 1918. (Reprinted several times through 1937. A good one-volume history, based on Altamira.)

Hume, M. A. S., *The Spanish People*. Cambridge, England, 1898. A good one-volume survey. Several editions, e.g., New York, 1909.

Lafuente, Modesto, *Historia general de España*. 25 vols. Several eds., e.g., Barcelona, 1887-1891.

On the recent history of Spain and the Spanish Civil War, there are hundreds of volumes and articles in periodicals. Among the best books are:

Acier, Marcel, *From Spanish Trenches*. New York, 1937. Vivid letters from Republican soldiers.

Alvarez del Vayo, J., *Freedom's Battle*. London, 1940. An account of the Civil War by the Spanish Republic's former Secretary of State.

Bernanos, G., *A Diary of My Times*. New York, 1938.

Cardozo, H., *The March of a Nation*. New York, 1937.

*Contemporary Europe*. New York, 1941. A symposium by thirty authors. The section on Spain and Portugal, pp. 274-294, is by Loren C. MacKinney.

Gil Robles, J. M., *Spain in Chains*. New York, 1937. A violent condemnation of the Republic by an arch-conservative Rightist.

Hamilton, Thos. J., *Appeasement's Child*. An Account of Franco's Spain. Definitely not good reading for Fascists.

Matthews, Herbert, *Two Wars and More to Come*. New York, 1938.

Mendizábal Villalba, A. M., *The Martyrdom of Spain*. New York, 1938.

Morrow, F., *Revolution and Counter Revolution in Spain*. New York, 1938.

Peers, E. Allison, *The Spanish Tragedy, 1930-1936*. New York, 1936. An objective account by a noted British Hispanist.

—— *The Spanish Dilemma*. London, 1940.


Several novels have the Spanish Civil War as their background, such as Ralph Bates' *Lean Men, The Olive Field* and *Sirocco* (short stories), Ernest Hemingway's *For Whom the Bell Tolls,* Eliot Paul's *The Life and Death of a Spanish Town,* Ramón Sender's *Seven Red Sundays* and *Counter-attack in Spain*.


## LITERATURE

### Chief histories of Spanish literature

Boggs, Ralph S., *Outline History of Spanish Literature*. Boston, New York, etc., 1937. Useful outline and brief comments.

Cejador y Franca, Julio, *Historia de la lengua y literatura castellana*. 14 vols., Madrid, 1915-1922. Extensive, disordered and not always trustworthy. Valuable if used with proper checking.

Fitzmaurice-Kelly, James, *New History of Spanish Literature*. Oxford, 1926. Brief, well written.

Ford, J. D. M., *Main Currents of Spanish Literature*. New York, 1919.

Henríquez Ureña, P., *Tablas cronológicas de la literature española*. New York, 1920. Useful tables.

Hurtado, J., and A. González Palencia, *Historia de la literatura española*. 3d ed., Madrid, 1932. The fourth edition, Madrid, 1940, is in two vols., on very poor paper. Extremely valuable for factual information and bibliography.

Mérimée, Ernest, and S. Griswold Morley, *A History of Spanish Literature*. New York, 1930. Professor Morley's translation, with corrections and valuable additional material of Mérimée's *Préçis de la littérature espagnole*.

Northup, George Tyler, *An Introduction to Spanish Literature*. Chicago, 1925. 2d ed., 1936. A standard brief but scholarly history.

Romera Navarro, M., *Historia de la literatura española*. New York, 1928. Good criticism. Contains illustrations and excerpts.

Ticknor, George, *History of Spanish Literature*. 6th ed., 3 vols., Boston [1891]. Except in cases where modern investigation has revealed new facts, this admirable history has not been superseded.

Valbuena Prat, A., *Historia de la literatura española*. 2 vols., Barcelona, 1937. Uneven, valuable for stimulating criticism.

A very large number of more specialized studies will be found referred to in the above works.

## ANTHOLOGIES AND COLLECTIONS OF TEXTS

*Biblioteca de autores españoles* (B. A. E.). 71 vols., Madrid, 1846-1880. Many volumes reprinted. Contains most of the best Spanish literature through the eighteenth century. Badly printed. Texts uncritical.

*Biblioteca Calleja*. Madrid, n.d. Small and useful volumes.

*Bibliotheca Hispanica,* ed. R. Foulché-Delbosc. 22 vols., 1900-1921. Reprints of early editions by the noted French Hispanist.

*Biblioteca Literaria del Estudiante*. Madrid, 1922- . Useful anthologies.

*Clásicos Castellanos.* Madrid, 1910-1936. 114 vols. Best modern series. Inexpensive, well edited and printed.

*Clásicos Olvidados.* Madrid, 1928- .

*Colección de libros españoles raros o curiosos.* 24 vols., Madrid, 1871-1896.

*Colección de los mejores autores españoles (Colección Baudry).* Paris, 1838-1872.

Fitzmaurice-Kelly, James, *The Oxford Book of Spanish Verse.* 2d ed., with material added by J. B. Trend, Oxford, 1940.

—— *Cambridge Readings in Spanish Literature.* Cambridge, England, 1920.

Ford, J. D. M., *A Spanish Anthology.* Boston, 1911.

Hills, E. C., and S. G. Morley, *Modern Spanish Lyrics.* New York, 1913.

Hurtado, J., and A. González Palencia, *Antología de la literatura española.* Madrid, 1926.

Menéndez y Pelayo, M., *Antología de poetas líricos castellanos . . .* 14 vols., Madrid, 1890-1916.

—— *Las cien mejores poesías (líricas) de la lengua castellana.* London and Glasgow, 1908.

Menéndez Pidal, R., *Antología de prosistas castellanos.* 2d ed., Madrid, 1920.

Pattison, Walter T., *Representative Spanish Authors.* 2 vols. in 1, New York, 1942.

Romera-Navarro, M., *Antología de la Literatura Española.* Boston, New York, etc., 1933.

*Sociedad de Bibliófilos Andaluces.* 51 vols., Seville, 1867-1907.

*Sociedad de Bibliófilos Españoles.* 44 vols., Madrid, 1866-1928.

*Sociedad de Bibliófilos Madrileños.* 11 vols., Madrid, 1909-1914.

## ART AND ARCHITECTURE; MINOR ARTS

Sections on Spain are included, of course, in general histories of art, architecture and sculpture, such as those of Cheney, Faure, Pijoán, Reinach, Cotterill, Gardner, Robb and Garrison, Fletcher, Statham, Whitaker, Short, Abbot, Orpen, Chase and Post, Michel.

*Arte y decoración en España.* 12 vols., Barcelona, 1917-1928.

Bevan, B., *History of Spanish Architecture.* London, 1938.

*Burlington Magazine Monograph II.* New York, 1927. On Spanish art. Ten contributors. Good bibliography.

Byne, Arthur, and Mildred Stapley (Byne), *Rejería of the Spanish Renaissance.* New York, 1914; *Spanish Ironwork.* New York, 1915; *Decorated Wooden Ceilings in Spain.* New York, 1920; *Spanish Interiors and Furniture.* New York, 1921; *Provincial Houses in Spain.* New York, 1925.

Caffin, Charles, *The Story of Spanish Painting.* New York, 1910.

Calvert, A. F., *Sculpture in Spain.* London, 1912.

King, Georgianna G., *The Way of St. James.* 3 vols., New York and London, 1920.

—— *Heart of Spain.* Cambridge, Mass., 1941.

Mayer, August L. (in translation), *La pintura española.* Barcelona, 1926.

Post, Chandler R., *A History of Spanish Painting.* 8 vols. in 12, Cambridge, Mass., 1930-1941. The most satisfactory history of Spanish painting.

Street, George E., *Some Account of Gothic Architecture in Spain.* 2 vols., London, 1865; ed. with notes by Georgianna Goddard King, London and Toronto, 1914.

Tormo, Elías, *La escultura antigua y moderna.* Barcelona, 1903.

## MUSIC

Chase, Gilbert, *The Music of Spain.* New York, 1941. Contains, in addition to a good bibliography, an extensive list of phonograph records of Spanish music of all epochs.

*Encyclopédie de la Musique et Dictionnaire du Conservatoire.* 1ère partie, vol. 4, Paris, 1919. On Spanish and Portuguese music, by Rafael Mitjana.

Pedrell, Felipe, *Diccionario biográfico y bibliográfico de músicos y escritores de música españoles . . .*, Barcelona, 1897.

Soubies, Albert, *Histoire de la musique: Espagne.* 3 vols., Paris, 1900.

Trend, J. B., *The Music of Spanish History to 1600.* Oxford, 1926.

—— *A Picture of Modern Spain, Men and Music.* London, 1921.

Van Vechten, Carl, *The Music of Spain.* New York, 1918.

Wolf, Johannes, *Historia de la música. Traducción de Roberto Gerhard. Con un estudio de la música española por Higinio Anglés.* Barcelona, 1934.

## FOLKLORE

*Biblioteca de las tradiciones populares españolas,* Director: Antonio Machado y Alvarez. 11 vols., Madrid and Seville, 1883-1886.

Espinosa, Aurelio M., *Cuentos populares españoles.* 3 vols., Stanford University, 1923-1926.

Demófilo [Antonio Machado y Alvarez], *Colección de enigmas y adivinanzas en forma de diccionario.* Halle and Seville, 1880.

*"Folklore" y costumbres de España.* 3 vols., Barcelona, 1931-1934. Various contributors. Good survey.

Palencia, Isabel de, *Regional Costumes of Spain.* Madrid, 1926.

Rodríguez Marín, Francisco, *Cantos populares españoles.* 5 vols., Seville, 1882-1883.

—— *21.000; 12.6000; 6.666; 10.700 refranes.* 4 vols., Madrid, 1926-1941.

## TRAVEL

### Standard Older Books

Amicis, Edmondo de, *Spagna.* Florence, 1873. Tr. by S. R. Yarnall as *Spain and the Spaniards.* 2 vols., Philadelphia, 1895.

Borrow, George, *The Bible in Spain.* London, 1843. Various other editions.

Gautier, Théophile, *Tra los montes.* Paris, 1843. Published as *Voyage en Espagne,* Paris, 1845. Tr. by Catherine Allison as *A Romantic in Spain.* New York and London, 1926 (Blue Jade Library).

Ford, R., *Gatherings from Spain.* London, 1846.

—— *A Handbook for Travellers in Spain.* 2 vols., London, 1845.

Hay, John, *Castilian Days.* New York, 1871.

Howells, W. D., *Familiar Spanish Travels.* New York and London, 1913.

### Recent Books of Travel

Martínez Ruiz, José (Azorín), *El paisaje de España visto por los Españoles.* Madrid. 1917.

Symons, Arthur, *Cities and Seacoasts and Islands*. London, 1918.

Trend, J. B., *Spain from the South*. London, 1928.

Maugham, W. Somerset, *Andalusia*. New York, 1920.

Hielscher, Kurt, *Das unbekannte Spanien*. Berlin, 1922. 304 unusually beautiful pictures.

Peers, E. Allison, *Spain. A Companion to Spanish Travel*.

Unamuno, M. de, *Por tierras de España y Portugal*. Madrid, 1911.

Meier-Graeffe, Julius, *The Spanish Journey*, tr. by G. Holroyd-Reece. New York (1926).

# Special Chapter Bibliographies

## CHAPTER I

For Chapter I, see also under *History*.

Ballester, R., *Geografía de España*. 2d ed., Gerona, 1918.

Madariaga, S. de, *Spain*.

Martín Echeverría, L., *España. El país y los habitantes*. Mexico, 1940.

Dantín Cerceda, J., *Ensayo acerca de las regiones naturales de España*. Madrid, 1922.

## CHAPTER II

See also under *History*.

Bourchier, E. S., *Spain under the Roman Empire*. Oxford, 1914.

Cartailhac, Émile, *Les âges préhistoriques de l'Espagne et du Portugal*. Paris, 1886.

Sutherland, C. H. V., *The Romans in Spain*. London, 1939.

D'Arbois de Jubainville, *Les Celtes en Espagne*. In *Revue Celtique*, 1893.

## CHAPTER III

See also under *History*.

Fernández Guerra, A., and others, *Historia de España desde la invasión de los pueblos germánicos hasta la ruina de la monarquía visigoda*. 2 vols., Madrid, 1890.

Pérez Pujol, E., *Historia de las instituciones sociales de la España goda*. 4 vols., Valencia, 1896.

St. Isidore, *Opera omnia*. Romae, 1797-1803. *Etymologies,* ed. Lindsay, 2 vols., Oxford, 1912.

Cañal, C., *San Isidoro*. Seville, 1897.

## CHAPTER IV

See also under *History*.

Dozy, R. P. A., *Spanish Islam: A History of the Moslems in Spain*. Tr. F. G. Stokes.

González Palencia, A., *Historia de la España musulmana*. 2d ed., Barcelona, 1929.

—— *Historia de la literatura arabigoespañola*. Barcelona, 1928.

Lane-Poole, S., *The Moors in Spain*. New ed., New York, 1911.

Renan, Ernest, *Averroès et l'averroïsme*. 4th ed., Paris, 1882.

Lévy, L., *Maïmonide*. Paris, 1911.

Münz, J., *Moses ben Maimon. Sein Leben und seine Werke*. Frankfurt am Main, 1912.

Graetz, H. H., *Geschichte der Juden* . . . 11 vols. in 13, Leipzig, 1897-1911. Vol. 8 is on the Jews in Spain. English tr., *History of the Jews,* 6 vols., Philadelphia, 1891-1898.

Saladin, H., and G. Migeon, *Manuel d'art musulman*. Paris, 1902.

Lampérez, V. *Historia de la arquitectura española en la Edad Media*. Madrid, 1908-1909.

## CHAPTER V

See also under *History*.

Watts, Henry Edward, *The Christian Recovery of Spain from the Moorish Conquest to the Fall of Granada*. New York, 1901.

Menéndez Pidal, R., *La España del Cid*. 2d ed., Mexico and Buenos Aires, 1939. Tr. as *The Cid and His Spain* by Harold Sunderland, London, 1934.

*Colección de las crónicas y memorias de los reyes de Castilla*. 7 vols. Madrid, 1779-1787.

Manuel Rodríguez, M. de, *Memorias para la vida del santo rey Don Fernando III*. Madrid, 1800.

## CHAPTER VI

See also under *History*.

López de Ayala, Pedro, *Crónicas* . . . , *B. A. E.* lxvi and lxviii.

Pérez de Guzmán, F., *Generaciones y semblanzas,* ed. J. Domínguez Bordona. Madrid, 1924 (Clas. Cast. 61).

## CHAPTER VII

Entwistle, *The Spanish Language.* New York, 1929.
Menéndez Pidal, R., *Orígenes del español.* 2d ed., Madrid, 1929.
—— *Poesía juglaresca y juglares.* Madrid, 1924.
—— *L'épopée castillane.* Paris, 1910.
—— *La leyenda de los Infantes de Lara.* Madrid, 1896.
—— *Cantar de Mío Cid.* 3 vols., Madrid, 1906-1911. Condensed ed. in *Clásicos Castellanos,* vol. 24, 1913.
Rose, R. S., and Leonard Bacon, *The Lay of the Cid.* Berkeley, 1919. Good verse translation.
*Fernán González,* ed. C. C. Marden. Baltimore, 1904.
*Alixandre,* ed. A. Morel-Fatio. Dresden, 1906.
Berceo, *Vida de Santo Domingo de Silos,* ed. J. D. Fitzgerald. Paris, 1904.
—— *Milagros de Nuestra Señora,* ed. A. G. Solalinde. Madrid, 1922.
Menéndez Pidal, R., *La primitiva poesía lírica española* (1919). In *Estudios literarios* (1920), pp. 251-344.
Michaëlis de Vasconcellos, Carolina, *Cancioneiro da Ajuda.* 2 vols., Halle, 1904. Text and study of the early Galician-Portuguese poems.
Ribera, J., *El cancionero de Abencuzmán.* Madrid, 1912.

## CHAPTER VIII

Solalinde, A. G., *Alfonso X el Sabio, Antología de sus obras.* Madrid, 1923.
*Las siete partidas,* ed. *Real Academia de la Historia.* 3 vols., Madrid, 1807.
Menéndez Pidal, R., ed. *La primera Crónica general.* Madrid, 1906 (N.B.A.E., vol. 5).
*Cantigas de Santa María,* ed. *Real Acad. Esp.* 2 vols., Madrid, 1889.
*Libro de los engannos* . . . , ed. A. Bonilla y San Martín (Bibliotheca hispanica, 1914).
*Calila et Dimna,* ed. J. Alemany. Madrid, 1915.
*Barlaam et Josaphat,* ed. F. Lauchert in *Romanische Forschungen,* VII (1893).

Petrus Alfonsi, *Disciplina clericalis,* ed. Hilka and Söderhjelm. Heidelberg, 1911.

Don Juan Manuel, *El Conde Lucanor,* ed. Knust-Birch-Hirschfeld. Leipzig, 1900; ed. E. Krapp, Vizo, 1898, 2d ed., 1902.

*El libro del cavallero Zifar,* ed. C. P. Wagner. Ann Arbor, 1929.

Wagner, C. P., *The Sources of El Caballero Cifar,* in *Revue Hispanique,* x, 1903.

*Libros de Caballerías,* ed. Gayangos, in B.A.E., xi; ed. Bonilla, in N.B.A.E., vi, xi.

Thomas, H., *Spanish and Portuguese Romances of Chivalry.* London, 1920.

Menéndez y Pelayo, M., *Orígenes de la novela.* 4 vols., Madrid, 1905-1915 (N.B.A.E., vols. 1, 7, 14, 21).

*Auto de los Reyes Magos,* ed. R. Menéndez Pidal, in *Revista de Archivos,* iv (1900). J. D. M. Ford in *Old Spanish Readings.* Boston, 1906.

Crawford, J. P. W., *Spanish Drama Before Lope de Vega.* Philadelphia, 1922.

## CHAPTER IX

Ruiz, Juan, *Libro de buen amor,* ed. G. Ducamin. Toulouse, 1901 (Paleographic edition).

—— ed. J. Cejador. Madrid, 1913 (*Clásicos Castellanos,* 14 and 17).

—— *The Book of Good Love.* Tr. by E. K. Kane, Privately Printed, 1933.

Puyol y Alonso, J., *El Arcipreste de Hita, estudio crítico.* Madrid, 1906.

Fitzmaurice Kelly, J., *The Archpriest of Hita,* in *Chapters on Spanish Literature.* London, 1908.

López de Ayala, Pero, *Poesías,* ed. A. F. Kuersteiner. New York, 1920.

*Danza de la muerte,* ed. R. Foulché-Delbosc (*Textos castellanos antiguos,* ii). Barcelona, 1907.

*Coplas del provincial,* ed. M. Menéndez Pelayo, *Antología,* vi.

*Coplas de Mingo Revulgo,* ed. M. Menéndez Pelayo, *Antología,* iii.

*Coplas de ¡Ay, panadera!,* ed. B. J. Gallardo, *Ensayo . . . ,* i.

## CHAPTER X

Foulché-Delbosc, ed., *Cancionero del siglo XV*. (N.B.A.E., vols. xix and xxii.) Good edition of most of the poems of the fifteenth century.

Bonilla y San Martín, A., *Antología de poetas de los siglos* xiii al xv. Madrid, 1917.

*Cancionero de Baena,* ed. P. J. Pidal. Madrid, 1852. Facsimile ed., Hispanic Society of America. New York, 1926.

Santillana, *Canciones e decires,* ed. V. García de Diego. *Clas. Cast.,* Madrid, 1913.

—— *Obras,* ed. J. Amador de los Ríos. Madrid, 1852.

Puymaigre, Comte de, *La cour littéraire de don Juan II* . . . , 2 vols., Paris, 1873.

Mena, Juan de, *El laberinto de Fortuna,* ed. R. Foulché-Delbosc. Mâron, 1904.

Manrique, Jorge, *Coplas,* ed. R. Foulché-Delbosc. Madrid, 1912.

Ballads: *Romancero General,* ed. A. Durán, B.A.E., x, xvi.

Wolf und Hoffmann, *Primavera y Flor de Romances*. Berlin, 1856.

Menéndez Pidal, R., *Flor nueva de romances nuevos*. Madrid, 1928.

Morley, S. G., *Spanish Ballads*. New York, 1911.

Entwistle, W. J., *European Balladry*. Oxford, 1939. Long section on Spain, with translations.

## CHAPTER XI

See also *Art* and *Architecture* and *Music*.

Lampérez y Romea, V., *Arquitectura civil española en los siglos I al XVIII*. 2 vols., Madrid, 1922.

—— *Historia de la arquitectura cristiana española en la Edad Media*. 2 vols., Madrid, 1908-1909.

Mayer, A. L., *El estilo gótico en España*. Madrid, 1929.

## CHAPTER XII

See also *History*.

Prescott, W. H., *History of the Reign of Ferdinand and Isabella the Catholic*. New York, 1938. New ed., 3 vols., Philadelphia, 1902.

Armstrong, Edward, *The Emperor Charles V.* 2 vols., London, 1910.

Branli, Karl, *Kaiser Karl.* Munich, 1937. Tr. C. V. Wedgwood, *The Emperor Charles V.* London, 1939.

Starkie, Walter, *Grand Inquisitor. Being an account of Cardinal Ximénez de Cisneros and His Times.* London, 1940.

Lea, Henry Charles, *History of the Inquisition in Spain.* 4 vols., New York and London, 1906-1907.

Walsh, William T., *Characters of the Inquisition.* New York, 1940.

Llorente, J. A., *Historia crítica de la Inquisición de España.* Barcelona, 1835-1836.

## CHAPTER XIII

Bell, A. F. G., *Notes on the Spanish Renaissance,* in *Revue Hispanique,* xxx (1930).

Radet, G., *La Renaissance en Espagne et au Portugal,* in *Revue Hispanique,* xiv.

Menéndez y Pelayo, M., *Historia de las ideas estéticas en España.* 9 vols., Madrid, 1883-1891.

—— *Historia de los Heterodoxos españoles.* 3 vols., Madrid, 1911.

—— *La ciencia española.* 3 vols., Madrid, 1887-1888.

Lemus y Rubio, P., *El Maestro Elio Antonio de Lebrija,* in *Revue Hispanique,* xxii, xxix.

San Pedro, Diego de, *Cárcel de amor,* ed. R. Foulché-Delbosc. *Bibliotheca hispanica,* xv; N.B.A.E., vii.

Matulka, Barbara, *The Novels of Juan de Flores and their European Diffusion,* New York.

Rojas, F. de, *Comedia de Calisto y Melibea,* ed. R. Foulché-Delbosc; *Bib. Hisp.,* i (1902). The two earliest editions known.

—— *La Celestina,* ed. J. Cejador, *Clas. Cast.,* 20, 23, Madrid, 1913.

*Palmerines,* ed. A. Bonilla. N.B.A.E., xi.

Encina, Juan del, *Teatro completo,* ed. M. Cañete and F. A. Barbieri. Madrid, 1913.

Torres Naharro, B., *Propaladia,* ed. M. Cañete and M. Menéndez y Pelayo, in *Libros de Antaño,* ix, x. Madrid, 1880, 1900.

Gil Vicente, *Obras,* ed. Mendes dos Remedios. 2 vols., Coimbra, 1907-1912.

Rueda, Lope de, *Obras,* ed. E. Cotarelo y Mori. 2 vols., Madrid, 1908.

—— *Teatro,* ed. Moreno Villa, Madrid, 1924 (*Clas. Cast.,* 59).

Cueva, Juan de la, *Tragedias y comedias,* ed. F. A. de Icaza, *Bibliófilos Españoles.*

Crawford, J. P. W., *Spanish Drama before Lope de Vega.* Philadelphia, 1922.

Boscán, Juan, *Obras,* ed. W. I. Knapp. Madrid, 1875.

Garcilaso de la Vega, *Works,* ed. H. Keniston. New York, 1925.

—— *Obras,* ed. T. Navarro Tomás. 2d ed., Madrid, 1924 (*Clas. Cast.,* 3).

Keniston, H., *Garcilaso de la Vega, A Critical Study of His Life and Works.* New York, 1922.

Castillejo, C. de, *Obras,* ed. J. Domínguez Bordona. Madrid, 1925-1928 (*Clas. Cast.,* 72, 79, 88, 91).

## CHAPTER XIV

See also *History.*

Prescott, W. H., *History of the Reign of Philip the Second.* 3 vols., Boston, 1855-1858. Philadelphia, 1916.

Hume, M. A. S., *Spain, Its Greatness and Decay (1479-1788).* 3d ed., Cambridge, England, 1925.

—— *Philip II of Spain.* London, 1897, 1911.

Walsh, William T., *Isabella of Spain, the Last Crusader.* New York, 1930.

—— *Philip II.* London and New York, 1937.

Loyola, St. Ignatius, *The Autobiography of . . . ,* tr. by J. F. X. O'Connor. New York, 1900.

Thompson, Francis, *Saint Ignatius Loyola.* London, 1909, 1910.

Castro, Adolfo de, *The Spanish Protestants and Their Persecution by Philip II.* London and Edinburgh, 1851.

Watson, Foster, *Luis Vives.* Oxford, 1922.

Bonilla, A., *Luis Vives y la filosofía del Renacimiento.* Madrid, 1903.

Castro, A., *Lo hispánico y el erasmismo,* in *Revista de Filología Hispánica,* III, IV.

Mariana, Juan, *Historia de España.* Published in 30 books, in Latin, 1605. He began publishing the Spanish translation in 1601. Various modern editions.

Cirot, Georges, *Mariana historien.* Bordeaux and Paris, 1905.

Ocampo, Florián de, *Crónicas,* ed. B. Cavo. Madrid, 1791.

Fernández de Oviedo, G., *Historia general y natural de las Indias,* B.A.E., 1.

Garcilaso de la Vega (El Inca), *Comentarios reales,* ed. H. H. Urteaga. 6 vols., Lima, 1918-1921.

Santa Teresa, *Escritos,* B.A.E., LIII, LV.

—— *Las moradas,* ed. T. Navarro Tomás. Madrid, 3d ed., 1922 (*Clas. Cast.,* 1).

Cunninghame-Graham, Mrs. G., *Santa Teresa: Her Life and Times.* 2 vols., London, 1894.

San Juan de la Cruz, *Obras,* B.A.E., XXVII, XXXV; ed. Padre Gerardo de San Juan de la Cruz. 3 vols., Madrid, 1912-1914.

—— *El cántico espiritual,* ed. M. Martínez Burgos. Madrid, 1924 (*Clas. Cast.,* 55).

Peers, E. Allison, *Studies of the Spanish Mystics.* New York and Toronto, 1927.

Rousselot, P., *Les mystiques espagnols.* Paris, 1867.

Lewis, D., *The Life of St. John of the Cross.* London, 1897.

Baruzi, Jean, *S. Jean de la Croix* . . . Paris, 1924.

## CHAPTER XV

Cetina, G. de, *Obras,* ed. J. Hazañas y la Rúa. 2 vols., Seville, 1895.

Figueroa, Fr. de, *Obras,* A. M. Huntington. New York (1903) (facsimile of 1626 ed.). *Poesías,* B.A.E., XLII.

León, Luis de, B.A.E., XXXV, XXXVII.

—— *Poésies originales,* ed. A. Coster. Chartres, 1923.

Coster, A., *Luis de León,* in *Revue Hispanique,* LVIII, LVIV.

Herrera, F. de, *Poesías,* B.A.E., XXXII. *Poesías,* ed. V. García de Diego. Madrid, 1914 (*Clas. Cast.,* 26).

Coster, A., *Fernando de Herrera,* el Divino. Paris, 1908.

Ercilla, A. de, *La Araucana,* ed. J. Toribio Medina, 5 vols., Santiago de Chile, 1910-1918.

Montemayor, J. de, *Diana,* ed. M. Menéndez y Pelayo, N.B.A.E., VII.

Rennert, H. A., *The Spanish Pastoral Romances.* Philadelphia, 1912.

Delicado, Fr., *La lozana andaluza.* Madrid, 1916.

*Lazarillo de Tormes,* ed. J. Cejador. Madrid, 1914 (*Clas. Cast.,* 25).

*Lazarillo de Tormes,* tr. by Louis How, with an introduction by C. P. Wagner. New York, 1917.

De Haan, Fonger, *An Outline of the History of the Novela Picaresca in Spain.* The Hague and New York, 1903.

Chandler, F. W., *Romances of Roguery.* New York, 1899.

*El Abencerraje,* ed. G. Le Strange. Cambridge, England, 1924.

## CHAPTER XVI

Alemán, Mateo, *Guzmán de Alfarache,* ed. S. Gili y Gaya. 3 vols., Madrid, 1927-1928 (*Clas. Cast.,* 73, 83, 90).

—— tr. into English by James Mabbe, *The Rogue,* 1623, reprinted London, 1924.

Several of the picaresque novels will be found in B.A.E., III, XVIII, XXXIII.

Quevedo, Fr. de, *Historia de la vida del Buscón,* ed. Foulché-Delbosc. New York, 1917; ed. Américo Castro. 2d ed., Madrid, 1927 (*Clas. Cast.,* 5).

—— *Obras completas,* ed. L. Astrana Marín. 2 vols., Madrid, 1932.

—— *Los sueños,* ed. J. Cejador. 2 vols., Madrid, 1916-1917 (*Clas. Cast.,* 31, 34).

Mérimée, E., *Essai sur la vie et les oeuvres de Francisco de Quevedo.* Paris, 1886.

Juderías, J., *Don Francisco de Quevedo y Villegas.* Madrid, 1923.

López de Ubeda, Fr., *La pícara Justina,* ed. J. Puyol y Alonso. 3 vols., Madrid, 1912 (*Bibliófilos Madrileños,* 7, 8, 9).

Espinel, V., *Marcos de Obregón,* ed. S. Gili y Gaya. 2 vols., Madrid, 1922-1923 (*Clas. Cast.,* 43, 51).

Salas Barbadillo, J. de, *Obras,* ed. E. Cotarelo. 2 vols., Madrid, 1907-1909.

—— *La hija de Celestina y la ingeniosa Elena,* ed. F. Holle. 2 vols., Strasbourg, 1912 (*Bibl. Romanica*).

—— *La peregrinación sabia* and *El Sagaz Estacio,* ed. F. A. de Icaza. Madrid, 1924 (*Clas. Cast.,* 57).

Castillo Solórzano, A. de, *Jornadas alegres, Tardes alegres, Noches de placer, Las harpías de Madrid, La niña de los embustes,* ed. E. Cotarelo. Madrid, 1906-1909.

Castillo Solórzano, A. de, *La garduña de Sevilla,* ed. F. Ruiz Morcuende. Madrid, 1922 (*Clas. Cast.,* 42).

Chandler, F. W., *Romances of Roguery.* Madrid, 1899; *The Literature of Roguery.* 2 vols., New York, 1907.

Pérez de Hita, G., *Guerras civiles de Granada,* ed. Paula Blanchard-Demouge. 2 vols., Madrid, 1913-1915.

## CHAPTER XVII

Ríus, L., *Bibliografía crítica de las obras de Miguel de Cervantes Saavedra.* 3 vols., Madrid, 1895-1904.

Ford, J. D. M., and Ruth Lansing, *Cervantes, a Tentative Bibliography.* Cambridge, Mass., 1931.

*Obras completas de M. de C. S.,* ed. Rudolph Schevill and A. Bonilla. Madrid, 1914-1929. Best texts.

*Don Quijote,* ed. F. Rodríguez Marín. 6 vols., Madrid, 1916-1917; 2d ed., 1927-1928. Very extensive commentary, published in somewhat reduced form in Rodríguez Marín's edition in *Clásicos Castellanos.* 8 vols., Madrid, 1911-1913.

The first English translation of *Don Quijote* was made by Thomas Shelton, 1st part, 1612 (?), 2d part, 1620. The best modern translations into English are those of Peter Motteux, London, 1700, John Ormsby, London, 1885, and H. E. Watts, London, 1888. Ormsby's translation is reprinted in *The Complete Works of M. de C. S.,* ed. James Fitzmaurice-Kelly, Glasgow, 1901-1903. The works are not complete, including only the *Galatea,* the *Quijote,* and the *Novelas ejemplares.*

Icaza, F. A. de, *Las novelas ejemplares de Cervantes.* Madrid, 1915. Study and criticism.

Schevill, R., *Cervantes.* New York, 1919.

Fitzmaurice-Kelly, James, *M. de C. S., A Memoir.* Oxford, 1913.

Savj-López, Paolo, *Cervantes.* Spanish tr. by A. G. Solalinde, 1917.

Fernández de Avellaneda, Alonso, *Segundo Tomo del ingenioso hidalgo Don Quixote de la Mancha.* Tarragona, 1614; in B.A.E., xviii.

## CHAPTER XVIII

Schack, A. F. von, *Geschichte der dramatischen Literatur und Kunst in Spanien*. 2d ed., 2 vols., Frankfurt a. M., 1854. Tr. E. de Mier, 5 vols., Madrid, 1885-1887.

Schaeffer, A., *Geschichte des Spanischen Nationaldramas*. 2 vols., Leipzig, 1890.

Creizenach, W., *Geschichte des neuen Dramas*. Vol. iii for Spain, 2d ed., revised by A. Hämel, Halle, 1923.

Díaz de Escobar, N., and F. de P. Lasso de la Vega, *Historia del teatro español*. 2 vols., Barcelona, 1924.

Rennert, H. A., *The Spanish Stage in the Time of Lope de Vega*. New York, 1909.

La Barrera, C. de, *Catálogo bibliográfico y biográfico del teatro antiguo español*. Madrid, 1860.

Rennert, H. A., and A. Castro, *Vida de Lope de Vega*. Madrid, 1919.

Schevill, R., *The Dramatic Art of Lope de Vega*. Berkeley, 1918.

Lope de Vega, F., Non-dramatic works. 21 vols., ed. Cerdá y Rico. Madrid, 1776-1779.

—— *Obras*, ed. Real Academia (vols. ii-xiii ed. M. Menéndez y Pelayo). 15 vols., Madrid, 1890-1913.

—— *Obras*, new ed., ed. E. Cotarelo for the Real Acad. Esp. 12 vols., Madrid, 1916-1931.

—— *Poesías líricas*, ed. J. F. Montesinos. 2 vols., Madrid, 1925-1926 (*Clas. Cast.*, 68, 75).

Téllez, Gabriel (Tirso de Molina), *Comedias*, ed. E. Cotarelo, N.B.A.E., iv, ix. *Comedias*, B.A.E., v.

—— *The Love Rogue* (English adaptation of *El burlador de Sevilla*, by Harry Kemp). New York, 1923.

Muñoz Peña, P., *El teatro del maestro Tirso de Molina*. Valladolid, 1889.

Gendarme de Bévotte, G., *La légende de don Juan*. Paris, 1906; ed. 2 vols., Paris, 1911.

Castro, G. de, *Obras*, ed. E. Juliá Martínez. 1925- .

—— *Las mocedades del Cid*, ed. V. Saíd Armesto. Madrid, 1913 (*Clas. Cast.*, 15).

Ruiz de Alarcón, J., *Comedias*, B.A.E., xx.

Ruiz de Alarcón, J., *Teatro* (*La verdad sospechosa* and *Las paredes oyen*), ed. A. Reyes. Madrid, 1918 (*Clas. Cast.*, 37).

Henríquez Ureña, P., *Don Juan Ruiz de Alarcón*. Havana, 1915.

Vélez de Guevara, L., *Comedias*, B.A.E., xlv.

Cotarelo, E., *Luis Vélez de Guevara y sus obras dramáticas*, in *Boletín de la Real Acad. Esp.*, iii, iv.

Rojas Zorrilla, Fr. de, *Comedias escogidas*, B.A.E., xliv, xlv.

—— *Teatro* (*Del rey abajo ninguno* and *Entre bobos anda el juego*), ed. F. Ruiz Morcuende. Madrid, 1917 (*Clas. Cast.*, 35).

Cotarelo, E., *Don Francisco de Rojas Zorrilla*. Madrid, 1911.

Calderón, Pedro, *Comedias*, B.A.E., vii, ix, xii, xiv.

—— *Comedias*, ed. J. G. Keil. 4 vols., Leipzig, 1827-1830.

There are numerous editions of one or a few of Calderón's plays or *autos*.

Cotarelo, E., *Ensayo sobre la vida y obras de don D. C. de la B.* Madrid, 1924.

Menéndez y Pelayo, M., *Calderón y su teatro*. Madrid, 1881.

Fitzgerald, Edward, *Six Dramas of Calderón Freely Translated*. London, 1853, 1903.

Moreto, A., *Comedias escogidas*, B.A.E., xxxix.

—— *Teatro* (*El lindo don Diego* and *El desdén con el desdén*), ed. N. Alonso Cortés. Madrid, 1916 (*Clas. Cast.*, 32).

Kennedy, Ruth Lee, *The Dramatic Art of Moreto*. Philadelphia, 1932.

## CHAPTER XIX

Thomas, A., *Le lyrisme et la préciosité cultistes en Espagne*. Halle, 1909.

—— *Gongora et le gongorisme* . . . Paris, 1911.

Kane, E. K., *Gongorism and the Golden Age*. Chapel Hill, N. C., 1928.

Carrillo, L., B.A.E., xlii.

Góngora, Luis de, *Obras poéticas*, ed. R. Foulché-Delbosc. 1921 (*Bibl. Hisp.*, xvi, xvii).

—— *Poesías* . . . Cambridge, England, 1942.

Artigas, M., *Biografía y estudio crítico de don Luis de Góngora*. Madrid, 1925.

Churton, Edward, *Gongora*. London, 1862. With translations.

Bernadete, M. J., *Gongora Revaluated,* in *Revista de Estudios Hispánicos,* 1 (1928).

Alonso, Dámaso, *La lengua poética de Góngora*. Madrid, 1935.

Góngora, L. de, *The Solitudes, translated into English Verse,* by E. M. Wilson. Cambridge, England, 1931.

Quevedo, Fr. de, *Obras completas,* ed. L. Astrana Marín. 2 vols., Madrid, 1932.

Saavedra Fajardo, Diego de, *República literaria,* ed. V. García de Diego. Madrid, 1923 (*Clas. Cast.,* 46).

—— *Idea de un príncipe político christiano,* ed. V. García de Diego. 2 vols., Madrid, 1927 (*Clas. Cast.,* 76, 81).

Gracián, Baltasar, *El criticón,* ed. M. Romera Navarro. 3 vols., Philadelphia, 1938-1940.

—— *Agudeza y arte de ingenio,* ed. E. Ovejero. Madrid, 1929.

Coster, A., *Baltasar Gracián,* in *Revue Hispanique,* XXIX.

Bell, A. F. G., *Baltasar Gracián,* Oxford, 1921.

## CHAPTER XX

See also *Art* and *Architecture* and *Music*.

Velázquez, R., *El barroquismo en arcquitectura,* in *Boletín del Instituto Libre,* 1903.

Cosío, M. B., *El Greco*. Madrid, 1908.

Phaedon Press editions, *El Greco*. Oxford Univ. Press, New York, 1938.

Villar, E. H. del, *El Greco en España*. Madrid, 1928.

Mayer, A. L., *Jusepe de Ribera* (*Lo Spagnoletto*). 2d ed., Leipzig, 1923.

*Masters in Art*. Boston, 1900-1909. Contains illustrated monographs on El Greco, Velázquez, Murillo, and Goya.

Justi, C., *Velázquez und seine Jahrhundert*. 2d ed., Berlin, 1903.

Mayer, A. L., *Diego Velázquez*. Berlin, 1924.

Bernete, A. de, *Velázquez*. Paris, 1908.

Minor, Ellen E., *Murillo*. London, 1882.

Salinas, Fr., *De Musica Libri Septem*. Salamanca, 1577.

Trend, J. B., *A Sixteenth Century Collector of Folk Songs* (Salinas), in *Music and Letters,* VIII.

—— *Luis Milán and the Vihuelistas*. London, 1925.

## CHAPTER XXI

See also *History*.

Coxe, W., *España bajo el dominio de . . . la familia de Borbón.* Tr. from French. 4 vols., Madrid, 1936-1937.

Danvila y Collado, M., *El reinado de Carlos III.* Madrid, 1891-1894.

Gómez de Arteche, *El reinado de Carlos IV.* Madrid, 1890-1892.

Addison, Joseph, *Charles the Third of Spain.* Oxford, 1900.

## CHAPTER XXII

Pellissier, R. E., *The Neo-Classic Movement in Spain during the XVIII Century.* Stanford Univ., 1918.

Luzán, I. de, *Poética.* 2 vols., Madrid, 1789.

Feijóo, B. J., B.A.E., LVI.

—— *Teatro crítico universal* (Selections), ed. J. Millares Carlo. 3 vols., 1923-1925 (*Clas. Cast.,* 48, 53, 67); *Cartas eruditas,* ed. J. Millares Carlo, Madrid, 1928 (*Clas. Cast.,* 85).

Iriarte, Tomás de, *Obras en verso y prosa.* 8 vols., Madrid, 1805. Also B.A.E., LXIII.

Cotarelo, E., *Iriarte y su época.* Madrid, 1897.

Jovellanos, G. M. de, B.A.E., XLVI, L.

Juderías, J., *Don Gaspar Melchor de Jovellanos.* Madrid, 1913.

Tadeo González, D., B.A.E., LXI.

Cadalso, José. *Obras.* 3 vols., Madrid, 1821. Also B.A.E., XIII, LXI.

Meléndez Valdés, Juan, B.A.E., LXIII.

—— *Poesías,* ed. P. Salinas. Madrid, 1925 (*Clas. Cast.,* 64).

Quintana, Manuel José, *Obras Completas.* Madrid, 1897-1898. Also B.A.E., VII, XIX, LXI, LXIII, LXVII.

—— *Poesías,* ed. N. Alonso Cortés. Madrid, 1927 (*Clas. Cast.,* 78).

Piñeyro, E., *Manuel José Quintana.* Paris and Madrid, 1892.

Moratín, Leandro Fernández de, *Obras,* B.A.E., II. *Obras póstumas.* 3 vols., Madrid.

—— *Teatro* (*La comedia nueva* and *El sí de las niñas*), ed. F. Ruiz Morcuende. Madrid, 1924 (*Clas. Cast.,* 58).

Cruz, R. de la, *Sainetes,* ed. E. Cotarelo. Madrid, 1915.

Cotarelo, E., *Don Ramón de la Cruz y sus obras.* Madrid, 1899.

Isla, Fr. de, *Obras escogidas,* B.A.E., XV.

Isla, Fr. de, *Fray Gerundio,* ed. D. E. Lindforss. 2 vols., Leipzig, 1885.

Torres, Diego de, *Obras.* 15 vols., Madrid, 1794-1799.

—— *Vida,* ed. F. de Onís. Madrid, 1912 (*Clas. Cast., 7*).

Stokes, H., *Goya.* London and New York, 1914.

Poore, Charles G., *Goya.* New York and London, 1938.

Araujo, C., *Goya.* Madrid, 1895.

Viñaza, Conde de la, *Goya: su tiempo, su vida, sus obras.* Madrid, 1887.

Calvert, A. F., *Goya, an Account of His Life and Works.* London and New York, 1908.

## CHAPTER XXIII

See also *History.*

Clarke, H. Butler, *Modern Spain, 1815-1898.* Cambridge, 1906.

Hume, M. A. S., *Modern Spain.* London, 1899.

White, G. F., *A Century of Spain and Portugal (1788-1898).* London, 1909.

Peers, E. Allison, *A History of the Romantic Movement in Spain.* 2 vols., Cambridge, 1940.

Tarr, F. Courtney, *Romanticism in Spain and Spanish Romanticism.* Liverpool, 1939. (Reprinted from the *Bulletin of Spanish Studies.*)

Blanco García, F., *La literatura española en el siglo XIX.* 2d ed., 3 vols., Madrid, 1899.

Piñeyro, E., *El romanticismo en España.* Paris [1904]. Tr. E. Allison Peers, as *The Romantics of Spain.* Liverpool, 1934.

Rivas, Duque de, *Obras.* 7 vols., Madrid, 1894-1904.

Peers, E. Allison, *Rivas and Romanticism in Spain.* Liverpool, 1923.

—— *Romances,* ed. C. Rivas Cherif. 2 vols., Madrid, 1912 (*Clas. Cast.,* 9, 12).

Boussagol, G., *Angel de Saavedra, Duc de Rivas.* Toulouse, 1927.

Martínez Ruiz, J. ("Azorín"), *Rivas y Larra, razón social del romanticismo.* Madrid, 1916.

Espronceda, José de, *Obras poéticas,* ed. J. Cascales Muñoz. Madrid, 1923.

—— *Poesías* and *El estudiante de Salamanca,* ed. J. Moreno Villa. Madrid, 1923 (*Clas. Cast.,* 47).

Espronceda, José de, *El diablo mundo,* ed. J. Moreno Villa. Madrid, 1923 (*Clas. Cast.,* 50).

Churchman, P. H., *Byron and Espronceda,* in *Revue Hispanique,* xx; idem, *An Espronceda Bibliography,* in *Rev. Hisp.,* xvii.

Zorrilla, José de, *Obras completas.* 4 vols., Madrid, 1905 (far from complete).

Alonso Cortés, N., *Zorrilla. Su vida y sus obras.* 3 vols., Valladolid, 1916-1920.

Arolas, Juan, *Poesías* . . . Valencia, 1883.

——*Poesías,* ed. J. Lomba y Pedraja. Madrid, 1929 (*Clas. Cast.,* 95).

Lomba y Pedraja, J., *El padre Arolas, su vida y sus versos.* Madrid, 1898.

Avellaneda, Gertrudis Gómez de, *Obras.* 4 vols., Havana, 1914-1918.

Williams, E. B., *The Life and Dramatic Works of G. G. de A.* Philadelphia, 1924.

Cotarelo, E., *La Avellaneda y sus obras.* Madrid, 1930.

Bécquer, G. A., *Obras.* 10th ed., 3 vols., Madrid, n.d.

Schneider, F., *G. A. Bécquer's Leiden und Schaffen.* Leipzig, 1914.

Castro, Rosalía de, *Obras completas.* Madrid, 1909.

González Besada, A., *Rosalía de Castro,* 1916.

Barja, César, *Rosalía de Castro.* New York, 1923.

Martínez de la Rosa, F., *Obras.* 3 vols., Madrid, 1861.

Sarrailh, Jean, *Un homme d'état espagnol: Martínez de la Rosa.* Bordeaux and Paris, 1930.

García Gutiérrez, Antonio, *Obras escogidas.* Madrid, 1866.

——*Venganza catalana* and *Juan Lorenzo,* ed. J. R. Lomba. Madrid, 1925 (*Clas. Cast.,* 65).

Adams, N. B., *The Romantic Dramas of García Gutiérrez.* New York, 1922.

Hartzenbusch, J. E., *Obras.* 5 vols., Madrid, 1887-1892.

Hartzenbusch, Eugenio, *Bibliografía de Hartzenbusch, formada por su hijo.* Madrid, 1900.

Corbière, A. S., *Juan Eugenio Hartzenbusch and the French Theatre.* Philadelphia, 1927.

Cotarelo, E., *Sobre el origen y desarrollo de la leyenda de los "Amantes de Teruel."* Madrid, 1927.

Bretón de los Herreros, M., *Obras.* 5 vols., Madrid, 1883-1884.

——*Teatro* (*Muérete y verás* and *El pelo de la dehesa*), ed. N. Alonso Cortés. Madrid, 1928 (*Clas. Cast.,* 92).

Molins, Marqués de, *Bretón de los Herreros*. Madrid, 1883.

Le Gentil, G., *Le poète M. B. de los H. et la société espagnole de 1830 à 1860*. Paris, 1909.

González Blanco, A., *Historia de la novela en España desde el romanticismo hasta nuestros días*. Madrid, 1909.

Churchman, P., and E. Allison Peers, *A Survey of the Influence of Sir Walter Scott in Spain*, in *Revue Hispanique*, LV.

Peers, E. Allison, *Studies in the Influence of Sir Walter Scott in Spain*, in *Revue Hispanique*, LXVIII.

Gil y Carrasco, E., *Obras*, ed. G. Laverde. Madrid, n.d. *Obras en prosa*, 2 vols., Madrid, 1883.

Lomba, J. R., *E. G. y C.: su vida y su obra literaria*, in *Revista de Filología Española*, II.

Samuels, D. J., *Enrique Gil y Carrasco* . . . New York, 1939.

Mesonero Romanos, R., *Obras*. 8 vols., Madrid, 1925-1926.

Pitollet, C., *Mesonero Romanos costumbrista*, in *La España Moderna*, Oct. 1903.

Estébanez Calderón, J., *Escenas andaluzas*. Madrid, 1883.

Cánovas del Castillo, A., *"El Solitario" y su tiempo*. 2 vols., Madrid, 1883.

Larra, M. J. de, *Obras completas*. Barcelona, 1886 (not complete).

——*Artículos* . . . , ed. J. R. Lomba. 3 vols., Madrid, 1923-1927 (*Clas. Cast.*, 45, 52, 77).

——*Postfígaro, artículos no coleccionados*, ed. E. Cotarelo. 2 vols., Madrid, 1918-1919.

Burgos, Carmen de, *"Fígaro."* Madrid, 1919.

Chaves, M., *Don M. J. de L.* Seville, 1898.

## CHAPTER XXIV

Campoamor, Ramón de, *Obras completas*. 8 vols., Madrid, 1901-1903.

——*Poesías,* ed. C. Rivas Cherif. Madrid, 1921 (*Clas. Cast.*, 40).

Hilton, R., *Campoamor, Spain and the World*. Toronto, 1940.

Núñez de Arce, G., *Obras escogidas*. Barcelona, 1911.

——*Obras dramáticas*. Madrid, 1879.

Tamayo y Baus, M., *Obras*. 4 vols., Madrid, 1898-1900.

López de Ayala, A., *Obras*. 7 vols., Madrid, 1881-1885.

Echegaray, José, *Obras dramáticas escogidas.* 2 vols., Madrid, 1884.

Antón del Olmet, L., and A. García Caraffia, L., *Echegaray.* Madrid, 1912.

Barja, César, *Libros y autores modernos.* New York, 1924.

Bell, A. F. G., *Contemporary Spanish Literature.* Rev. ed., New York, 1933.

Vézinet, F., *Les maîtres du roman espagnol contemporain.* Paris, 1907.

Gómez de Baquero, E. ("Andrenio"), *Novelas y novelistas.* Madrid, 1918.

——*De Gallardo a Unamuno.* Madrid, 1926.

Madariaga, S. de, *The Genius of Spain and other Essays.* Oxford, 1923.

Böhl de Faber, C. ("Fernán Caballero"), *Obras completas.* 17 vols., Madrid, 1893-1914.

Trueba, Antonio de, *Obras completas.* 11 vols., Madrid, 1907-1915.

Valera, Juan, *Obras completas.* 46 vols., Madrid, 1905-1917.

——*Pepita Jiménez,* ed. M. Azaña. Madrid, 1927 (*Clas. Cast.,* 80; has bibliography).

Alarcón, P. A. de, *Obras completas.* 19 vols., Madrid, 1899.

Pardo Bazán, Emilia, *Obras completas.* 47 vols., Madrid, 1888-1922.

Andrade Coello, A., *La condesa Emilia Pardo Bazán.* Quito, 1922.

Pereda, J. M. de, *Obras completas.* 17 vols., Madrid, 1894-1906.

——*Pedro Sánchez,* ed. R. E. Bassett. Boston, 1907. Extensive introduction.

Palacio Valdés, A., *Obras completas.* Madrid, 1894.

——*Obras escogidas,* ed. L. Astrana Marín. 2d ed., Madrid, 1940. Includes sixteen novels, 2061 pages.

Cruz Rueda, A., *Armando Palacio Valdés.* Jaén, 1924.

Alas, Leopoldo ("Clarín"), *La Regenta.* 2 vols., Madrid, 1884.

Sáinez Rodríguez, P., *"Clarín" y su obra,* in *Revista de las Españas,* 11 (1927).

Pérez Galdós, B., *Obras.* Madrid, various dates.

Menéndez Pelayo, M., *D. B. P. G. considerado como novelista,* in *Estudios de crítica* 5^ta serie, Madrid, 1908.

Antón del Olmet, L., and A. García Caraffia, *Galdós.* Madrid, 1911.

Walton, L. B., *Pérez Galdós and the Spanish Novel of the Nineteenth Century.* 1928.

Dendariena, G., *Galdós, su genio, su espiritualidad, su grandeza.* Madrid, 1922.

Blasco Ibáñez, V.: his numerous novels are current in Spanish and most of them in English translation.

Pitollet, C., *V. B. I.: ses romans et le roman de sa vie.* Paris, 1921.

Gasco Contell, E., *V. B. I.* Paris, 1928.

## CHAPTER XXV

See *History* above, including the titles on the Spanish Civil War. For Spain just before the Second Republic, Salvador de Madariaga's *Spain,* New York, 1930, is particularly to be recommended.

## CHAPTER XXVI

The works of the authors mentioned in this chapter are mostly current and can be found in at least the larger libraries.

Bell, A. F. G., *Contemporary Spanish Literature.* Rev. ed., New York, 1933.

Madariaga, S. de, *The Genius of Spain and Other Essays.* Oxford, 1923.

Cansinos Assens, R., *La nueva literatura.* 4 vols., Madrid, 1917-1927.

Casares, J., *Crítica profana.* Madrid, 1916.

Cassou, Jean, *Panorama de la littérature espagnole contemporaine.* Paris, 1929.

Balseiro, José A., *Nueve escritores españoles contemporáneos juzgados por un crítico angloamericano.* Havana, 1926.

González Blanco, A., *Los contemporáneos.* 1$^{ra}$ serie, 2 vols., Paris, 1907; 2$^{da}$ serie, Paris, 1908; 3$^{ra}$ serie, Paris, 1910.

Petriconi, H., *Die spanische Literatur der Gegenwart.* Wiesbaden, 1926.

Barja, César, *Libros y autores contemporáneos.* Madrid, 1935.

Salaverría, J. M., *Retratos.* Madrid, 1926.

——*Nuevos retratos.* Madrid, 1930.

Valbuena Prat, A., *La poesía española contemporánea.* Madrid, 1930.

Critical material concerning all the authors mentioned in this chapter will be found in some or all the works listed above.

Costa, J., *Obras.* 5 vols., Madrid, 1911-1915.

Fernández Almagro, M., *Vida y obras de Ganivet.* Madrid, 1925.

León Sánchez, M., *Angel Ganivet, su vida y su obra.* Mexico, 1927.

Azaña, Manuel, *Plumas y palabras.* Madrid, 1930.

Navarro Lesdesma, F., Unamuno, "Azorín," and C. Román Salero, *Angel Ganivet.* Valencia, 1905.

Unamuno, Miguel de, *Ensayos.* 7 vols., Madrid, 1916-1918.

—— *Essays and Soliloquies,* tr. J. E. Crawford Flitch. New York, 1925.

—— *The Tragic Sense of Life,* tr. by J. E. Crawford Flitch. London, 1928. Good "Introductory Essay."

Romera Navarro, M., *Miguel de Unamuno.* Madrid, 1928.

Martínez Ruiz, José ("Azorín"), *Obras completas.* Madrid, 1919- .

Mulertt, Werner, *Azorín.* Halle, 1926. Tr. Juan Carandell and A. Cruz Rueda, Madrid, 1930.

Gómez de la Serna, Ramón, *Azorín.* Madrid, 1930. Unsystematic, stimulating.

Darío, Rubén, *Obras completas.* 22 vols., Madrid, 1917-1919.

Marasso, Arturo, *Rubén Darío y su creación poética.* La Plata, 1934.

Díaz Plaja, G., *Rubén Darío.* Barcelona, 1930.

Torres Ríoseco, A., *Rubén Darío: americanismo y casticismo de su obra.* Cambridge, Mass., 1931.

Mapes, E. K., *L'Influence française dans l'œuvre de Rubén Darío.* Paris, 1925.

Villaespesa, Francisco, *Obras completas.* 12 vols., Madrid, 1916-1918.

Machado, Manuel, *Obras completas.* Madrid, 1922- .

—— *Antología.* Buenos Aires—Mexico, 1940.

Machado, Antonio. *Campos de Castilla.* Madrid, 1912.

—— *Páginas escogidas.* Madrid, 1917.

—— *Poesías completas.* 3d ed., Madrid, 1933.

—— *Obras,* ed. J. Bergamín. Mexico, 1939.

Jiménez, Juan Ramón, *Obras.* Madrid, 1918- .

—— *Poesías escogidas,* ed. P. Henríquez Ureña. Madrid, 1923.

—— *Segunda antolojía poética.* Madrid and Barcelona, 1920.

Gabriel y Galán, J. M., *Obras completas.* 4th ed., Madrid, 1921.

Revilla Marcos, A., *J. M. G. y G., su vida y sus obras.* Madrid, 1921.

Benavente, Jacinto, *Teatro.* Madrid, 1904- .

——*Plays,* tr. John Garrett Underhill. 3d series, New York, 1917-1923.

Onís, F. de, *Benavente.* New York, 1923.

Starkie, Walter, *Jacinto Benavente.* Oxford, 1924.

Martínez Sierra, G., *Obras completas.* Madrid, 1920- .

Linares Rivas, Manuel, *Obras completas.* Madrid, 1913- .

Alvarez Quintero, S. and J., *Teatro completo.* Madrid, 1923- .

Martínez Ruiz, J. ("Azorín"), *Los Quinteros y otras páginas.* Madrid, 1925.

Baroja, Pío, novels published mainly by M. Caro Roggio, Madrid, 1900- .

——*Paradox, Rey,* ed. Claude E. Anibal. New York, 1937. Good introduction and bibliography.

——*Páginas escogidas.* Madrid, 1918.

Valle-Inclán, Ramón María del, *Opera omnia.* Madrid, 1912- .

*La Pluma,* IV, Jan. 1923. Whole issue devoted to Valle-Inclán.

Miró, Gabriel, *Obras completas.* Madrid, 1926- .

Pérez de Ayala, R., *Obras completas.* Madrid, 1911- .

Agustín, Francisco, *R. P. de A., su vida y obras.* Madrid, 1927.

León, R., *Obras completas.* Madrid, 1919- .


## CHAPTER XXVII

See also *Art.*

Colmena Solís, J., *Contemporary Spanish Painting,* in *The London Studio,* October 1926.

Sorolla, J. *Notice biographique et bibliographique,* in *L'Amour de l'Art,* Paris, Nov. 1934.

Zuloaga, I. *Modern Masters at Barcelona,* by Mrs. S. Erskine, in *Apollo,* Jan. 1930.

——*Notice biographique et bibliographique,* in *L'Amour de l'Art,* Paris, Nov. 1934.

McGreevey, T., *Ignacio Zuloaga, Painter of the Pittoresque,* in *The London Studio,* XVII.

## CHAPTER XXVIII

Gómez de la Serna, Ramón, works mainly published at Madrid, from 1904 onward. Lately in Buenos Aires.

García Lorca, Federico, *Obras completas*. 6 vols., Buenos Aires, 1938.

—— *Poeta en Nueva York*. Mexico, 1940.

—— *Lament for the Death of a Bullfighter and Other Poems*. Original in Spanish, translation by A. L. Lloyd. London and New York, 1937.

—— *The Poet in New York and Other Poems*. Spanish text, and English translations by Rolfe Humphries. New York, 1940.

—— *From Lorca's Theatre*. Five Plays in the Authorized Translation by Richard L. O'Connell and James L. Graham. New York, 1941.

# Index